Bribery Beyond Borders

Bribery Beyond Borders:
The Story of the Foreign Corrupt Practices Act

How scandal, courage, and world politics redefined corporate ethics—and what the origins of the FCPA reveal about our ongoing fight against corruption

Severin Wirz

Bribery Beyond Borders: The Story of the Foreign Corrupt Practices Act
Copyright © 2025 by Severin Wirz

All rights reserved. No part of this publication may be reproduced, distributed or transmitted in any form or by any means, including photocopying, recording or other electronic or mechanical methods, without the prior written permission of the publisher, except in the case of brief quotations embodied in critical reviews and certain other noncommercial uses permitted by copyright law.

CCI Press

Fort Worth, Texas

www.corporatecomplianceinsights.com

ISBN: 978-1-7350285-9-0

Publisher: Sarah Hadden

Editor: Emily Ellis

Front cover artwork: Luis Martinez

Book design: Jennifer L. Gaskin

Author photo: Ken Koeberlein

PRAISE FOR SEVERIN WIRZ AND *BRIBERY BEYOND BORDERS*

"The story of the most important U.S. law against corporate corruption reads like a mystery, with suicides and with dirty cash spilling into the coffers of foreign leaders. Never before has the history of the FCPA been told in such detail and with such verve."
—**Frank Vogl**, author of *Waging War on Corruption* and *The Enablers*

"Severin Wirz has produced an exhaustively researched history of U.S. anticorruption law packaged as a thriller. Tracing long-standing concerns in U.S. history about domestic and foreign corruption as well as countervailing concerns about regulatory overreach, he provides an invaluable resource for anyone interested in reimagining the global anticorruption regime."
—**Kevin E. Davis**, Beller Family Professor of Business Law, NYU Law

"In a world in which corrupt government remains a gargantuan problem, Severin Wirz explores the origins of America's legal quest to stop it in an absorbing and grippingly told story. Coupling his excavation of the progressive origins of the Foreign Corrupt Practices Act with a call for a pluralistic approach now, Wirz's investigation of the past is indispensable for reformers present and future."
—**Samuel Moyn**, Kent Professor of Law and History, Yale Law School

"A meticulously researched and eminently readable history of the U.S. struggle to combat corporate bribery and corruption overseas. Featuring larger-than-life politicians and their rivalries, innovative civil servants, falling foreign governments, suicides, fixers, and schemes to hide and disguise illicit payments, Severin Wirz's *Bribery Beyond Borders* reads more like a thriller than a legislative history. A must-read for anyone interested in corporate governance, compliance, and international business."
—**Lucinda Low**, Board Chair of the Coalition for Integrity and former president of the American Society of International Law

"This couldn't be a timelier and more important reminder of the significance of the crown jewel of the U.S. anticorruption framework: the Foreign Corrupt Practices Act. If past is prologue, this engaging and meticulously detailed story provides a clear warning of the dangers of returning to a world before rules existed to rein in the worst impulses of the unethical when partnering with the corrupt."
—**Gary Kalman**, Executive Director of Transparency International U.S.

"Severin Wirz has produced a timely and deeply researched history of the Foreign Corrupt Practices Act. As the global anticorruption landscape shifts, *Bribery Beyond Borders* lays a historical foundation for thinking critically about the statute's next chapter. The book's insights into the FCPA's origins provide a crucial perspective on current debates over the future of transnational anticorruption enforcement."
—**Jessica Tillipman**, Associate Dean, The George Washington University Law School

To my wife, Sarah, who saw this through
with me—and me through it.

CONTENTS

Introduction — 1

Chapter One: The Ghost of Eli Black — 8

- A CEO's Downfall — 9
- Can a Sensitive Man Survive? — 13
- The SEC Takes Notice — 16
- Bananagate: The Honduran Bribe — 20
- The SEC Story: From Campaign Cash to Corporate Bribes — 22
- Turbulence at CAB — 27
- Gulf Oil's Hidden Millions — 30
- Journalists Connect the Dots — 32
- El Pulpo — 38
- The Road to Reform — 41

Chapter Two: Rise of the Antibribery Ethic — 47

- An Ethic Born — 48
  - The Progressive Awakening (1904-1921) — 48
  - Pressure Builds Under Teapot Dome (1921-1929) — 54
- An Ethic Realized — 62
  - Organized Crime and Corruption (1930s-1970s) — 62
  - Nixon and Campaign Finance (1960s-1970s) — 70
- An Ethic Explained — 82
  - Post-Watergate Morality — 82
  - A Bipartisan Ethic — 85
  - Constructing Memory — 87
  - Echoes of the Past — 89

Chapter Three: Of Profits and Patriotism — 93

The Young Senator from Idaho — 95
Church's Investigative Platform — 99
The ITT Investigation: Sabotage and Subpoenas — 105
Corporations Without Borders — 109
Crisis of Confidence — 112
Peril and Opportunity for Church — 119
Gulf Oil in the Hot Seat — 122
From Confession to Crisis — 129

Chapter Four: Bloodletting — 137

Northrop in the Crosshairs — 137
Fallout in Paris — 143
Lockheed Under Pressure — 148
Secrets and Suicides — 154
The Informant's Diary — 160
The Black Curtain — 164
Japan Erupts — 174
Ford Moves to Contain the Scandal — 181
The '76 Democratic Nomination — 185
Shockwaves in Tokyo — 191
The Global Reckoning — 197

Chapter Five: Legislating Morality — 203

H.R. 7539: A Freshman's Ambitious Start — 204
S. 3133: The First Comprehensive Bill — 211
S. 3379: Sunlight is the Best Disinfectant — 214
S. 3418: The SEC Weighs In — 222
S. 3741: Ford Responds — 226
S. 3664: The Composite Compromise — 232
Amendment 2292: The Last Stand for Disclosure — 237
Enter Jimmy Carter — 241
S. 305: The Foreign Corrupt Practices Act Emerges — 244
H.R. 3815: The Unlawful Corporate Payments Act — 252
Public Law 95-213: The FCPA Becomes Law — 256

Epilogue — 263

The FCPA: From Dormant Law to Global Blueprint — 263
The Rise of "FCPA Inc." — 267
Leveling the Playing Field — 269
The Brazilian Crucible — 273
Fractures in the Global Order — 276
End of the Road — 278
Reimagining the Fight Against Corruption — 282
The Way Forward — 287

Acknowledgments — 293

Notes — 297

Index — 335

About the Author — 343

About CCI Press — 344

They that take the bribe shall perish by the bribe,
Dying of dry rot, ending in asylums,
A curse to children, a charge on the state.
But still their fears and frenzies infect us;
Drug nor isolation will cure this cancer:
It is now or never, the hour of the knife,
The break with the past, the major operation.

—Cecil Day Lewis, "Consider These,
for We Have Condemned Them" (1933)

Introduction

The United States has long sought common ground with other countries in the fight against international corruption. Collaboration between governments to counter corruption makes sense in a global economy characterized by the ease with which money travels seamlessly from one country to the next. If bribery extends beyond borders, then anticorruption efforts to combat it must do the same, often operating at the intersection of foreign diplomacy, economic relations, and international law.

The question we face now is how these coordinated efforts will survive in an emerging new world order. Declining U.S. hegemony, ebbing faith in the benefits of globalization, rising authoritarianism, and the overall breakdown of the liberal, rules-based system have already undone decades of work in the anticorruption field. No single event more clearly marks this incredible transformation than when

Donald Trump, early in his second term as president, announced a pause on enforcement of the Foreign Corrupt Practices Act, the U.S. law at the heart of global efforts to combat corruption over the past half century.

When enacted in 1977, the Foreign Corrupt Practices Act (FCPA) was the first-ever attempt by any country to criminalize bribery outside of its own borders. The statute grew out of a series of embarrassing revelations involving U.S. companies caught bribing high-level public officials around the world. Core to American national identity at the time was the promotion of democracy abroad, both in newly independent countries of the Global South and in established democratic strongholds across Western Europe. Congress worried that U.S. multinational corporations, if left to their own devices, could undermine these key foreign policy interests while simultaneously providing fodder for communist propaganda about the evils of American capitalism. The end result was a statute intended to bolster the reputation of the United States and the free market economy by applying long-standing principles of American anticorruption law to its international business dealings.

In the years following its passage, however, the FCPA has been the subject of continuous iteration, being reimagined and repurposed to reflect America's changing role on the world stage. In the 1980s, mounting U.S. trade deficits would lead to calls for the statute's repeal, but the fall of the Soviet Union by the following decade and the emergence of the United States as the world's sole remaining superpower imbued the FCPA with renewed importance.

Curbing corruption was soon reframed as part of America's efforts to create a truly globalized economy of the future, with focus shifting away from the abuse of power by U.S. companies to the entrenched backwardness of the foreign countries in which those companies now sought to do business. The statute's moral justifications also morphed, becoming less about applying U.S. law to American businesses operating overseas than spreading neutral concepts of the rule of law around the world.

In a post–Cold War context, America initially saw enormous success in achieving both of these objectives. International organizations like the Paris-based Organization for Economic Co-operation and Development (OECD) helped "level the playing field" for U.S. businesses by serving as vehicles through which the language of the FCPA could be grafted onto foreign legal codes and criminal statutes the world over—so much so that by the early 2000s, the FCPA could no longer be described simply as a U.S. law with international applications; it had become a kind of international law unto itself. America's aggressive, extraterritorial legal system proved equally suitable for bringing multimillion-dollar actions against corporations involved in bribery schemes across the globe. This meant vigorous enforcement not only against U.S.-based companies, but also, increasingly, against foreign entities caught in America's jurisdictional crosshairs. By the 2010s, the FCPA had become a multipurpose tool of American overseas legal power, as important to President George Bush's war on terror as it was to President Barack Obama's human rights agenda.

Yet by decade's end, it became clear that efforts to create a truly multinational, FCPA-centric anticorruption legal regime were losing momentum. While almost all countries by then had FCPA-style laws on their books, few had made any progress in enforcing them. Treaties and international summits notwithstanding, the United States largely stood alone in prosecuting transnational corruption, and as enforcement became ever-more concentrated at home, the corporations subject to the long arm of the FCPA were increasingly located abroad. Frustrations mounted on both sides, with American pro-business advocates seeking greater global parity, while detractors outside the United States accused America of engaging in double standards and politicizing the statute for domestic gains. Declining U.S. power and a growing backlash against neoliberal, economic policies further diminished the statute's moral underpinnings, prompting what many came to recognize as a crisis of legitimacy for global anticorruption efforts altogether.

Donald Trump's reelection in 2024 brought this crisis to a head in more ways than one. His February 2025 executive order pausing enforcement of the FCPA to realign the statute with his "America First" policies both signaled an abrupt change to America's approach in combatting corruption over the last several decades and effectively stripped the statute of any of its remaining moral justifications. The Trump administration may yet find use in the FCPA, but only so long as it conforms to the president's narrow, zero-sum view of the world. This includes using the FCPA more overtly as a weapon to punish those perceived as adversaries to the United States. Anticorruption advocates reeling from the demise of the rule-of-law-based FCPA they once knew must now look abroad to wonder if the vestiges of the legal regime created by the United States has legs enough to go on without it.

All this points to the fact that there likely has never been a better time to revisit the origins of the Foreign Corrupt Practices Act. Much as at the advent of the FCPA, we now find ourselves in a global debate about competing systems of governance, and America once again must redefine its place in the world. For fifty years, the statute has been a bellwether for the U.S. government's influence abroad, as well as its on-again, off-again relationship with regulating large corporations here at home. Concerns around authoritarianism, oligarchic rule and democratic erosion all signal that global corruption will continue to pervade our political lives for years to come. Yet what constitutes corruption remains as contested a concept as it was in 1977—as does the moral righteousness of those fighting against it.

My hope in writing this book, then, is not to monumentalize the FCPA, but to revive its radical aspirations to meet our current challenges. Just as today we have no assurances of the statute's future, it is worth remembering that the path leading to passage of the FCPA some fifty years ago was itself without guarantees. At the time, some of the world's most powerful corporations used every lever available to them within the federal government to prevent the public from being made aware of overseas bribery. The story of the FCPA is about how those truths came to light, how their exposure gripped a nation, and how they formed a narrative that profoundly changed the way we think about corruption in other parts of the world. Readers looking to find meaning in the statute's history today should, therefore, seek to understand not only the policies and ideas that informed the statute, but also the very ways in which those ideas first took root in the imagination of the American public.

In the pages ahead, you will find both heroes and anti-heroes: journalists, executives, bureaucrats, and politicians who jointly defied the odds and faced great personal risks in bringing forth an entirely new legal concept. Together, the motivations that drove them, the sins that dogged them, and the historical milieu in which they existed—in effect, the drama of their lives—evidence the small miracle that is democracy when operating in real time. The vitality of the statute's legacy today lies as much in the vision of America they once represented as in the black letter law they actually produced. As inheritors of this idea, may their stories grant the FCPA new meaning at a time when the nation, once more, seeks to ensure that its democratic principles endure.

The Pan Am Building in Manhattan seen from Park Avenue in 1980. Five years earlier, United Brands CEO Eli Black had an office on the forty-fourth floor.

Credit: Roger Wollstadt, Creative Commons license (https://creative-commons.org/licenses/by-sa/2.0/)

CHAPTER ONE

The Ghost of Eli Black

*He loved many people...
It was the one way to hurt everybody.*

Philip Fuchs, nephew of Eli Black[1]

A CEO's Downfall

On the evening of February 1, 1975, two days before taking his own life, Eli Black accompanied his wife and two children for a night out at the movies. The family had settled on *Murder on the Orient Express*, a whodunit flick featuring the peculiar talents of Agatha Christie's famously mustachioed Belgian detective, Hercule Poirot. While traveling from Istanbul to London aboard the Orient Express, Poirot is tasked with solving the murder of fellow passenger Samuel Ratchett, a rich American businessman who is killed in his compartment in the middle of the night. As Poirot pieces together a motive, each seemingly random stranger on the train becomes a suspect. Poirot's first big clue comes when he learns that Ratchett was not a retired businessman who'd made his millions selling baby food, as he'd claimed at the beginning of the journey, but rather a brutal gangster hiding from a former life of crime. A man like that, Poirot remarks, will always have enemies—and so too will his past eventually catch up with him.

But unlike Samuel Ratchett, Eli Black was an actual businessman whose trade was bananas, not baby food. He was also among the top CEOs in the country and a respected philanthropist. His company, United Brands, was the largest producer and marketer of bananas worldwide. In 1974, Black's company was ranked in *Fortune* magazine among the top 100 companies in the world, a veritable food conglomerate, with revenues exceeding $2 billion and operations that included processed foods, fast-food chains, and meatpacking. Even so, like Ratchett, Eli Black had his share of secrets.[2]

The family was gathered at the Blacks' weekend home in Westport, Connecticut. Eli's wife, Shirley, a professional artist whose work hung in local galleries and small museums, was there, along with their daughter, Judy Nadler, who had come to visit with her husband, Allen, a vice president for a large New York securities firm. Also present was their son, Leon, a twenty-three-year-old student at Harvard Business School who, fifteen years later, would go on to found Apollo Global Management, one of the largest private equity firms in the world. Father and son were close, and before going to the movies, Eli bought Leon a sweater which his son repaid by paying for his father's haircut. On Sunday night, the Nadlers drove Eli and Shirley back to the Blacks' apartment on Manhattan's Upper East Side, and, instead of going back to Westport, the young couple decided to spend the night on her parents' living room couch.

The next morning—the morning of his death—Black woke early. In fact, he was already showered and dressed in a dark blue suit and patterned tie by 7:00 a.m. Passing his daughter and son-in-law, who were still asleep on the living room couch, Eli slipped into the study and reached for some of the heavier books on his bookshelf, placing them into his oversized, brown attaché case. He then walked downstairs where his company chauffeur, James Thomson, was already waiting for him. It had rained the night before, and the early-morning sky was overcast and dark. Mr. Thomson opened the back door of the company's Cadillac Fleetwood sedan, and Eli greeted him warmly: "Hello, Jim! How was your weekend?"

From Black's apartment on East 79th Street, James Thomson drove the thirty-five blocks down Park Avenue to United Brands' headquarters in the Pan Am building. At its completion in 1963, the building stood as the largest commercial office space in the world and a dominant feature of the Manhattan skyline. Positioned above Grand Central Terminal, the building sits like a giant blockade between two halves of the city: Uptown are the Upper East Side, Central Park, and the luxury shops lining 5th Avenue; downtown, the view stretches toward Union Square, Chinatown, and the tip of Manhattan. After taking over United Brands in 1970, Eli had the company headquarters relocated from Boston to New York and made the iconic building its main office. Mr. Thomson stopped the car in front of the building and opened the door for Black.

"Will this be an 'in-day' or an 'out day', then?" asked the chauffeur, so he'd know whether to park the car. "This will be an 'in day,'" Black said.

It was still before 8:00 a.m., and Black rode the elevator alone. When he got out on the forty-fourth floor, the reception area was quiet, dark, and empty. He slid the crossbar to lock the large, double wooden doors behind him and deadbolted a second, emergency door next to it. Then he walked down the hallway to his corner office and locked both of those doors as well.

Like its proprietor, Eli Black's office was modest and unassuming. Whereas most CEOs of large multinational companies could reason to give themselves correspondingly generous salaries, Black had set his yearly salary at $200,000, less than half of what most CEOs in his position were making at the time. In the center of the office sat a large, reddish brown wooden desk, behind which rested a photograph of his son, Leon. The walls were decorated with Shirley's abstract watercolors and oil paintings. Eli removed his coat and hat and placed them neatly on the chair beside his desk. He walked over to the window behind the desk and raised the venetian blinds, revealing a jumble of rooftops, skyscrapers, and water towers. Then, in a single gesture, Eli picked up his large, brown attaché case, heavy with the books he'd packed that morning, and crashed it into the plate glass office window. He swung again, and then again, until the hole was three to four feet wide—large enough for him to squeeze through. Using his hands, he carefully removed some of the more jagged pieces of glass that stuck out, and then flung his suitcase out the window and watched it fall. Five hundred feet below, Grand Central Station buzzed with the arrival of morning commuters. Eli climbed through the opening and stood on the window ledge. In a moment, he twisted around and let go, his body hurtling forty-four floors to an elevated section of northbound Park Avenue below.[3]

Can a Sensitive Man Survive?

Why on earth had Eli Black killed himself? Mary Bralove, a young reporter from the *Wall Street Journal*, was tasked with answering that question for her next article. A week had passed since February 3, and the *Journal* wanted a longer feature on what may have driven Black to his death. Black left no suicide note, only a paper found in the briefcase by his body on which he had scrawled "Early retirement—55," leaving Mary searching for clues.

In the newspapers, tributes for Eli Black had poured in from all around. César Chavez called Black a "just and honest man," and reports told how five years earlier, when no other lettuce grower would even acknowledge Chavez's weakening United Farm Workers Union, Black had personally negotiated a collective bargaining agreement with the labor leader. After signing the contract, Black invited Chavez and other union leaders to accompany him to Rosh Hashanah services in Westport, where Chavez had been asked to read a prayer. Journalist Norman Cousins, who had known Black personally through Black's work on the board of the *Saturday Review*, extolled Black's "insight, leadership and sense of conscience," which he said "created an exciting and new ideal for the multinational corporation."

Born Elihu Blachowicz in Poland, Eli emigrated to America with his parents as a young boy. He grew up in what was then a poor, Orthodox Jewish neighborhood in Manhattan's Lower East Side. Like ten generations in his family before him, he'd studied to become a rabbi, graduating magna cum laude from Yeshiva University and afterward assuming his own congregation in the hamlet town of Woodmere, Long Island. But after three years, Black felt compelled to pursue another calling: business. He anglicized his name, left the rabbinate, and began attending business school at Columbia University. After graduation, Black went to work for Lehman Brothers, the former investment banking firm. By the age of 32, he had left Lehman Brothers, taken over a small, ailing milk-bottle cap manufacturer called American Seal-Kap Corp., and begun nursing the company back to health. With the company expanding, Black's breakthrough on Wall Street would come ten years later in the heady bull market of the late 1960s. In the first in a series of gutsy moves, Black bought John Morrell & Co., the fourth-largest meatpacking company in the country and an organization twenty times larger than his own. A short time later, Black aggressively merged that company with the United Fruit Company, the established banana titan, in what was at the time one of the largest share deals in the history of the United States stock market.

Black, the newly appointed head of a billion-dollar company, continued to maintain deep ties with his religious roots. He remained close friends with Rabbi Jonathan Levine, often spending Saturday afternoons together in Black's garden discussing both spiritual and intellectual problems involved in developing new forms of Jewish worship. Black also generously donated to countless Jewish organizations, although most of the time he did so anonymously. When he wasn't working at United Brands, he sat on the board of several nonprofit organizations, including the Federation of Jewish Philanthropies and the Jewish Museum.[4]

The more Mary Bralove learned about Eli Black, the more confounding and wondrous the tragedy of his death seemed to her. Not only was suicide completely against Black's strong Judaic faith, but the spectacular manner in which he'd chosen to end his life seemed utterly inconsistent with his character. To his friends and family, Eli was a fundamentally private, cautious person—someone who shunned the limelight so much that for years he refused to even allow a picture of himself to be shown in United Brands' annual report. This was not the typical profile of someone who would throw himself out of a forty-four-story window.

For her article in the *Wall Street Journal*, Mary eventually settled on the inner tension she believed Eli Black must have felt in trying to straddle two conflicting worlds—one that valued moral and spiritual well-being, and the other that demanded steadily increasing earnings. Published on February 14, Bralove's article asked what, to her, was the fundamental question surrounding Black's death: "Can a sensitive man, a man with high moral standards, survive in an uncompromising financial world?"[5] This, like much else surrounding Eli Black's death, was yet another question with no apparent answer.

The SEC Takes Notice

Mary Bralove wasn't the only person trying to understand why Eli Black had killed himself. In the Washington, D.C. office of the Securities and Exchange Commission, Stanley Sporkin, head of the Commission's Enforcement Division, wondered the same thing. Created in 1934 in response to the Great Crash of 1929, the SEC has served as the government's primary regulatory agency to oversee the securities industry and the rest of Wall Street. Holding in his hands a newspaper announcing Black's suicide the previous day, Sporkin telephoned Ralph Ferrara, one of his brightest young investigators, and asked him to come immediately to his office.

Sporkin had first met Ferrara at a lecture he'd given at George Washington University a few years earlier. During the question-and-answer portion of the lecture, Ferrara had impressed Sporkin so thoroughly with his knowledge of securities law that Sporkin asked him on the spot to come work for the SEC.[6] At that time, Sporkin had already served for ten years at the Commission under former SEC Enforcement Director Irving ("Irv") Pollack. Together, Pollack and Sporkin had aggressively applied the securities laws during the 1960s and made more than a few enemies on Wall Street in the process.⁷ When Pollack was promoted to Commissioner in 1974, Sporkin replaced him as director and soon earned himself his own reputation as a tough-as-nails investigator. Described as "direct, vigorous and salty," Sporkin ran the Enforcement Division with the style of a burly basketball coach.⁸ In many ways, he was the antithesis of Agatha Christie's small, fastidious, and obsessively tidy character, Hercule Poirot. Sporkin's plain, fourth-floor office was largely barren except for stacks of boxes and papers strewn over an old, decrepit couch patterned in yellows, greens, and blacks—a sofa one of his colleagues once described as "the ugliest piece of furniture ever created by man."⁹ But what Sporkin lacked in tidiness he made up for in a drive to ferret out fraud and insider trading on Wall Street. Within his first year as head, Sporkin's no-nonsense approach had already earned him a reputation as "the terror of the securities industry."¹⁰

Sporkin showed Ferrara the newspaper headline of Black's death and quickly made his point: "Ralph, guys like this don't drop out of windows for no reason. I want you to call up and find out what's going on." Never having even heard of Eli Black, Ferrara struggled to understand what was being asked of him. Sporkin's instructions were simple: "figure it out."¹¹

Ferrara guessed that the best place to start might be to simply call United Brands' people directly and ask them to come meet with him. But when Ferrara called up United Brands' headquarters in New York, no one answered the phone. Almost the entire office, along with hundreds of relatives and friends—some of whom had flown in from Israel—were at Manhattan's Riverside Chapel attending Black's funeral.[12] The following day, a representative from United Brands returned Ferrara's phone call. The young SEC investigator asked all of United Brands' senior management, including its general counsel, chief financial officer, and president, to meet with him as soon as possible. Surprisingly, or perhaps simply because they sensed the urgency of the situation, the officers agreed. They would fly to Washington, D.C. and meet with Ferrara that very same week.

In New York, things had gone from bad to worse at the United Brands offices. Black's death had sparked an internal battle of succession that had been brewing for months. At a board of directors meeting the day after Black's funeral, directors could be heard shouting at each other from the hallway. On one side of the dispute was United Brands' Chief Operating Officer, Edward Gelsthorpe, with whom Black had increasingly clashed and reportedly wanted to fire, partly because Black believed Gelsthorpe had made important decisions behind his back and was turning other employees against him. Since September, Gelsthorpe had begun openly questioning Black's ability to manage the company. Rumors had even begun circulating that Black was on drugs. The conflict eventually escalated into a rivalry between offices, with Gelsthorpe winning the allegiance of United Brands' Boston office (the headquarters of United Fruit prior to its acquisition by Black) and Black maintaining the allegiance of the New York office.[13]

Those still loyal to Black refused to make Gelsthorpe CEO after Black's death, but the board failed to reach a consensus on a replacement. Forced to settle on an interim solution, they appointed J.E. Goldman, one of United Brands' directors and group vice president of Xerox Corp., to head the executive and management committees while Gelsthorpe ran the day-to-day business of the company.[14] What hadn't been resolved, though, and what still lay buried beneath the surface when representatives from United Brands flew to Washington, D.C. to meet with the SEC, was a matter that Black had felt truly made him vulnerable—information he believed, if in the wrong hands, could be used to oust him.[15] After Black's death, United Brands' directors feared worse: that the information, if leaked, might land a crippling blow to the entire company.

In the Washington offices of the SEC, Ralph Ferrara met with United Brands' representatives for an entire day, peppering them with questions as to why Black might have killed himself. The company had been under all kinds of stress over the past year—a hurricane that had devastated most of the banana crop in Honduras, a falling stock price, mounting bank debts, and the reluctant sale of a profitable subsidiary—any of which could have contributed to Black's death, and none of which were illegal. As the meeting wore on, Ferrara could think of only one final question: "You know, you guys do business in Latin America. Do you know if anybody was bribing anybody in Latin America, in a way that could have . . . was about to be exposed, and drove him out of the window?"

The question had come to Ferrara spontaneously and without reason. Not only did the SEC not investigate foreign bribes, but bribes to foreign officials were not even clearly illegal under U.S. law. More often, they were simply not discussed. "No," answered one of United Brands' representatives. And with that, the interview was over.

Bananagate: The Honduran Bribe

"What did you do yesterday?" Sporkin shouted at Ferrara over the phone when he arrived at his desk the following morning. Ferrara recounted the interview, admitting that he hadn't gotten any further in uncovering what had happened with Black. "Well, the Chairman wants to see us in his office, okay?" In SEC Chairman Ray Garrett's office stood United Brands' general counsel, along with Samuel Butler, United Brands' outside counsel from the prestigious law firm of Cravath, Swaine & Moore. Lying to an SEC investigator is a criminal offense, and United Brands had come back to say that they had not correctly recalled the answer to Ferrara's last question. The correct answer—the one that Gelsthorpe already knew and that Black had feared could be used against him—involved a $1.25 million bribe the company had paid seven months earlier to one of the Honduran government's highest officials.

United Brands' lawyers explained the backstory. In early 1974, amid increasing worldwide oil prices, various countries in South and Central America had formed the Union of Banana Exporting Countries, a cartel modeled after the success of OPEC among oil-producing countries.

In an effort to artificially raise the price of bananas, the governments of Costa Rica, Guatemala, Honduras, Panama, Ecuador, Nicaragua, and Colombia signed the Panama Agreement in March 1974, agreeing to jointly increase taxation on banana exports. In April, Honduras followed up on the agreement by imposing a fifty-cent tax on each forty-pound box of bananas leaving its borders.[16] For United Brands, the tax was potentially disastrous. In 1974 alone, the company had exported more than 30 million boxes of bananas from Honduras, which amounted to over 35 percent of United Brands' total banana supply. Already facing stiff competition from rivals Standard Fruit and Del Monte, the additional cost to export the fruit meant that United Brands would have to pass the tax onto its consumers and risk losing an even larger share of the market.

In August, company representatives met with Honduran Economic Minister Abraham Bennaton Ramos at the Fontainebleau hotel in Miami to try to work out a deal. Bennaton Ramos matter-of-factly told them that he could lower the tax if the company agreed to pay him $5 million.[17] United Brands' representatives said they would need time to consider the offer, but a few weeks later, the company publicly announced it had reached an "understanding" with Honduras to lower the tax to twenty-five cents per box, with yearly increases beginning in 1975. Unofficially, company officials, including Eli Black, had quietly agreed to pay half of what Bennaton Ramos had asked—$2.5 million to be paid in two equal installments—to have the tax lowered.[18] The money was paid in U.S. dollars and was transferred through the Paris branch of the Chase Manhattan Bank in which United Brands' Dutch subsidiary maintained an account. The Paris bank sent an international cable in September to Chase's New York office, directing the New York branch to transfer $1.25 million—the first installment—into an account in the name of Credit Suisse in Zurich.[19] On their books, United Brands recorded the payoff as "the cost of European sales."[20]

Sporkin listened carefully to United Brands' story. For the top enforcer at the SEC, the bribe to Honduras presented a novel problem. It wasn't that he'd never dealt with political payments before (he was, by then, well versed in dealing with political corruption); rather, the SEC had never prosecuted a company for bribes paid to a politician *outside* the United States. Foreign bribery was not even clearly illegal under U.S. law. Legal questions aside, the Honduran revelations were coming at a particularly bad time for Sporkin and the SEC, raising sensitive political issues that some felt might better be left undisturbed.

The SEC Story: From Campaign Cash to Corporate Bribes

A year earlier, after returning from a vacation to Spain, Stanley Sporkin had turned on his television and began watching what it seemed like everyone else in America was watching at the time: the Senate Watergate hearings. The hearings had captured the public's attention, and the attendance of celebrities like John Lennon added a circus-like feel to the entire inquiry. But what interested

Sporkin most about the hearings was not the botched burglary, the mysterious "Deep Throat," or even President Nixon's fall from grace; it was the allegations of wrongdoing by some of the president's corporate backers. When looking into hush money paid to the Watergate burglars, Archibald Cox, the special prosecutor appointed by the Senate to investigate Watergate, also revealed that Nixon's Committee to Re-elect the President (CRP) had solicited millions of dollars in illegal campaign contributions from major U.S. corporations. In a moment of remarkable clarity and creativity, Sporkin realized that companies that had failed to properly disclose these campaign contributions to investors in their annual reports had probably also violated the disclosure requirements of the 1934 Securities and Exchange Act.[21]

Under U.S. securities law, companies making statements regarding the purchase or sale of their securities are obligated to disclose all information considered "material" to a reasonable investor. On March 8, 1974, the SEC released its first statement on the Nixon political contributions scandal, noting that the Commission intended to treat any conviction against a corporation or one of its officers for an illegal campaign contribution as a "material fact" that the company would have to disclose publicly.[22] But Sporkin believed that the payments themselves, not just any convictions resulting from them, should have to be disclosed to investors. After all, executives who paid illegal bribes were jeopardizing the health of their companies, a fact that would certainly be of material importance to investors. Sporkin's argument convinced enough people at the SEC for the Commission to create the "Management Fraud Program," a specialized unit within the SEC aimed at detecting managers who used corporate profits for the purpose of engaging in illegal political activity.[23] Under the program, Sporkin's team filed motions to obtain grand jury transcripts of the Watergate prosecutor's investigations and also made direct requests to Leon Jaworski—who by then had replaced Cox as head of the Watergate special prosecutor's investigation—asking that his staff be granted access to any information regarding corporate payments to the CRP.[24]

On October 16, the SEC brought its first bribery-related case against American Ship Building Company and owner George M. Steinbrenner III.[25] Steinbrenner, who had just bought the Yankees baseball team a year earlier, failed to disclose to investors information regarding close to $120,000 in corporate funds paid to Nixon's 1972 presidential campaign.[26] It was the first of many cases the Enforcement Division would bring over the course of the next several months related to illegal payments to the 1972 campaign, and Sporkin would become the face of those efforts.[27] But not everyone at the Commission welcomed the Enforcement Division's sortie into the world of Watergate. Although the cases generated headlines, some believed that the bribery investigations were evidence of SEC overreach and that the cases were compromising the Commission's long-standing credibility among professionals in the business community.[28] After all, was bribery really a Securities problem? "The one we had to convince was Ray," remembered Sporkin, referring to Ray Garrett, Chairman of the SEC at the time.[29] Irv Pollack also recalled the challenges in persuading the chairman: "Garrett's view was, you know, this goes on all the time, bribery and this other stuff. You can't get too excited about that."[30]

So now, on top of the general misgivings about the Watergate cases, there was this additional problem presented by United Brands: whether to go after a company for paying bribes overseas. Not only was foreign bribery not considered illegal under U.S. law, United Brands wasn't even the first company Sporkin had found paying bribes abroad.

Ten months earlier, Thomas Jones, President and CEO of Northrop Corporation, pleaded guilty to having illegally contributed over $30,000 to the CRP during the 1972 Presidential election. In the aftermath of that investigation, the SEC received a copy of a report by its external auditors detailing how Northrop had, for many years, been paying off governments all over the world. But Northrop successfully convinced the Department of State to intervene on its behalf, and the SEC agreed not to investigate or publish any section of the report mentioning the overseas payments. Revealing those facts, the State Department explained, risked too much diplomatic embarrassment to the United States.[31]

It is no surprise, then, that United Brands' team of lawyers tried making a similar diplomatic plea to Sporkin. For years, mostly under Eli Black's tenure, the company had worked diligently to distance itself from the legacy of United Fruit's colonialist past and transform the image of the company in Latin America. The company built a medical center in Guatemala and provided key relief in Nicaragua after an earthquake in 1972 leveled much of the capital of Managua.[32] A *New York Times* article written at that time even sang high praise for United Brands' efforts in Honduras:

> [I]n a region filled with the incipient change of rising nationalism, where American business-men talk nervously of expropriation and where Latins accuse Americans of meddling in governmental affairs, United Fruit has won considerable acceptance and even a measure of goodwill from the more than 12,500 Hondurans on its payrolls.[33]

In fact, only a few weeks after Black's death, in its March 1975 issue, *Business Management Review* ran a feature article on United Brands with the following tagline: "The people who brought you the banana republics present the hottest game in town: social responsibility."[34] If the Honduran bribes were exposed now, United Brands claimed, the fallout would undo all of that progress. Worse, the Honduran government might use the scandal to expropriate all 28,000 acres of the company's land in the country.

Stanley Sporkin listened to United Brands' story but promised nothing. Under SEC regulations, the Commission would have to conduct an independent hearing to determine whether to keep the bribe confidential. If Northrop was any indication, however, foreign bribes were simply too politically volatile to pursue. For the time being, the matter would have to remain under wraps, and United Brands' officers would be allowed to go back to New York to try to run their company.

Turbulence at CAB

As it turned out, the SEC was not the only agency in Washington, D.C. that February to have stumbled into the world of corporate corruption abroad. Across town, William Gingery, Chief of Enforcement at the Civil Aeronautics Board (CAB), was unraveling a corporate cover-up of his own. In late February, Gingery was asked to represent CAB before the Senate Subcommittee on Administrative Practices and Procedures for a routine hearing on CAB's regulatory policies for airlines. While preparing for the hearing, Gingery uncovered something hidden in CAB's files that took him by surprise. Three documents showed that CAB had opened investigations into several airline companies regarding illegal bribes and campaign contributions, and then, for reasons Gingery could not understand, CAB mysteriously closed the investigations.

The discovery shook Gingery to his core. By all accounts, the man was a workaholic who loved his job. At thirty-four years old—just seven years out of law school—he'd already clerked for the Washington State Supreme Court, worked at a Seattle law firm, and been made chief of enforcement at CAB, the federal agency in charge of regulating all commercial aviation. Bewildered and distraught by what he'd found in the agency's files, Gingery went home on February 17 to his one-bedroom apartment in Fairfax, Virginia and began frantically typing a letter addressed to the Senate Judiciary Subcommittee. At times disjointed and rambling, the missive came to twenty pages in length and expressed Gingery's own sense of failure that he hadn't discovered the closed files earlier. Likely already wrestling with depression, the guilt overpowered Gingery, and two days later, police entered his apartment to find him lying in a pool of blood, with a self-inflicted rifle shot to the head.[35]

After his death, newspapers published parts of Gingery's letter to the Senate Judiciary Subcommittee and referred to it as a "suicide memo."[36] Unlike Black, Gingery had been forthcoming, even profuse, in giving the press a motive behind why he'd chosen to end his own life. The memorandum also successfully re-raised questions of corporate corruption in the airline industry, which, like other industries, had been implicated in the Watergate scandal.[37] But even more than awakening old suspicions, Gingery's memo hinted at something new, something *foreign*. He'd written that the political contributions were "merely symptoms of a disease involving subterranean services of money extracted by management for illicit purposes, including payments in foreign countries to nationals of these countries."[38] Suddenly, the ghost of Eli Black was no longer the only specter haunting Washington with tales of bribery and corruption in foreign lands.

Gingery's death spurred CAB to action; three weeks later, on March 12, the agency charged both Braniff Airways and American Airlines with using corporate slush funds for illegal purposes.[39] What made the CAB suit unique from other political slush-fund cases at the time was the way in which it detailed how Braniff had been making bribes overseas. In order to compete with foreign airlines in South America, Braniff had offered $749,000 worth of free and discounted trips to South American ticket agents. The company disguised the payments on its account books by improperly recording actual ticket purchases and siphoning purchase payments into a secret account.[40]

It is worth mentioning, however, that neither Gingery's death nor the Braniff suit ever made major front-page news. This is not all that surprising; the idea of bribing ticket agents was really quite tame and irrelevant to most Americans at the time, so the story quickly faded from the public eye. It is nonetheless an important marker in the FCPA story: The Braniff complaint marked an initial step in the direction of prosecuting foreign bribery. It was a bellwether of a changing mood in Washington toward illicit uses of offshore accounts, and by putting those bribes onto the legal radar, the complaint also succeeded in drawing the attention of the SEC.

Seven days after CAB filed its complaint against Braniff, Sporkin's team requested from the Department of Justice any information it might also have regarding illegal payments by Braniff or American Airlines, as well as other airlines, including Continental and Flying Tiger Line.[41] The "subterranean services" Gingery had warned of were finally beginning to see the light of day.

Gulf Oil's Hidden Millions

Since its case against George Steinbrenner and American Ship Building Company in October, Sporkin's Management Fraud Program had been bringing a steady stream of cases against companies that had failed to disclose payments they had made to Nixon's reelection campaign. There was a request for information sent to Ashland Oil in January, then suits against the Minnesota Mining and Manufacturing Company (3M) in February and Phillips Petroleum Company in early March.[42] Around the same time as the SEC learned of the Braniff Airlines case, it had also just brought one of its biggest slush-fund cases to date: a suit alleging that Gulf Oil had falsified records to hide a $10.3 million secret slush fund in the Bahamas.[43] The $10.3 million number set new records: It was by far the largest corporate political slush fund alleged to exist by any law enforcement agency since disclosures of illegal corporate campaign contributions began a few years earlier. The size of the fund even drew the attention of other governmental agencies, including the Internal Revenue Service, which soon opened its own investigations into the company for tax evasion.[44]

The Gulf Oil fund also gave Stanley Sporkin and his team a first-hand, up-close look at the underbelly of corporate bribery abroad. Previously, with the Northrop case, Sporkin had only learned of bribery abroad indirectly, through the company's auditors. But with Gulf, Sporkin got to question top officials directly and learn how the bribes worked. Sporkin eventually learned how Gulf wanted to capitalize the payments in order to avoid having to make income tax deductions in the United States. They had therefore conceived of the idea of making two secret accounts linked to a shell company in the Bahamas. The whole setup was a complicated way to bypass Gulf's outside auditors and also slip past the IRS. Sporkin later recalled this fact as "the diabolical aspect" behind these secret funds—"that they knew exactly what they were doing and that they were violating the law."[45]

But while Sporkin might have begun to understand some of the mechanics behind how these bribes worked, foreign bribery was still off limits. The SEC's complaint against Gulf was therefore mostly vague as to its foreign activities, preferring to focus instead on the $5.4 million from the fund that was "returned to the United States for political contributions and related expenses, a substantial portion of which was unlawful."[46] As an aside, the SEC noted in its complaint that the remainder of the $10.3 million "was distributed overseas in cash by Gulf and others," a little detail that went largely unnoticed by the general public and the press.[47] The SEC had given no specifics as to who handled the money abroad, what purpose it had been used for, or even whether the money had been distributed illegally. Nor did it help that Gulf, hoping to deflect attention away from itself as quickly as possible, agreed to settle the SEC suit the very same day.

Similarly, in late March, United Brands publicly filed its annual 10-K report with the SEC, intentionally leaving out any mention of its problem in Honduras. Buried deep in an audit letter accompanying the report written by the independent accounting firm PriceWaterhouse was a description of the Panama Agreement and the Honduran tax, as well as the following statement:

> Certain information has been omitted from this Annual Report on Form 10-K and is being filed separately with the Securities and Exchange Commission, together with an application to the Commission for a determination that such information be kept confidential....[48]

It was the kind of sentence that would signify almost nothing to anyone reading it outside the company. In fact, most of Wall Street focused instead on the company's disconcerting losses that year, which totaled $71.3 million.[49]

To the general public, then, the United Brands' annual report—much like the Braniff Airways suit and the SEC's complaint against Gulf Oil—gave little hint of any larger underlying problem that companies might be engaged in bribery overseas. Perhaps to the careful observer, clues were starting to appear, but no one could have predicted that in a matter of just a few more days, the whole affair would blow wide open.

Journalists Connect the Dots

On a weekend in late March, on a beach somewhere in Southern California, Stephen Sansweet, a reporter for the *Wall Street Journal*'s Los Angeles office, was enjoying a favorite pastime: flying his kite. Accompanying Sansweet was an old friend who now worked in public relations but had once been a well-established journalist in Washington, D.C. As the two watched Sansweet's kite rise higher into the sky, their conversation turned to Eli Black. Even though Sansweet wrote mostly about Hollywood and the gaming industry, he had been fascinated by Mary Bralove's article on Black's death and wondered aloud to his friend what might have driven Black to such despair.

"Well," replied the friend, "when are they going to report about the bribes?"[50] Sansweet, dumbfounded, was soon told what was already common gossip among many inside the D.C. beltway: Eli Black's death had led the SEC to uncover bribes to a high official in the Honduran government, and the company was seeking help from the State Department to keep the payments secret. "Holy shit!" Sansweet remembered thinking years later. After coming home from the beach, he rushed to contact an anonymous source he knew who lived in Washington, D.C., a lawyer friend who also had contacts with the State Department and the SEC. The story checked out: In late February, lawyers from United Brands had contacted the Department of State about the Honduran bribe and asked the Department to assist in persuading the SEC to keep the bribes a secret.[51]

Sansweet next called Mary Bralove in New York, and very quickly, the puzzle pieces began to fit together. Bralove had recently read PriceWaterhouse's letter accompanying United Brands' annual report and questioned what the company might be hiding. Together, Sansweet and Bralove reached out to Kenneth Bacon, one of the *Journal*'s most respected reporters in Washington, D.C. Bacon had people he could talk to deep within the Department of Defense and elsewhere in government, and was able, once more, to confirm the story. All three journalists had pieced together enough to know that the bribe was for $1.25 million and had been made to one of Honduras' highest governmental officials, including possibly President and General Oswaldo López Arellano himself. They also knew that it had been paid in order to lower the banana tax. The reporters presented their findings to the *Journal*'s editors, who immediately realized the story's probable significance: This was something new, something foreign, something bound to make huge headlines. They also knew that very soon, they would have to confront United Brands with what they had.

*

Back in New York, United Brands' seventeen-member board of directors was still struggling to appoint Black's successor. The situation was quickly becoming dire, with the company teetering on the edge of managerial collapse. At least one board member who tried to act as a peacemaker had quit out of frustration. Another reportedly had ripped a telephone out of the wall when a third director had called into a meeting unannounced to cast a vote.[52] Amid the tumult, the company was wholly unprepared to answer any calls from the *Wall Street Journal*, let alone any concerning Honduras.

Largely leaderless and desperate for help, the company stonewalled the *Journal*'s questions and once more reached out to the State Department. For weeks, the Department had quietly been agreeing with United Brands' lawyers: Allowing the bribes to go public *would* be too diplomatically damaging. But the Department had yet to actually go on record with the SEC on the company's behalf.[53] Now, the fact that the *Wall Street Journal* knew about the bribes changed everything; once the story went public, the entire reputation of the United States government in Latin America would be jeopardized. In a wire sent from Secretary of State Henry Kissinger to several State Department embassies in Latin America on March 31, Kissinger wrote:

> I have reason to believe a story may break here within the next few days regarding secret seven-figure payments made or promised by United Brands to Honduran Chief of State General López . . . I also have reason to believe the story is substantially correct . . .[54]

The telegram went on to warn the ambassadors that they might soon be forced to explain the U.S. government's position to foreign counterparts and that they should stress that the U.S. position was "that we did not know of the payment and that we condemn such behavior utterly."[55] American Ambassador Phillip V. Sanchez, dismayed by the news, responded to Kissinger the following day that the story, if published, would be played locally as yet another example of American "Dollar Diplomacy." "We are braced and will try to pick up the pieces here," were the Ambassador's last words.[56]

A few days later, on April 3, Assistant Secretary of State William Rogers wrote United Brands' counsel to make the separation official. Rogers told United Brands that the State Department would not only refuse to help the company conceal the payment, but that it would openly condemn such bribes as against the interests of the United States.[57] It was clear now, under the weight of public scrutiny, that United Brands was toxic and that no government agency would defend it.

In Washington, the SEC, equally aware of the *Journal's* imminent story, began to view the situation with more urgency. Sporkin instructed his lawyers to start drafting a complaint against United Brands for violating the 1934 Securities and Exchange Act. Although foreign bribes in and of themselves were not illegal under U.S. securities law, the Commission could charge United Brands with failing to disclose the payments to its shareholders—the same theory Sporkin had used in the Nixon CRP cases. But before bringing any formal suit, Sporkin still needed authorization from the SEC's commissioners. These five men remained conflicted as to what precedent the SEC might set in extending its jurisdiction into foreign activities.[58] "I have never seen the commission and the staff so divided over an issue," one insider at the SEC later told a reporter.[59] Regardless, the *Wall Street Journal's* scoop had turned the issue into a ticking time bomb. Eli Black and the entire United Brands-Honduras problem was about to be splashed across the headlines of every major newspaper in the country. The SEC needed to respond, and quickly.

*

On the morning of April 9, the story finally broke. In bold typeface, the *Wall Street Journal*'s front-page headline read: **"Buying Favor: United Brands Paid Bribe of $1.25 Million to Honduran Official**."[60]

Authored by Bacon, Bralove, and Sansweet, the article detailed the SEC's investigation following Eli Black's death, hinted that the bribe's recipient might have been General López, and also told of the company's efforts to keep the bribe a secret. The reporters even interviewed the president of Castle & Cooke, the parent company of United Brands' rival Standard Fruit, who called the bribe "deplorable" and promised that his company had never resorted to such behavior in conducting its business abroad.

The afternoon the story went public, the SEC filed a civil complaint against United Brands. But unlike with Gulf Oil, the SEC this time made explicit its allegations of foreign bribes.[61] In addition to the $1.25 million payment in Honduras, the SEC revealed an additional $750,000 illegal payment to a foreign government in Europe, which it had discovered from United Brands' auditors.[62] The complaint alleged that the company had not only failed to disclose material information to its shareholders, but also that it had engaged in substantive fraud under U.S. securities law. United Brands and PriceWaterhouse were forced to revise their previous investor filings in order to explicitly reference the Honduran payment, and the SEC took the further, more drastic step of freezing all trading action on United Brands' stock for five days in order to give the market enough time to digest the news.[63]

The overall result would prove a stunning blow for the company. Federal prosecutors in New York soon opened their own investigation to determine whether United Brands could be charged criminally,[64] and on the New York Stock Exchange, the price of United Brands' shares declined by 21 percent over the course of the next thirty days.[65] It did not go unnoticed that the SEC brought a suit against United Brands only after the *Wall Street Journal* had already made the story public; at least one columnist at the *Boston Globe* openly questioned how the SEC could have allowed investors to trade close to 900,000 shares of United Brands stock in March while clearly already aware of the payments.[66]

But nowhere did the news of United Brands' bribe have a bigger impact than in Honduras.

El Pulpo

On the morning the *Wall Street Journal* story went public, the Honduran government made its own broadcast on national radio, announcing that news reports in the United States claimed United Brands had bribed a high-ranking official in the Honduran government. By the afternoon, local daily newspapers were running front-page headlines asking if General López had been the recipient. By that evening, Honduras' council of ministers had organized a seven-member independent commission to investigate the allegations.[67]

The scandal could not have come at a worse time for General López, who had assumed control of the country in 1972 but had recently begun to see his power wane. In late December 1974, a cadre of young, left-leaning lieutenant colonels began demanding changes in the government. Seeking radical agrarian reform, the young colonels viewed López as too conservative to implement the group's goals, and they began to execute a series of political maneuvers to oust older colonels from all key troop commands. By the end of March, a week before the *Wall Street Journal* published its story, López had been forced to step down as commander in chief of the armed forces, although he would be allowed to maintain his title as Head of State.[68]

So, in the immediate aftermath of the United Brands announcement, López was left clinging to his post and vehemently defending his innocence. Honduras's attorney general even announced that the government was prepared to sue the *Journal* for making false accusations against it.[69] Meanwhile, student groups and labor unions marched in the streets demanding that the government nationalize United Brands' properties. Inside the Honduras Maya Hotel in Tegucigalpa, Stephen Sansweet, who had been sent by the *Journal* to continue reporting on the United Brands story, was told to return home.

General López, for his part, tried to project the appearance of control. One *New York Times* reporter who asked a López aide if speculation about the general might further weaken his standing with the army was told defensively, "everything's normal here. There's no danger of anything."[70] In the end, though, López's fate would be tied to the findings of the independent commission created by Honduras' council of ministers, which required all top members of the Honduran government to grant the commission authority to investigate their foreign bank accounts. General López's refusal to cooperate provided all the justification needed for the army's younger soldiers to take matters into their own hands.[71]

On April 22, nine hours after the commission announced that López had refused to cooperate, the army's supreme council ordered "Operation Honesty" to depose him.[72] By 10:00 a.m., Honduran radio had announced that the transition had been bloodless and that Colonel Juan Alberto Melgar Castro was the new chief of state. López was allowed to remain at his country home seven miles outside of the capital city but was prohibited from leaving the country.[73]

*

The toppling of General López in Honduras would provide a stunning counterweight to the defenestration of Eli Black: Two men, exactly the same in age, entangled in a single bribe. But even the high drama provided by the Honduran coup failed to provide closure to the larger

United Brands scandal. Instead, it only prompted further questions into the company's activities in other parts of Latin America.

News agencies soon reported that United Brands might also have been paying bribes in Costa Rica and Panama, causing Costa Rican President Daniel Oduber Quirós to threaten to ban all United Brands operations in the country permanently unless the company publicly came forward with the identity of the recipients of the bribe.[74] Meanwhile, the *Wall Street Journal* reported that United Brands' $750,000 bribe in Europe—first mentioned in the SEC complaint—had been paid to someone inside the Italian government, setting off an internal crisis of confidence in that country as well.[75] Despite all efforts, the United Brands scandal just would not go away.

In "La United Fruit Co.," Chilean poet Pablo Neruda wrote of a company that "attracted the dictatorship of flies." The United Brands scandal had seemingly reawakened the mythical United Fruit of old, which had so often been referred to derisively by locals in Latin America simply as "El Pulpo"—the octopus. How many more governments were ensnared within the tight grip of El Pulpo's far-reaching tentacles was still unknown.

The Road to Reform

Back home, the United Brands scandal was sending shockwaves throughout the U.S. government. A day after the *Wall Street Journal* published its story, Senator Frank Church, a Democrat from Idaho and Chairman of the

Senate Subcommittee on Multinational Corporations, announced that his staff was exploring whether to hold closed-door sessions with officials from United Brands to study the problem of "questionable foreign payments."[76] The Subcommittee also announced that it hoped to interrogate officials from Gulf Oil, whose offshore Bahamas account now appeared more ill-boding than when first discovered by the SEC in early March.[77] On April 18, Senator Church sent a letter to SEC Chairman Ray Garrett asking that his congressional staff be granted full access to any information the Commission had regarding United Brands and Gulf Oil.[78] Four days later, the Watergate Special Prosecution Office, which had closed its investigation of Gulf Oil in late 1973, announced that it too would reopen its investigation of the company.[79]

At the SEC, the United Brands case seemed to have cleared a path for Sporkin and his team to bring other cases involving bribery in foreign lands. On April 16, the Commission at last brought its suit against Northrop Corporation regarding the company's offshore account.[80] And while the SEC upheld its earlier promise to the State Department not to reveal the countries where Northrop had paid bribes nor to make public the Ernst & Ernst report detailing those bribes, it could not resist naming the foreign consultant Northrop had used in Paris to launder its money, nor publishing the report's table of contents, which tantalized reporters with such headings as "Special Payment to Iranian Attorney" and "Unusual Payments to Third Parties."[81] Together with the fact that Northrop's settlement statement admitted that the company was studying its payments and sales commissions to foreign agents, most observers, including the *New York Times*, realized "that Northrop, like United Brands, against which the SEC filed a suit last week, might be accused of illegal or unethical actions in foreign countries." [82]

And so it was that between United Brands, Braniff Airways, Gulf Oil, and Northrop, the American public was finally being made to take stock of a new chapter in the saga of corporate political scandals: bribery beyond America's borders. "Investigations by the Securities and Exchange Commission into corporate political slush funds have uncovered another area of possible widespread misuse of corporate funds—payoffs to foreign government officials to secure sales or favorable business treatment abroad," announced syndicated reporter Jack Egan in the *Los Angeles Times*.[83] In the spring of 1975, within the span of just a few weeks following the death of Eli Black, the narrative regarding illegal corporate campaign contributions had shifted dramatically from bribery at home to bribery on a global scale.

That shift continued over the course of the next several months and years, during which time revelations about the number of companies that had offered bribes and the number of foreign officials who had accepted them would both mushroom to dizzying proportions. Scandal begat more scandal. Investigations into Northrop by Congress unearthed even bigger bribes made by Northrop's rival, Lockheed Corporation. Revelations about United Brands in Italy prompted investigations into corrupt payments made there by oil giants Gulf Oil, Exxon, and Mobil. Even Castle & Cooke, United Brands' rival that was quoted in the *Wall Street Journal* deriding their behavior as "deplorable," would eventually disclose that it, too, had paid hundreds of thousands of dollars in bribes to government officials throughout Latin America.[84]

By the end of the summer, governments in Bolivia, Italy, Germany, Korea, and Saudi Arabia had all been entangled in accusations of accepting major bribes from U.S. corporations. Within a year, that list also included serious allegations involving the governments of the Netherlands, Sweden, Indonesia, the Philippines, and Japan, leading to embarrassing scandals for heads of government and royal families across Europe, the Middle East, and Asia.

Gingery was right: Corporate corruption was like a disease, and it had spread from the halls of the White House to the doorstep of every presidential palace in the world. In response, Congress would conduct over fifty days of public hearings pertaining to foreign bribery and introduce more than two dozen separate pieces of legislation, culminating eventually in the passage of the Foreign Corrupt Practices Act in December 1977. Those unsavory foreign agents who for decades had lived in obscurity, quietly greasing palms for corporate benefactors, would finally be drawn into the light of day. Agreements made halfway across the world that had once been confined to the privacy of corporate boardrooms and covered up by sophisticated accounting tricks were now, at long last, open to public scrutiny. In one single leap, America's moment of reckoning with foreign corrupt practices had begun.

CHAPTER TWO

Rise of the Antibribery Ethic

> Legislation unquestionably generates legislation. Every statute may be said to have a long lineage of statutes behind it ... once begin the dance of legislation, and you must struggle through its mazes as best you can to its breathless end,—if any end there be.
>
> Woodrow Wilson, *Congressional Government* (1885)

Curiously, the dramatic events surrounding the death of Eli Black and the true origins of the Foreign Corrupt Practices Act seem to be largely lost to history. The few contemporary books addressing the statute insist its origins are found squarely in the Watergate era when the SEC "discovered" foreign bribery in its investigations and that Congress first sought to outlaw overseas corruption as a reaction purely to that scandal. It's generally assumed that the U.S. government felt compelled to criminalize the practice out of a sense of post-Watergate morality.[85] One academic writing on the law's origins in 2013, for example, conjectures that "an enduring effect of Watergate on American political life has been a tendency to overreact to corruption scandals by introducing increasingly strict anticorruption laws."[86]

The reality is that the FCPA arrived at the tail end of decades-long anticorruption reform efforts in America, and like most laws, it is steeped in U.S. legal tradition. Public concerns about bribery date as far back as the drafting of the Constitution itself, and worries about politicians abusing their powers for personal gain are well documented throughout the 1800s.[87] Precipitous economic growth in the latter half of the nineteenth century drew the public's attention to the particularly corrupting role of modern corporations, and backlash against corporate corruption gave birth to a powerful anticorruption ethic in America that grew over the course of the first half of the twentieth century, peaking sometime around the late 1970s. Understanding why Americans cared about corporate corruption overseas at that time, then, first requires an understanding of how they came to view corporate corruption here at home.

That story begins with the presidential election of 1904.

An Ethic Born
The Progressive Awakening (1904–1921)

By all outward appearances, the outcome of the race between Republican candidate Theodore Roosevelt and Democratic candidate Alton B. Parker was a foregone conclusion. Early polling put Roosevelt, a popular incumbent who had stepped into the presidency following the assassination of President William McKinley, well ahead of Parker. But troubles for Roosevelt began in early February when Joseph Pulitzer, wealthy owner of the newspaper the *New York World*, published a series of articles accusing Roosevelt of corruption. Pulitzer decried what he called "the great moral issue of the campaign"—whether the presidency could "be bought for Mr. Roosevelt by the great corporations and special interests."[88]

At issue was Roosevelt's appointment of George Cortelyou as his campaign manager. Cortelyou had been Roosevelt's Secretary of Commerce and Labor during his first term; during that time, the regulation of large corporations was among Roosevelt's top initiatives. In fact, Cortelyou had been Roosevelt's primary appointee tasked with breaking up the large corporations and trusts engaging in anticompetitive behaviors. Now, as his campaign manager, it appeared as if his only qualification was that he was well placed to extort large contributions from those very same corporations that were being investigated. The appointment "has all the appearance of deliberate preparation for partisan blackmail," challenged Pulitzer in an open letter to the president, to which the *New York Times* responded, denouncing Cortelyou's appointment as "a national disgrace" and the Republican party as that of special interests.[89]

The danger presented by industrial capitalism and the wealthy elite was an idea that would animate activists throughout the Progressive Era, the period beginning around the turn of the twentieth century. Popular intellectuals, writers, and policymakers of the day sought to apply modernizing principles to fix what many decried as a broken political and social system that had grown out of the excesses of America's Gilded Age. Reining in corporate corruption became a central theme, first presented in the election of 1896 by populist candidate William Jennings Bryan and newspaper magnate William Randolph Hearst, and subsequently explored by journalists like Pulitzer, Lincoln Steffens, Charles E. Russell, and Ray Stannard Baker—soon to be termed "muckrakers"—who exposed under-the-table dealings across a wide range of industries.[90] Progressive reforms were not limited to regulating business either; academics in the newly created field of political science inspired by European forms of government advocated overhauling American electoral laws more generally, including proposals that would allow for the direct election of senators, the introduction of referenda and ballot initiatives, and the use of primary elections. These democratizing ideas gained traction alongside popular movements such as women's suffrage to offer a completely reimagined view of what democracy in America might look like.

As president, Roosevelt had been sympathetic to many of these ideas, indeed promising to break up large monopolies and loosen their stranglehold on the levers of government power. With "Cortelyouism"—a *mot du jour* that briefly entered American popular vocabulary—he now found himself on the wrong side of the issue, with the claim not merely that he was being influenced by corporate interests, but that he'd been bought by them entirely. Alton Parker, Roosevelt's opponent and a well-respected federal judge, seized upon the topic, warning in a speech delivered outside his home in upstate New York of "a government whose officers are practically chosen by a handful of corporate managers."[91]

Roosevelt ultimately survived the accusations, winning the election by a solid margin several months later. But a shadow of doubt had been cast, only to be elongated the following year when Charles Evans Hughes, future presidential candidate and Chief Justice of the U.S. Supreme Court, was commissioned by the New York State legislature to investigate the allegations. Hughes' final report proved that Pulitzer's suspicions had been largely correct. The New York Life Insurance Company, one of the corporations previously under investigation for antitrust violations, had donated $48,000 to the Republican National Committee, a substantial sum for any political donation, let alone one made by a corporate entity. That amount was soon eclipsed, however, when it emerged that Standard Oil, which Roosevelt had personally sought to break up, had given his campaign a stunning $125,000 (roughly $4.5 million today).[92]

Eager to regain public credibility, Roosevelt vowed to make combating corporate influence a central theme of his 1906 State of the Union address and his "Square Deal" with the American people. Roosevelt stressed that legislation should be introduced immediately to prohibit all forms of corporate campaign contributions:

> I again recommend a law prohibiting all corporations from contributing to the campaign expenses of any party ... Let individuals contribute as they desire; but let us prohibit in effective fashion all corporations from making contributions for any political purpose, directly or indirectly.[93]

A year later, Congress answered the call by passing the Tillman Act, rendering it "unlawful for any national bank, or any corporation organized by authority of any laws of Congress, to make a money contribution in connection with any election to any political office."[94] Named after its main sponsor, Senator Benjamin "Pitchfork" Tillman of South Carolina, the law ultimately proved more bark than bite, as the $5,000 penalty was too small to serve as a proper deterrent and the law's wording was rife with loopholes. While the statute prohibited corporations from making a "money contribution in connection with any election" to politicians, companies were still permitted to make noncash payments, such as stock transfers. Others picked apart the phrase "in connection with any election," arguing that the statute did not cover payments *after* elections. Either way, individual officers and directors could still make personal contributions to candidates of their choosing, often using corporate coffers to reimburse themselves afterward.

Yet Roosevelt didn't stop there; in fact, the issue of corporate corruption hardened into a lifelong mission for him.

After leaving office, he regularly championed the cause, including during a 1910 visit to Osawatomie, Kansas, where he delivered his "New Nationalism" speech and declared emphatically that "[t]here can be no effective control of corporations while their political activity remains. To put an end to it will be neither a short nor an easy task, but it can be done...."[95]

Congress once more answered the call, passing the Federal Corrupt Practices Act later that year.[96] The statute's name was borrowed from the 1883 British "Corrupt-Practices Act," which itself followed on the heels of one of the most expensive British parliamentary elections in history to that point. Like its predecessor, which increased penalties for bribing voters and limited the amount candidates could spend on campaigns, the American version imposed spending limits on candidates and required that contributions to national elections be publicly reported.[97] In 1911, Congress extended the law to apply to national primaries as well.

Yet in actual practice, the Federal Corrupt Practices Act, like the Tillman Act before it, proved difficult to implement. With both political parties now fully reliant on corporate donations to help fund their campaigns and Congress left in charge of investigations, the Federal Corrupt Practices Act had left the foxes to guard the hen house.

Even so, progressive reforms carried into the next decade, albeit with a different emphasis under the administration of Woodrow Wilson. As the first U.S. president ever to visit Europe while in office, Wilson sought to replicate in the

U.S. the British model of increased bureaucratization and transparency in government. As his attention increasingly turned toward a looming war overseas, however, Wilson would be forced to abandon many of those reform efforts.[98] Then, in 1921, the reform movement was dealt another blow; the Supreme Court ruled in the case of *Newberry v. United States* that Congress did not have authority to restrict campaign finance contributions in primary elections. That decision effectively bookended early-twentieth century anticorruption measures and foreshadowed the laissez-faire economics that would soon follow.[99]

Nonetheless, the passage of the Tillman Act and the Federal Corrupt Practices Act were important milestones, and when viewed together, amounted to a burgeoning legal norm. Americans recognized that for democracy to function, they needed government to step in and limit the influence of money in politics.[100] Much of this was thanks to a news media that exposed corporate corruption, galvanized public sentiment, and pressured Congress to do something about it. As history would show, this remained a winning formula for fighting corruption until passage of the FCPA some fifty years later.

Pressure Builds Under Teapot Dome (1921–1929)

In the summer of 1920, a heat wave descended on Chicago just as the city was to host nearly 900 delegates for the Republican National Convention in the Chicago Coliseum. But those long summer days passed without a decision from the delegates on a nominee for the upcoming presidential election; that is, until the party elite took it upon themselves to break the deadlock inside a few smoke-filled rooms of the nearby Blackstone Hotel. The only certainty was that after eight long years of the Wilson presidency and a World War, the party needed a candidate who promised to restore a sense of peace and national prosperity. So it was that among the dozen or so candidates entered in the race, Warren Harding, a previously unremarkable senator from Ohio, emerged the nominee.

Warren's greatest attributes were apparently that he "looked like a president" and that his campaign slogan promised a "return to normalcy." Once he became the nominee, Harding's first order of business was to make clear that he would be a friend to business, committing to deregulate industry if elected. His campaign soon attracted a long line of corporate suitors, and over the course of the next several months, the RNC fund expanded to a sizable $8.1 million (equal to roughly $127 million today).[101] The Federal Corrupt Practices Act, by then long abandoned, proved no obstacle, and Harding's impressive financial advantage permitted him to coast to victory come November.

A mere three months after taking office, however, Harding's corporate skeletons began rattling from the closet. Harding's troubles began in mid-April, when a story by the *Wall Street Journal* reported that the Department of the Interior had secretly leased land containing Navy petroleum reserves to private corporations. Harry Slattery, a conservationist and Washington lawyer, had learned of the lease from a source inside the Interior Department and then leaked the information to the newspaper.[102] The land was in a remote area of Wyoming known as "Teapot Dome" that had originally been set aside by Presidents Taft and Roosevelt to provide the U.S. Navy with wartime fuel in case of an emergency. The scandal was that they were now apparently being secretly sold away to the Sinclair Oil Corporation for private profit.[103] A few days later, the Department of the Interior transferred use of two more Navy petroleum lands—in Elk Hills and Buena Vista, California—to the Pan American Petroleum Corporation, another big oil company.

Wyoming Senator John Kendrick and the eminent progressive Wisconsin Senator Robert La Follette soon called for a full-scale investigation of the leases. Due to logistical hurdles, however, the hearings were delayed for another two years. By then, President Harding had died in office, and Teapot Dome, which appeared to essentially be a complicated federal land-rights deal gone awry, held little public interest. The hearings were handed down to the unknown Senate Public Lands and Survey Committee to be investigated by the equally unknown Montana Senator, Thomas Walsh.

Despite the circumstances, Walsh did an admirable job of bringing the facts of the case to life. In exchange for substantial campaign contributions, Harding was shown to have promised several oil companies drilling rights to federal land, which his Interior Secretary, former New Mexico Senator Albert Fall, secured from the Secretary of the Navy, Edwin Denby. Harry Sinclair, founder of

Edward Doheny, owner of Pan American Petroleum, right, testifies before a 1924 Senate committee investigating the Teapot oil leases.

Credit: Library of Congress via Wikimedia Commons

Sinclair Oil, paid Fall several hundred thousand dollars in the form of Liberty bonds—issued in support of the U.S. effort in World War I—as well as personal gifts and favors in exchange for the leasing rights to drill in both Teapot Dome and Wyoming's Salt Creek Oil Field. Edward Doheny, owner of Pan American Petroleum, similarly promised personal favors to Fall, including upward of $100,000 toward renovations to Fall's ranch in New Mexico in exchange for the right to drill in the California reserves in Elk Hills and Buena Vista.

That the Teapot Dome affair became a true national fiasco, however, had less to do with the bribes themselves as the way in which they had been masked and the public spectacle by which they were revealed. First, Fall was repeatedly caught lying before the Walsh Committee about who had given him the funds to purchase additional land in New Mexico.[104] Then, in the middle of the investigation, Archibald "Archie" Roosevelt, decorated war veteran and son of President Theodore Roosevelt, suddenly quit his job at Sinclair Oil to make a surprise visit before the Walsh Committee to testify against his former employer. Archie Roosevelt revealed that Sinclair had paid thousands of dollars to Fall to gain access to the reserves in Wyoming and that days earlier, he'd even sought Archie's assistance in fleeing to Paris. One reporter wrote at the time that Roosevelt's testimony turned the investigation "almost overnight [into] a throbbing drama of politics, high finance, and intrigue."[105]

The timing of the revelations was also important, and as the country readied itself for the election of 1924, Teapot Dome became an indictment of not only Fall, but the entire previous administration. Other investigations had shown that Harding's cabinet had been accepting bribes left and right: An inquiry into Attorney General Harry Daugherty found that he'd taken money to drop cases against alcohol sellers during prohibition, and Harding's former head of the Veterans Bureau, Charles Forbes, was found to have solicited over $200,000 in exchange for improperly awarding government contracts.[106]

Buoyed by this steady drip of misconduct, the Teapot Dome scandal lasted a full decade, spanning three administrations, multiple Senate committees, a special executive branch investigative team, and several Supreme Court decisions. The U.S. government eventually succeeded in canceling both leases to Sinclair Oil and Pan American Petroleum, and all three major government actors—Denby, Dougherty, and Forbes—were eventually forced to leave public office in disgrace. Fall, however, would take the lion's share of the punishment with a $100,000 fine and a one-year prison sentence—marking the first time in American history that a member of the president's cabinet had ever gone to prison for his actions while in office.

Teapot Dome also gave the American public its first glimpse into how domestic companies engaged in corruption abroad. By the turn of the century, oil companies in North America had begun exploring farther afield, and, as the hearings revealed, Sinclair Oil applied largely the same playbook used in Teapot Dome to acquire land in Russia, Iran, Angola, and many countries across Latin America. One witness at the time noted that Sinclair's technique in each country was simply to "approach the government of the country with the flyleaf of his checkbook showing."[107] The Walsh Committee also revealed that Albert Fall, while Chairman of the Foreign Relations Subcommittee on Mexican Affairs, manufactured anti-Mexican sentiments and had even overseen efforts to break diplomatic ties with Mexico—the first step to a more formal declaration of war—simply to protect Pan American Petroleum's extensive oil interests in the state of Tampico.[108] Bribing foreign governments was one thing, but coaxing America to war simply to suit particular private interests vaulted corporate wrongdoing to a new magnitude of malevolence.

A few years later, similar stories emerged in another set of congressional investigations that came to be known as the "Senate Munitions Inquiry." Beginning in 1934 in the specter of another looming conflict in Europe, those investigations focused on the general business practices of the American armament industry. Sir Basil Zaharoff, a knight of the British Empire, admitted before the Senate panel to paying bribes made to look like "commissions" to dozens of Balkan government officials on behalf of British arms manufacturer Vickers. There were others too, like Adolph Lissner, "the German Jew," who could be counted on to bribe officials in Argentina, or the man known simply as "Mr. Klawe" in Europe, who was suspected of paying off weapons inspectors in Poland. In China, there was the Shanghai chemical engineer "Dr. C. Y. Wang," who had been arrested and hanged on suspicion of paying bribes on behalf of the DuPont chemical company to the Chinese Army in Nanking.[109]

Soon enough, all of the big arms manufacturers—including Remington Arms, Colt, American Armament, Boeing, Douglas, and Electric Boat—admitted to paying bribes to secret agents, military generals, and political officials of foreign governments around the world, from Japan and China to Poland, Mexico, the Bahamas, and Brazil. It was said the U.S. State Department was well aware of these practices and had been turning a blind eye for years.[110] Committee leader Senator Gerald Nye of North Dakota was quick to point out how bribes contributed to destabilizing foreign governments, including countries that were once the seat of instability in Europe and the locus of the outbreak of the first World War.[111] Ultimately, however, the Senate investigation into widespread corruption in the armaments industry was unable to translate outrage into law, and several bills introduced in Congress during the 1920s seeking to criminalize both domestic and foreign forms of commercial bribery died without ever making it out of committee.[112] In the end, the goals of the Committee had more to do with peace building and regulating the arms industry than fighting corruption.

Congress nevertheless did revisit the long-abandoned Federal Corrupt Practices Act, amending the statute in 1925 in the wake of the Teapot Dome scandal. Those amendments required candidates and large political committees to report contributions of $100 or more and prohibited offers of bribes to politicians, although Congress again left itself responsible for enforcing the law's spending limits.[113] Unsurprisingly, over the span of almost seventy years, the statute was only enforced twice: first against Republican Frank Smith of Illinois in 1928 and a year later against Republican William Vare of Pennsylvania.[114]

Even so, the anticorruption ethic had proved itself remarkably resilient. What began at the turn of the century with Courtelyouism had extended into the interwar period with the Teapot Dome scandal and the Senate Munitions Inquiry. The exposure of influence peddling and overseas corruption had laid bare the threat corporations posed to both U.S. national security and foreign peace efforts. And while the laws passed to rein in this newly identified ill were plainly insufficient, they evidenced that the anticorruption movement had gained a foothold as an established legal norm, something to be honed by Congress over the next quarter-century.

An Ethic Realized
Organized Crime and Corruption (1930s–1970s)

During the New Deal, perceptions about corruption in America again changed as President Franklin Roosevelt's use of the Works Progress Administration to ferret out claims of waste in the distribution of public funds—particularly in the construction industry—meant fewer headlines involving corrupt politicians and corporations.[115] Focus shifted instead to the power newly wielded by organized labor unions, and concerns about contributions made by the United Mine Workers to President Roosevelt's 1936 reelection campaign precipitated passage of the Smith-Connally Act of 1943. Post war, the role organized labor played in local elections in cities like Chicago and New York led to passage of the Hobbs Anti-Racketeering Act in 1946 and the Taft-Hartley Act in 1947.[116] As Hollywood aptly captured in the classic movie *On the Waterfront*, corruption in the public imagination of the time was comprised primarily of mobsters, henchmen, and union bosses, not upper-crust politicians and businessmen. By the late 1950s, many in Washington had abandoned anticorruption reform as a larger policy agenda.

Anticorruption reform efforts would reemerge a few years later, however, with the appointment of Robert F. "Bobby" Kennedy as Attorney General in 1961. Though only thirty-four years old, Kennedy was no newcomer to Washington and had served on several prominent Senate investigations, including most notably as Chief Counsel to the Senate Select Committee on Improper Activities in the

Labor or Management Field—better known as the McClellan Committee. In that post he'd gone toe-to-toe with Jimmy Hoffa, the lively Teamsters Union head, and squared off against some of the biggest names in the mafia, including Vito Genovese, leader of the Genovese crime family, and Carlos Marcello, the Louisiana crime boss. Kennedy had seen the harm caused by organized crime firsthand, and at his confirmation hearing in January, he pledged that if made Attorney General, he would continue the fight.[117]

Once in office, Kennedy quickly restructured the Justice Department's Organized Crime and Racketeering Section and tripled the number of attorneys working in the Crime Section. He understood from his time on the McClellan Committee that traditional state law enforcement agencies were no longer equipped to take on modern criminal organizations and brought the FBI to work alongside the Treasury Department, the IRS, the Federal Bureau of Narcotics, and the U.S. Customs Service to jointly tackle the problem.

Yet the federal government still lacked jurisdiction in most cases to prosecute local matters, and Kennedy understood that in order to really address the problem, Congress would have to empower the Justice Department with the authority to go after the mob bosses and corrupt city officials directly. Ronald Goldfarb, an attorney who worked at the DOJ at the time, recalled the considerable opposition Kennedy initially faced, noting that "[t]here was a widespread but misguided attitude that vice was inherent in people and ought to be left alone, that the government couldn't legislate and shouldn't enforce morality, and that those who advocated doing so were overreaching moralists if not misguided hypocrites."[118] "In their hearts," law professor Craig M. Bradley wrote about the period, "most citizens at least tolerated such organized criminal activities."[119] Apart from the mostly inane allegations of match-fixing in sports or on popular TV game shows, what went on between labor unions, businesses, and local government was widely viewed as "politics as usual."

But with John F. Kennedy in the White House and a changing American electorate more hopeful for change, the young Attorney General pressed on. On May 17, 1961, just five months into his tenure, Bobby Kennedy testified before the House Judiciary Committee in support of a new criminal statute that would give federal law enforcement officials the power to go after organized crime syndicates directly, and, crucially, to prosecute any government officials involved with those criminal organizations. "As has been pointed out so often, gambling, liquor violations, narcotics, bribery and corruption of local officials and labor racketeering and extortion go hand in hand," Bobby Kennedy told the committee.[120] "When racketeers bribe local officials to secure immunity from the law," he later wrote in an editorial published in the *New York Times*, "the cost of corruption—incalculable in dollars—is borne, again, by the public."[121]

Four months later, on September 13, the president sat beside his younger brother in the Oval Office and signed into law the Interstate and Foreign Travel or Transportation in Aid of Racketeering Enterprises Act, commonly referred to as the "Travel Act." The Travel Act proved an invaluable tool for federal prosecutors in combatting organized crime and corruption. In the entire Eisenhower era, from 1953 through 1960, the U.S. government secured only 148 extortion and bribery convictions, all pursuant to the Hobbs and Taft-Hartley Acts, and all related to labor unions.[122] But within just the first six months of 1963, federal law enforcement officials had indicted 171 people on racketeering and corruption-related charges under the Travel Act alone and went on to successfully convict 160 of those within the first ten months.[123]

Towns with long-standing mafia ties and embedded corrupt politicians were gutted entirely. In the city of Newport, Kentucky, long known as a scourge for wide-open gambling and prostitution, federal prosecutors indicted council members, the sheriff, numerous policemen, and even the city mayor.[124] Political affiliation mattered little. In Gary, Indiana, federal prosecutors indicted Mayor George Chacharis, a Greek immigrant who had played an active role in John F. Kennedy's presidential nomination and had since been selected to serve as the next ambassador to Greece. Chacharis was sentenced to two years in jail after the Justice Department proved that he'd skimmed over $200,000 in city contracts.[125] Jay Goldberg, the prosecutor in charge of the Chacharis case, remembered discussing it with Bobby Kennedy after the guilty verdict: "He sat with his feet up on the desk, with drawings by his kids on the walls, and he said to me, 'You know, Jay, my brother said that if we don't stop locking up Democrats he's gonna have to put me on the Supreme Court.'"[126]

Emboldened by its victories, the DOJ even began experimenting with new legal theories. In the summer of 1963, federal prosecutors charged John Kubacki, the mayor of Reading, Pennsylvania, with extortion "under color of official right" pursuant to the Hobbs Act.[127] Until then, the statute had only been used to prosecute labor leaders; *Kubacki* was the Justice Department's first-ever application of the statute against an elected official. For the DOJ, the advantages of prosecuting under the Hobbs Act were obvious: To prove a violation under the Travel Act, prosecutors had to show that the offense actually involved travel across state lines, whereas under Hobbs, they need only show that the bribe had an *effect* on interstate commerce "in any way or degree."

The Kubacki case exemplified how far the federal government was now willing to intrude into local politics. Kubacki had grown up in Reading, a town of 100,000 about an hour's drive northwest of Philadelphia, where he'd been a star athlete at his high school and then gone on to play quarterback at Bucknell University, just two hours away. Now middle-aged, the local mayor was charged with accepting relatively minor bribes of $10,000 in cash and a grandfather clock worth $800 from two companies that had won contracts to install parking meters around the city.[128] Although prosecutors were initially able to secure a guilty verdict, the district judge reversed the jury's decision on grounds that the government had failed to show that payments to Kubacki had been made out of sufficient "duress." Kubacki, the quintessential friendly, hometown politician, was too well-liked, it seemed, to have been able to actually extort money from the corporations who'd paid him. Perhaps to the judge, the payments had been voluntary. Or perhaps Kubacki was simply too well-entrenched within the political system to be convicted. Either way, he would be brought to trial two more times on related charges of corruption, each time unsuccessfully.

Vindication for the Department of Justice came six years later in another Hobbs Act case brought against Mayor Hugh Addonizio of Newark, New Jersey. On December 17, 1969, the DOJ indicted Addonizio alongside fourteen others on charges of extorting over $1.5 million from Newark city contractors.[129] The DOJ at the time was headed by President Nixon's new Attorney General, John Mitchell. After the tumultuous summer of 1968, Nixon had entered the White House promising a tough-on-crime approach that would restore law and order to American cities. Shortly after his inauguration, he'd asked Congress to double the funding used to fight organized crime, and Mitchell, in turn, had expanded the DOJ's Organized Crime and Racketeering Section from 65 to 252 agents.[130]

After a trial lasting seven weeks, Addonizio was found guilty and sentenced to ten years in prison, marking the Justice Department's first political corruption win under the Hobbs Act.[131] Three months later, the DOJ successfully prosecuted Jersey City mayor John Kenny for extorting over $180,000 from city contractors.[132] Legal scholars would later hail *Addonizio* and *Kenny* both as key achievements in the advancement of antibribery law in America, and over the course of the next several years, the federal government would continue to use the Hobbs Act to prosecute hundreds of state officials, including a former attorney general of Alabama, an Oklahoma governor, a Chicago alderman, and a South Carolina county councilman.[133] "With *Kenny*," remarked John Noonan, Jr., a former Senior Circuit Judge for the Ninth Circuit Court of Appeals, "[t]he federal policing of state corruption had begun."[134]

In the autumn of 1970, Congress would further expand those efforts, passing the Organized Crime Control Act.[135] The law had been drafted by Senator John McClellan (the Arkansas Democrat for whom the 1950s committee tasked with uncovering corruption in organized labor was named), and the statute's key corruption provisions, known as the Racketeer Influenced and Corrupt Organizations Act (RICO), made any repeated act or threat involving bribery or extortion under state law into a federal crime.[136] Notably, RICO applied to anyone who committed the proscribed acts, regardless of whether the individual was a member of organized crime, giving federal prosecutors broad authority to go after both the giver of the bribe and its recipient. Whether it was the small-time cigarette smuggler, the private corporation, or the governor of a state, all forms of corruption were now prohibited under one federal statute.[137]

What is especially remarkable about this period is the cooperation and resolve that both political parties showed in passing anticorruption legislation. The movement that began with Bobby Kennedy nine years earlier as a campaign to combat organized crime had become a bipartisan cause célèbre to stamp out corruption in its various forms across America. Alongside RICO, Congress passed the Banks Records and Foreign Transactions Act (better known as the Bank Secrecy Act) in 1970, granting the federal government the ability to regulate the use of secret foreign bank accounts for money laundering and other illegal purposes.[138] Around the same time, the IRS launched a special program aimed at examining the international transactions of multinational corporations to detect illegal payments made through foreign affiliates.[139] Prosecutors also applied the mail fraud statute, a law dating back to 1872, in novel ways to charge former Illinois Governor and federal judge Otto Kerner, Jr. with accepting bribes. When Kerner argued on appeal that he'd committed no fraud because there was no evidence that the bribes had affected his ability to govern, the Seventh Circuit upheld the conviction, noting that the former governor had committed fraud by depriving the citizens of Illinois of the governor's "honest and faithful service."[140] The decision marked just how far the anticorruption ethic now reached across all three branches of government.

Even so, when Congress revised the Tax Code in 1973 to prohibit tax deductions for any "illegal bribe, kickback or other illegal payment," few could have imagined that the law would soon be applied to indict Vice President Spiro Agnew for failing to disclose $29,000 in kickbacks he'd received from state contractors while serving as governor of Maryland. The vice president eventually resigned after striking a deal with prosecutors to plead no contest, marking the first time a vice president had been forced to leave office under duress. Agnew's fall, of course, was only the beginning; enforcement of the antibribery ethic had yet to reach the highest echelons of the White House—President Richard Nixon himself.

Nixon and Campaign Finance (1960s–1970s)

Understanding Watergate, both as a political scandal and as an important precursor to the Foreign Corrupt Practices Act, begins with a brief review of campaign finance law. In 1952, total candidate expenditures for national, state, and local elections was an estimated $140 million. By 1972, the increased use of television advertising in campaigns meant that expenditures had tripled, running well over $400 million.[141] The $5,000 federal spending limit still applicable under the 1925 Federal Corrupt Practices Act was treated by both political parties as some archaic remnant from the medieval era.

A series of embarrassing revelations of personal cupidity by several public officials, however, pressured Congress to make at least some overtures at reform. In 1963, Robert "Bobby" Baker, former secretary to the Senate Democratic Majority and close associate of President Lyndon Johnson, was convicted on charges of tax evasion and defrauding the government after it was revealed that he'd funneled large corporate donations into his personal bank accounts.

Six months later, the House of Representatives began an investigation against veteran representative Adam Clayton Powell, Jr. (D-NY) regarding Powell's use of congressional funds for personal expenses that included lavish trips to beach resorts in the Caribbean. The Baker and Powell cases led Congress to form the Senate Select Committee on Ethics in July 1965 and the House Committee on Standards of Official Conduct in April 1967. Soon after, Senator Thomas J. Dodd (D-CT) became the subject of the Senate Committee's first investigation, eventually receiving a censure for using $116,000 in campaign funds as personal income. It was only the sixth time in its history that the Senate had used the power of censure to punish one of its own.

In response to these rapid-succession political scandals, President Lyndon Johnson promised to finally revise the rules on campaign contributions, calling the forty-year-old Federal Corrupt Practices Act "more loophole than law."[142] In his 1966 State of the Union Address, the president committed to introduce new legislation on campaign finance reform, and in May, Johnson presented Congress with the Presidential Election Campaign Financing Act of 1966. Johnson told Congress that the bill was intended to ensure that wealthy interests would no longer be "permitted to affect—or even appear to affect—the conduct of government through their largesse."[143] But in the middle of a midterm election year, Congress was in no rush to amend the rules governing campaign fundraising, and Johnson's law died without ever even making it out of committee.

The following year, the law was reintroduced by Senate Majority Leader Mike Mansfield (D-MT) and amended by Senator Albert Gore (D-TN), where it was sent to the Senate Finance Committee.[144] While the Committee promised to carefully consider a more comprehensive overhaul of federal election law, one newspaper aptly commented at the time that "members of Congress are notoriously reluctant to clean their own house."[145] Instead, Congress went about trying to offer a piecemeal solution, aiming its sights at smaller targets. The Federal Anti-Nepotism law, which prohibited public officials from hiring relatives into public office, was passed in 1967, and a few years later, Congress passed the Political Broadcast Act, designed to limit the amount candidates could spend on television ads. President Nixon vetoed the latter bill, claiming that it plugged "only one hole in a sieve" and did not do enough to lower overall campaign costs.[146] Many saw the veto as a shrewd political move, however, and few believed that comprehensive modernization of campaign finance law was possible.

In the end, outside public interest groups served as the needed catalyst for reform. In the summer of 1970, John W. Gardner, former Secretary of Health, Education, and Welfare in the Johnson administration, founded the non-profit organization Common Cause, a nonpartisan citizens' lobby whose goal was to force political reform on issues like rising campaign costs and corruption in government. "Campaign spending has gotten wildly out of hand" wrote Gardner in a November *New York Times* op-ed piece; "many of our public officials are being bought and paid for."[147] In January 1971, Common Cause brought the first of a series of several highly significant lawsuits to enforce America's little-used campaign-finance laws. The case was a class-action lawsuit on behalf of the group's members against both the Democratic and the Republican national committees, alleging that both parties were blatantly guilty of violating the $5,000 contribution limit under the 1925 Federal Corrupt Practices Act.[148] "It is time we found out whether the law means what it appears to say" said Gardner at the time.[149] To the surprise of many, the court granted Common Cause standing.[150]

That success fueled the group's growing popularity, and in its first eleven weeks, Common Cause attracted 20,000 new members and received up to 1,200 pieces of mail a day. In just six months, its membership swelled to over 50,000.[151] Part-businessman, part-professor, and part-motivational speaker, Gardner appeared to be more than just another empty policy wonk: Here, finally, was a man of action. His group offered concrete, nonpartisan solutions outside the traditional avenues of policy reform and galvanized a growing sense of contempt and frustration many Americans shared for politicians and the electoral process.

Then, in December 1971, Representative John Dowdy, a nineteen-year veteran of Congress from East Texas, was found guilty in federal court of taking a $25,000 bribe from a Maryland home improvement company. Dowdy was the first sitting congressman to be convicted of a felony in over fifteen years, and his conviction dovetailed with the public's growing outrage against corruption in Washington. "If this is the first sitting congressman in fifteen years to be convicted," said the chief federal prosecutor Stephen H. Sachs after the verdict was read, then "I don't think he's the first congressman in fifteen years to take a bribe."[152]

With Common Cause driving a grassroots campaign and Congress still in the throes of the Dowdy scandal, the moment for legislative action was finally at hand. As the year came to a close, both parties agreed on a more comprehensive campaign reform bill called the Federal Election Campaign Act of 1971 (FECA). The bill was approved in the Senate by a margin of 88–2 and was signed into law by Nixon shortly thereafter.[153] Like the Organized Crime Control Act of 1970, FECA had been proposed by a Democratic Congress and ratified by a Republican president. Nixon, on signing the new law, had this to say:

> The Federal Election Campaign Act of 1971 is a realistic and enforceable bill, an important step forward in an area which has been of great public concern. Because I share that concern, I am pleased to give my approval to this bill.[154]

After almost half a century of abortive efforts, FECA was the first law to fundamentally revise the structure of campaign financing. The law not only limited campaign expenditures for media advertising and tightened previous expenditure limitations, but also required all political committees to make full disclosures of contributions to the General Accounting Office, which was newly created to serve as a more independent bookkeeping arm of Congress. It was also the first time that political parties had to specifically identify contributions from corporate executives by name, address, and principal place of business.[155]

Like the effect RICO had on curbing both public and private forms of bribery, it is difficult to overstate the importance FECA has played in American electoral transparency. Almost all of FECA's early significance, however, is owed to one of its more seemingly anodyne provisions. When Congress passed the bill, it included a built-in ninety-day delay before the law would go into effect. Introduced by House Democrats, the proviso would become a key element for Republicans in the upcoming 1972 presidential election.[156]

Maurice Stans, finance chairman of the Committee to Re-Elect the President (first known as the CRP and later nicknamed "CREEP") along with Herbert Kalmbach, Nixon's personal lawyer, quickly set about approaching corporations and asking them for large donations to Nixon's campaign. Just as Teddy Roosevelt had once put Cortelyou in charge of his fundraising efforts, Stans had previously been Nixon's Secretary of Commerce and was similarly well placed to exert pressure on potential corporate donors. John Mitchell, Nixon's attorney general, stepped down from his official duties to help run CRP's efforts, and because of the ninety-day window set by FECA, much of their energy was spent on a five-and-a-half-week blitz of intense phone calls and meetings intended to raise as much money as possible between the close of the Federal Corrupt Practices Act reporting period and the effective start date of FECA on April 7, 1972. Unabashedly, Stans personally asked hundreds of business executives for $100,0000 each, promising that their identities would be kept secret so long as they contributed before the FECA cut-off date.[157] The approach worked, and in short order, corporate donations to the CRP reached a sizable $19.9 million.[158] Nixon's campaign ultimately raised and spent a then-record sum of $60 million.[159]

Public interest groups, many of which had only just formed, soon tried to intervene in the frenzy. In January 1972, Ralph Nader's Public Citizen, Inc. filed a suit alleging that the president had offered to support price increases for dairy products in exchange for contributions from various dairy producers.[160] In March, Nader, along with the National Committee for an Effective Congress, jointly filed a petition asking the SEC to force corporations to disclose their campaign contributions in the upcoming election.[161] Notably, the SEC ignored Nader's request, as the issue of illegal campaign contributions was not nearly as pressing for the Commission as it would later become. As a result, many in the CRP believed they were free under the auspices of the old Federal Corrupt Practices Act to continue to use these corporate monies however they saw fit.

It is within this context that the CRP paid five burglars on June 17 to break into the Watergate office building, headquarters of the Democratic political campaign. Their plan, to take pictures and fix a malfunctioning wiretap, was thwarted by a security guard who called the police after noticing that the lock on a basement door had been taped open. Within the hour, all five men were apprehended and driven to the D.C. police station in handcuffs. The next morning, the *Washington Post* ran a front-page story of the break-in, but had yet to make the connection between the burglary and the CRP or Nixon. The White House denied any ties to the incident and accused Democrats of intentionally sensationalizing the story in order to gain political advantage in the upcoming election. Nixon's strategy, almost from the beginning, was to make it seem as if the Watergate operation was a CIA matter, using the pretext of national security as a shield against further inquiries.

Meanwhile, the Nixon administration was still dodging questions about its campaign-finance tactics. In August 1972, James H. Duffy, counsel on the Senate Subcommittee on Privileges and Elections, gave an interview with the *Washington Post* accusing the Nixon team of violating the old 1925 Federal Corrupt Practices Act by refusing to disclose its donors prior to the April 7, 1972 date.[162] Public lobbying group Common Cause, no stranger to the Federal Corrupt Practices Act, once more brought suit to shed light on the identity of Nixon's campaign contributors. The court stayed the case until after the 1972 election (which Nixon won in a landslide over Democratic challenger George McGovern), but then later sided with Common Cause and ordered the CRP to release the names of its donors. The fallout was widespread: American Airlines, Ashland Oil, Gulf Oil, and Minnesota Mining and Manufacturing, among many others, were all found to have donated in excess of $500,000 to Nixon's 1972 campaign. The old 1925 Federal Corrupt Practices Act which had been so rarely been used in its forty-year lifespan, was now working posthumously to uncover political corruption at the highest levels of government. It would later come to light that almost a third of Nixon's campaign donations had been contributed illegally by corporations.[163]

Around the same time, in the ongoing trial of the Watergate burglars, Judge John Sirica, a conservative Republican known for his harsh sentences, voiced his growing suspicion about the whole affair.[164] Sirica admonished the prosecutors for not doing more to find out who was behind the break-in and why, for example, the burglars had been in possession of almost $6,000 in cash on the night of the affair.[165] For that matter, why was a $25,000 cashier's check earmarked for the Nixon reelection campaign tied to a Mexican bank account of one of the burglars? As it would turn out, that money was connected to an even larger campaign slush fund used to finance such other covert political activity as the break-in of the psychologist's office of Daniel Ellsberg, the whistleblower who had leaked the Pentagon Papers.

By winter of 1973, Congress had seen enough to suspect that mischief was afoot more broadly and voted unanimously to begin public hearings to investigate the Watergate break-in. In the spring, Attorney General Elliot Richardson appointed Harvard Law School professor Archibald Cox to become special Watergate prosecutor and to independently look into all abuses of power stemming from the affair.[166] One of Cox's first announcements in July 1973 was that he would create an amnesty program aimed at encouraging corporations to voluntarily come forward with information of campaign contributions made illegally during the 1972 presidential election, effectively picking up where the Common Cause lawsuit had left off.[167]

Soon, a cascade of other accusations surrounding the president came out. Nixon had used the Internal Revenue Service to harass all sorts of political enemies. He'd established a "plumbers" unit of covert ex-CIA officers to go after leaks to the media. He'd even used government funds to make improvements to his homes in Florida and California.[168] Not long after, John Dean, Nixon's former White House counsel and lynchpin to the Watergate coverup, came forward with evidence that linked the president directly to the break-in. As the Watergate coverup began to unravel, Nixon was left with fewer and fewer options, and by the time the Supreme Court ordered the release of White House tapes in the Summer of 1974 showing that the President had tried to use the CIA to hinder the FBI's investigation into the break-in, the curtain had essentially fallen on his political career. As the full House of Representatives readied itself to begin impeachment proceedings, Nixon appeared on national television on August 8 to announce his resignation.

The next day, Gerald Ford took the presidential oath of

office in the East Room of the White House and thereafter delivered a televised speech to the American public in which he declared that America's "long national nightmare" had finally come to an end. Yet the end of the Watergate saga was far from the end of the nation's corruption troubles. Anticorruption efforts, which began well before Watergate, only gained steam after Nixon's resignation. Just ten months after he left office, a California state grand jury returned an indictment against Congressman Andrew Hinshaw (R-CA) for taking bribes from an electronics manufacturer in his home state.[169] Before 1970, only ten members of Congress had ever been convicted of bribery, but between 1970 and 1979, seventeen members of Congress would be charged with bribery or with violating campaign finance laws, and eleven would go on to be convicted.[170] Others were charged with tax evasion, mail fraud, and similar financial crimes.[171] In those nine years, a total of 634 federal public officials were convicted on corruption-related charges.[172]

State and local officials fared even worse. By mid-decade, over 300 state officials were being prosecuted annually under the Hobbs Act alone.[173] Under RICO, forty-three mayors, forty-four state judges, sixty state legislators, and 260 sheriffs or local police officers were federally indicted for corruption; most of them were convicted.[174] In total, over 800 state and local officials were convicted of corruption-related charges in just five years after Nixon's resignation.[175]

Corporations were also targeted, and twelve months after Nixon's resignation, the Watergate Special Prosecution

Force had already successfully prosecuted sixteen companies for making illegal campaign contributions during the 1972 election.[176] Over several filibuster attempts, Congress eventually passed significant amendments to FECA, creating both additional limitations to the amount companies could contribute to candidates and forming the Federal Election Commission to monitor and enforce all federal election finance legislation.[177]

Even the judiciary, traditionally more insulated from political currents, would be impacted by reform efforts. At the 1971 proceedings of the Judicial Conference of the United States, an annual meeting of federal judges, the American Bar Association presented for the first time ever a Code of Judicial Conduct requiring judges to report their finances and prohibiting their participation in business activities.[178] A year later, the Supreme Court issued a decision in *United States v. Brewster* that removed any constitutional immunity for members of Congress who took bribes to vote on legislative matters. When, in 1976, Senator James Buckley (R-NY) filed a lawsuit claiming that FECA's new requirements were unconstitutional, the Supreme Court again came down on the side of the antibribery advocates, upholding the law's restrictions on campaign contributions and stating that eliminating both corruption "or appearance of corruption" were legitimate goals of the federal government.[179] Fordham University law professor Zephyr Teachout would later describe *Buckley* in her book *Corruption in America* as a seminal case that "elevated corruption and gave it a designated place in our constitutional framework."[180]

The anticorruption ethic, already reified *de jure* in the courts, was by then firmly a de facto part of American popular culture—its legal codification serving only to confirm the point. There were journalist-heroes Bob Woodward and Carl Bernstein, of course, but there were also lesser-known journalists, like Pulitzer-winning James Risser, whose exposé of widespread bribery in America's grain exporting trade prompted passage of the United States Grain Standards Act of 1976.[181] The same year, actor Al Pacino was nominated for an Oscar for his portrayal of Frank Serpico, the real-life police officer who'd revealed graft and kickbacks within the New York City Police Department.[182] On television, the bestselling potboiler book *The Moneychangers* about corruption and greed in the banking industry was turned into a four-part miniseries starring Kirk Douglas.

Former Ninth Circuit Judge John Noonan once wrote that for bribery as a legal concept to exist, it must first "be alive in minds other than those of politicians."[183] In tenor, Americans in the 1970s displayed a morbid fascination with corruption; in tone, they exhibited equal determination in exorcising themselves of the evil once and for all.

An Ethic Explained
Post-Watergate Morality

What caused the widespread success of anticorruption efforts in the 1970s? After resigning from office, former Vice President Spiro Agnew offered one explanation in claiming to have been the victim of a new moral standard in the country, something he bitterly described as a "post-Watergate morality."[184] Indeed, in the fifty years since, Watergate is often remembered for having ushered in a new ethos in American politics. But as Judge Noonan correctly notes in his treatise entitled *Bribes*, Watergate was less a "moral watershed" than the antibribery ethic conforming to a "traditional pattern."[185] And as Princeton historian Julian Zelizer writes, "Nixon's scandal reverberated in the context of a preexisting coalition that was seeking to enforce new laws … [He] embodied the corruption that reformers had attacked since the 1960s."[186]

In fact, prior to Watergate, Nixon's own administration had willingly promulgated this very antibribery agenda. While Kennedy passed the Travel Act, Nixon demonstrated an even deeper commitment to the cause by signing into law both RICO and FECA, two of the most significant anticorruption and campaign finance laws of the twentieth century. RICO, in fact, had been hugely popular on both sides of the aisle, sweeping the Senate vote by a margin of 73–1. At the signing ceremony inside the Justice Department's Great Hall, President Nixon basked in the glow of television cameras and enthusiastically claimed the statute as his own. Turning to FBI Director J. Edgar Hoover and Attorney General John Mitchell, Nixon exclaimed, "Gentlemen, I give you the tools—you do the job!"[187]

There is an irony to the story of Attorney General John Mitchell that helps in explaining the antibribery ethic around the time of Watergate: Mitchell was indicted by a federal grand jury in 1974 because of his involvement in the CRP coverup, going on to serve nineteen months in prison and becoming the first and only U.S. Attorney General to be convicted and imprisoned. Before Watergate, however, Mitchell had been Nixon's right-hand man at the Department of Justice, earning the nickname "Mr. Law and Order" by *Time Magazine* because of his oversight of the government's aggressive push against crime during Nixon's first term. As head of the DOJ, he targeted corrupt politicians and mobsters, doubling the number of organized crime strike forces at the Department and indicting half the top gang bosses of the nation's two dozen largest organized crime syndicates. He was also the first to propose that RICO allow for actions to be brought against "legitimate businesses," and he successfully expanded the federal government's reach under the Hobbs Act.[188] By securing a win against Jersey City Mayor John Kenny, Mitchell accomplished what Bobby Kennedy had failed to do seven years earlier in the *Kubacki* case.

Newly appointed Republican U.S. Attorney Frederick Lacey spoke to reporters on the steps of the federal courthouse moments after successfully bringing down Kenny: "This once again shows that we're going to move against allegations of corruption no matter how powerful those under investigation are supposed to be," he told reporters.[189] Without knowing it, the young prosecutor was prophesying the very fate of the attorney general who'd just appointed him.

A Bipartisan Ethic

Mitchell's story is a reminder that despite its deeply political consequences, the anticorruption movement had become quite apolitical. In very real terms, Agnew, like Mitchell, fell victim to a legal regime of his own creation, and he was ultimately indicted under the same tax code his party had helped revise only a few years earlier. In fact, despite coining the term "post-Watergate morality," the vice president was under investigation by federal prosecutors well before most people in America had even heard the word "Watergate."[190] In 2003, George Beall, the U.S. Attorney for the District of Maryland responsible for that investigation, spoke about the case in an event marking the thirtieth anniversary of the former vice president's resignation. When asked what had led him to pursue the investigation, he responded as follows:

> My motivation was generated by others around the country who were doing similar work. In New Jersey, there was a U.S. Attorney named Herbert Stern who became a federal judge thereafter, who conducted very sweeping investigations like this. In Illinois, the U.S. Attorney uncovered high levels of corruption on the part of the governor... What I was doing was not novel. Regrettably, it was part of an ongoing process involving attempts to purge the system.[191]

Herbert Stern, who Beall mentions as a source of inspiration, had in fact been named by Lacey as his chief assistant after both were courtroom adversaries in a New Jersey corruption case involving Bechtel Corporation.[192] After winning a series of high-profile corruption cases in the late 1960s, Stern and Lacey were each rewarded by Nixon with appointments to the federal bench.

History shows us, then, that the idea of a "post-Watergate morality" is more construct than reality. It was used as a rhetorical tool by those opposed to anticorruption efforts to portray those efforts as both politically motivated and overly puritanical. In 1975, when Congress set its sights on foreign corruption, conservatives would borrow this idea to similarly argue against any further reforms. Among them was Milton Gwirtzman, the one-time speech writer for the Kennedys, who authored a *New York Times* 1975 editorial entitled "Is Bribery Defensible?" to make his point:

> In the United States, this traditional way of doing business abroad has become food for scandal because of the new climate of openness and honesty that former Vice President Agnew ruefully but accurately called in his resignation speech the 'post Watergate morality.' [Congress' desire to legislate a solution is] the export of the new morality born of the Watergate tragedy.[193]

Post-enactment, critics of the FCPA continued to portray the statute as a consequence of this moral exceptionalism.[194] By 1982, two leading lawyers would describe the law's origins this way: "Given the ... Watergate scandal ... the revelations of foreign payments were widely perceived as yet another symptom of the moral decay infecting the nation [and a] reasoned approach to the foreign payments problem was lost beneath the presumed need to eradicate these symptoms at any cost."[195] By 2000, academics writing about the FCPA's origins would say that it had resulted "from a political bandwagon effect ... [and] statutory action seemed mandatory to Congress in the grip of a post-Watergate morality."[196] Monomania regarding the singular role played by Watergate on the passage of the FCPA has approached modern day dogma and is now firmly part of the FCPA lore.[197]

Constructing Memory

One reason the post-Watergate explanation has been so popular may lie with the statute's own historiography. Scholars and FCPA practitioners, in writing about the FCPA's origins, often point exclusively to the SEC's investigation into Watergate.[198] These accounts largely ignore, however, the fact that foreign bribes discovered by Sporkin and his team would likely have been suppressed if not for the work done by the *Wall Street Journal* to expose bribes paid by United Brands. In other words, most explanations about the history of the FCPA do not account for the fact that Watergate alone can't explain the sequence of events that eventually led to the public's awareness of overseas corruption.

Another answer may lie in the way collective memories are constructed. Michael Schudson, author of the book *Watergate in American Memory: How We Remember, Forget, and Reconstruct the Past,* suggests that America's memory of the Watergate scandal has been simultaneously conventionalized and mythologized, both distorting and cementing the way we see other events surrounding it.[199] The enormity of the scandal was akin to an emotional shock of the collective conscience, Schudson argues, and like most trauma, the result is a kind of short-term memory loss. This certainly helps explain why Watergate came to eclipse RICO, the Travel Act, and all manner of preceding anticorruption reform, and why, in our collective minds, Watergate has been yoked to the FCPA as well.

Surprisingly, legal historians and other academics offer little to dispel this memory fog. As Frank Anechiarico and James B. Jacobs, two professors of criminology, write in *The Pursuit of Absolute Integrity,* "[w]e know of no systematic scholarship devoted to explaining why norms about government ethics became stricter in the 1960s and 1970s in the United States . . ."[200] The authors suggest that the war on drugs, the rise of the religious right, and diminished public confidence in government officials were all possible root causes, although no one rationale is wholly convincing.[201] Former judge and Catholic theologian John Noonan suggests that the focus on corruption during the late 1960s may have been caused by loosening sexual mores. "[A]s one type of purity regulation declined," he writes, "a compensating increase took place in insistence on the purity of governmental conduct."[202] The decade between

1963 and 1973 certainly had its share of political sex scandals, from Fanne Foxe to Chappaquiddick.[203] And as Zelizer writes, "the media fully embraced an expanded understanding of corruption that included the personal relationships of politicians."[204] By themselves, however, these too seem unable to account for such an expansive popular and political shift against corruption in both the criminal and commercial arenas.

Echoes of the Past

A more satisfying explanation of America's dramatic anticorruption transformation in the 1970s likely requires us to look further afield and also reach further back to earlier precedents in American history. In the fall of 1976, Senator Frank Church did just that when he delivered a speech before the Harvard East Asian Society after leading a series of investigative hearings on foreign corruption. The senator had just finished questioning Carl Kotchian, then second-in-command at Lockheed Corporation, about a $20 million bribe that Kotchian paid to Japan's former Prime Minister, Kakuei Tanaka. After the hearings, Kotchian was fired by Lockheed's board of directors and returned to his home in Southern California to volunteer for the Salvation Army and tend to a small alfalfa farm.[205] Although he mostly avoided the public eye, he granted one interview to the *New York Times* in which he, like Agnew, blamed his fate on a new "post-Watergate morality."[206]

But before the Harvard audience, Church saw Kotchian's fate quite differently, indicating that something far more conventional was at hand. The former Lockheed executive had "set in train the events which were to lead to . . . the most profound reconsideration in the United States of corporate morality, power and influence since the Teapot Dome scandal of the early 1920s," Church told the audience.[207] In referencing Teapot Dome, the Senator made clear that Kotchian was no harbinger of some new moral hazard in America, but merely a reminder of an existing one, no different from Sinclair Oil's Harry Sinclair or Pan American Petroleum's Edward Doheny.

Church wasn't the only one making these sorts of connections. For those living through the corruption landscape of the 1960s and 1970s, the long road to anticorruption legal reform in America remained a constant backdrop. "Talk of bribery and corruption, such as the Northrop Corporation's recent admission," wrote *Times* reporter Louis Heren in 1975, "and most Americans immediately think of Teapot Dome."[208] One witness before the Committee on Commerce in 1976 observed, "[t]he activity of firms like Lockheed and Boeing in bribing overseas officials" is "nothing new," recalling also "the old 'Merchants of War' hearings that Senator Nye held in 1934."[209] And as journalist Anthony Sampson observed in a March 1976 article, Lockheed's dealings in Europe were throwbacks to Sir Basil Zarhoff's mixture of spycraft, salesmanship, and diplomacy in Europe prior to World War I.[210] Whether it was because of warmongering in Europe or organized crime in American cities, the notion of stopping political corruption was a reformist idea that had been appearing and reappearing over the course of seventy years in American political theater.

While perhaps unmatched, then, the corruption reforms of the 1960s and 1970s were certainly not unprecedented, achieving much of their success through internal forces that gained traction over several decades. Common Cause brought to light the illegal campaign finance practices of the 1972 presidential election only through recycling the once discarded Federal Corrupt Practices Act of 1925. With each new scandal, reformers, buoyed by an active media and public opinion, laid forth the corrosive effects of business on politics, convincing the U.S. government that this wrong could—and should—be curbed through legislative action, political will, and legal enforcement. This "traditional pattern," as Noonan once described it, would become a formula for success in the passage of numerous laws addressing corruption.

"Legislation unquestionably generates legislation," wrote Woodrow Wilson in 1885, and "every statute may be said to have a long lineage of statutes behind it." Even in name, the Foreign Corrupt Practices Act owes a debt to its precursor, the Federal Corrupt Practices Act, which itself borrowed from its British ancestor, the Corrupt-Practices Act. The Tillman Act, the Hobbs Act, the Travel Act, RICO, and FECA were likewise each the regulatory offspring of a growing antibribery ethic in America. In the spring of 1975, that ethic would come into full focus as Congress set its sights on corporate corruption abroad.

CHAPTER THREE

Of Profits and Patriotism

> We no longer live in a world of nations and ideologies, Mr. Beale. The world is a college of corporations, inexorably determined by the immutable bylaws of business.
>
> Arthur Jensen, *Network* (1976)

Three months after the death of Eli Black, on a cloudy Friday morning inside the Dirksen Senate Office Building, Idaho Senator Frank Church gaveled to order the Subcommittee on Multinational Corporations' first hearing on overseas corruption. The date was May 16, 1975, and the Subcommittee was set to hear testimony from CEO and Chairman of Gulf Oil Bob R. Dorsey.

Public hearings such as this one were held in the Senate Committee on Foreign Relations room, an impressive hall with ceiling-high stone pillars and walls decorated with world maps and dark wood paneling. With seating capacity for over 100 people, the room had borne witness to the Committee's most infamous proceedings, including John Kerry's televised testimony against the Vietnam War just a few years earlier. For especially crowded hearings such as that one, journalists and TV reporters were ushered into an anteroom, and the hall's wood panels were raised to reveal a glass divider, behind which the press sat. Conversely, when a hearing was poorly attended, as this one was, the room's tall ceilings and rows of empty seats only highlighted the sparseness of the onlookers. The enormous U-shaped table on the rostrum at the front of the room normally sat nineteen senators; today, only two sat beside Church, flanked by a few of the Subcommittee's most senior staff. In the media section, Frank Vogl, a journalist for the *London Times*, noted how very few other journalists sat beside him.[211]

"What we are concerned with is not a question of private or public morality," Church began, "what concerns us here is a major issue of foreign policy of the United States." The idea that multinational companies were eroding America's foreign interests was a familiar theme for Church, but as the Subcommittee prepared to interview Dorsey, its status was less clear than ever; a draft Foreign Relations Committee report issued a few months earlier had called for termination of the Subcommittee on Multinational Corporations in order to fund a new subcommittee on foreign assistance and economic policy, to be headed by Minnesota's powerful senator and former Vice President Hubert Humphrey.[212] Three years earlier, Church had promised that his Subcommittee would reveal whether multinational corporations were hindering America's foreign policy—a daunting task and one that Humphrey argued had gone on too long with too little to show for itself. Now, just as the Subcommittee was on the cusp of something potentially great, Church felt the rug being pulled out from under him.

Had the Subcommittee's fate been in the hands of anyone else, the American public would likely never have learned the full extent of corporate corruption overseas. But the senior senator from Idaho had spent his entire career fighting—for his life, for his beliefs, and for his job. He would persist once more until a compromise was reached that allowed both Humphrey's Subcommittee and his own to continue, although just barely. Church had just one more year of funding to demonstrate his Subcommittee's worth. Everything, it seemed, now depended on the success of the bribery hearings and the testimony to be heard from Gulf Oil's CEO.

The Young Senator from Idaho

Born in Boise, Idaho, in July 1924, biographers describe Frank Church's childhood as one marked by a precocious and independent spirit. His political interests were cultivated early on in debates around the kitchen table with his more conservative father on the merits of Roosevelt's New Deal. Church leaned Democrat, but his childhood hero was the late Republican Senator William E. Borah, the venerated "Lion of Idaho." Borah had been a conspicuous figure in Washington, both because he liked to sport a ten-gallon cowboy hat and because of his antiestablishment, maverick tendencies. Growing up solidly middle class, Church, like Borah, developed early on a strong suspicion of moneyed elites.[213]

His prowess on the high school debate team led him to national contests and a college scholarship, but the war cut his studies short, and in 1942, he enlisted as a private in the Army, going on to serve as a military intelligence officer in China. His passion remained in politics, however, and in letters to his high school sweetheart (later, his wife), Church refrained from the typical romantic bromides of wartime correspondence and wrote instead about how rising economic demands would soon goad the United States to follow in Europe's missteps in Asia.[214]

After returning home, he enrolled at Harvard Law School, but excruciating back pains would lead to a midsemester transfer to Stanford University, where he hoped California's sunnier weather would ease his troubles. The birth of his first son a few months later was soon overshadowed by the discovery that he had testicular cancer, a diagnosis he was told was fatal. Following an experimental treatment that whittled his six-foot frame down to just eighty pounds, Church somehow beat the odds and was pronounced cured. "I'd had a sentence of death passed upon me," he later recalled, "a sentence that had been lifted." [215]

Marked by his early brush with mortality, Church returned to Boise to run for public office. Undeterred by early losses in several state races, he announced his unlikely candidacy in 1956 to become Idaho's next Democratic Senator to Congress. It was a bold move for someone who'd never held elected office, had almost no funds, and whose campaign manager was his high school best friend. But the gifted orator found his audience, logging thousands of

Senator Frank Church alongside Senator John McClellan and McClellan Committee Chief Counsel Bobby Kennedy in 1958. A couple of years later, Church was invited to deliver the keynote address at the 1960 Democratic National Convention.

Credit: Special Collections and Archives, Albertsons Library, Boise State University

miles crisscrossing Idaho to deliver fiery speeches in which he railed against the "back scratching for big business" that he said epitomized Idaho's Republican party—a tactic he'd borrowed from his old political idol, Borah.[216]

Church's hard work soon paid off: He defeated former Senator Glen Taylor in the Democratic primary and then went on to easily defeat Republican incumbent Herman Welker in the general election by a margin of nearly three to two. Quite suddenly, the man who few thought had any chance of doing either both celebrated his thirty-second birthday and became Idaho's newest senator-elect within the same year.

In fact, Church had become the youngest senator in the 85th Congress and the fifth-youngest in the Senate's history. He was so often mistaken by Capitol guards for a page boy during his first term that it's said he was forced to give up wearing navy-blue suits for brown ones.[217] Yet despite his youthful appearance, Democrats saw in their junior colleague a prodigious debater— someone who could be trusted to help lead important investigations.

With those talents in mind, Church was appointed early in his tenure to the McClellan Committee to work alongside Bobby Kennedy on the labor union racketeering investigations. Three years later, the silver-tongued senator from Idaho was selected to deliver the coveted keynote speech at the 1960 Democratic National Convention in Los Angeles, where Kennedy's older brother, John, was elected the party nominee. Favorable press after the Convention helped Church win reelection in November, teaching him that national exposure was key to altering his image from a traditionally conservative state's young, liberal politician to that of a more senior statesman.

Following Borah's example, Church's next step was the "Foreign Relations track."[218] Ever since his wartime stint in China, he'd harbored strong opinions about the role America should play overseas. He believed that Cold War dynamics and revolutionary ferment in much of Africa, Asia, and the Middle East made it more important than ever for the United States to show restraint in respecting the independence of nascent, postcolonial democracies. As soon as the first slot opened on the Senate's prestigious Committee on Foreign Relations, Church let it be known that he wished to fill the post. But to secure the appointment above other, more senior-ranked Democrats, Church would have to strike a bargain with the powerful Texas Senator Lyndon Johnson. In the end, Church got the seat, and Johnson got a vote in favor of a controversial amendment to the 1957 Civil Rights Act.[219]

By the time Johnson became president a few years later, however, his relationship with Church had soured. Church disagreed with Johnson about Vietnam and the executive branch's power to order troops into war without congressional consent, prompting the President to start referring to him derisively as Frank "Sunday School" Church. By decade's end, Church had moved firmly away from his party's inner circle, and his press secretary would later recall that he'd begun cultivating an image, much like Borah, as "a proud loner who kept his own counsel."[220]

Yet by the early 1970s, that reputation would start to pay dividends as the Democratic party itself began to shift leftward. Church's longtime opposition to Vietnam was suddenly viewed as an asset, and when Democratic presidential nominee George McGovern's running mate Tom Eagleton dropped out of the 1972 election after revelations that he'd undergone electroshock therapy for depression, McGovern called Church to ask if he would serve as Eagleton's replacement. Church declined, believing that McGovern, a South Dakotan, gained little by adding another Western Democrat to the ticket, but the offer was a testament to Church's ascendency within the party. After fifteen long years in Washington, the proud outsider was now, undeniably, very much an insider.

Church's Investigative Platform

Early in the spring of 1972, Church's rising stature

within the Senate led to his being named chairman of the new Subcommittee on Multinational Corporations, which was formed to investigate the impact of multinationals on U.S. foreign policy. An exposé published by syndicated journalist Jack Anderson claimed that Connecticut-based International Telephone and Telegraph Company (ITT) had conspired with the U.S. government to sabotage Chile's 1970 presidential election.[221] Chilean President Salvador Allende was the world's first democratically elected Marxist leader, and The Anderson Papers, which included portions of both State Department and internal ITT corporate memos, tapped into widely held suspicions that the United States was intervening in the affairs of left-leaning governments across Latin America. J. William Fulbright, Arkansas Senator and Chairman of the Committee on Foreign Relations, sought to quickly convene an investigative subcommittee with a sufficiently broad mandate to prevent any other congressional inquiries from stealing the spotlight.[222]

Frank Church was Fulbright's obvious choice to head the Subcommittee on Multinational Corporations. He was already experienced in leading investigations into business activities as chairman of the Subcommittee on the Western Hemisphere, and was, according to later biographers LeRoy Ashby and Rod Gramer, "ideologically and temperamentally predisposed to pursue the multinationals investigation aggressively."[223] Since his first Senate campaign in 1956, he'd viewed large corporations with studied distrust; as head of the Subcommittee, he could now merge those suspicions with his innate interest in U.S. foreign policy.

As for the Subcommittee's other members, Fulbright proposed a bipartisan assembly that included Democrats Stuart Symington of Missouri and William Spong of Virginia, as well as Republicans Clifford Case of New Jersey and John Sherman Cooper of Kentucky.[224] For Church, the composition was optimal: He had worked across the aisle with both Cooper and Case—the former on a 1970 amendment limiting expansion of the Vietnam War into southeast Asia, and the latter a few years later as cosponsor of a bill that would have ended funding for the war altogether.

Not everyone on the Foreign Relations Committee liked the configuration, however; especially Minnesota Senator and former Democratic Vice President Hubert Humphrey. Humphrey complained to Fulbright that the Subcommittee, to be credible, would need more pro-business members. To rectify that imbalance, Humphrey offered himself alongside New York Senator Jacob Javits, a well-known Rockefeller Republican.

Church welcomed neither. On a personal level, his misgivings about Humphrey dated back to his early days in the Senate when Humphrey had abandoned him on civil rights issues.[225] And, like others in the left wing of the Democratic party, Church believed that Humphrey had squandered too much goodwill as vice president courting Wall Street and turning his back against his earlier liberal principles.[226] When Humphrey was selected as the party's candidate in 1968, Church was reportedly "extremely unhappy" with the decision and noted that the vice president was a hypocrite who extolled "the politics of happiness" all the while supporting the war in Vietnam.[227] Four years later, when Church turned down McGovern's offer for the vice presidency, he hoped that whomever McGovern chose, it wouldn't be Humphrey. "It's not that I don't trust Hubert," Church told an aide at the time, "but I don't."[228] As for Javits, Church feared that the pro-business Republican would torpedo the Subcommittee's work. Not only did Javits have reservations about corporate oversight, but he would later say in reference to global corruption that "you have to have these enterprises to hurdle the stupidities and parochialism of the nationalities of the world."[229]

Be that as it may, the two senators held considerable sway in the Senate, and by late March, Fulbright had no choice but to add both to the Subcommittee's roster. With Humphrey and Javits wielding sufficient power to undermine any of the Subcommittee's findings they found disagreeable, Church understood he would be chairman in name only. To add to his troubles, Church's Republican ally, Cooper, who was aging and increasingly deaf, declared that he would not seek reelection in November and was soon replaced by Republican Senator from Illinois Charles Percy.

With Percy's addition, any lingering doubts as to the Subcommittee's anti-business stance were now firmly put to rest. Percy was a millionaire former businessman who had once worked with Harold Geneen, ITT's CEO, and would later say that he viewed Geneen as a mentor of sorts. His presence also meant that the Subcommittee had become a proving ground for some of the Senate's most ambitious members. As one aide remembered it, Percy, Church, and Humphrey all "smelled that they were heading towards the 1976 election together."[230]

Officially established in March 1972, the Subcommittee's first order of business was to select its staff, a task that fell to Pat Holt, Deputy Chief of Staff of the Foreign Relations Committee. For chief counsel, Holt chose Jerome Levinson, a New Yorker who'd once worked for the Kennedy administration's aid program in Latin America and someone Church immediately took a liking to. The son of Russian immigrants, a product of New York City's public schools, and a Harvard grad who had attended law school on full scholarship, Levinson shared Church's own personal story of pulling himself up by his bootstraps.

Next came Jack Blum, a trusted Capitol Hill staffer who'd served as an assistant counsel to the Senate Judiciary Committee and brought with him practical experience investigating corporations on antitrust matters.[231] Others soon to join included Bill Lane, Jeff Shields, and John Henry—a tight-knit group of recent Ivy League law school graduates. Occupying a nondescript office space inside an old hotel near the Capitol Building, they began gathering as much information on ITT's overseas activities as they could.

Their efforts were rewarded within a matter of weeks when a former ITT employee approached Levinson with potentially explosive new information. Anderson's articles noted that ITT solicited the CIA for help in Chile, but the tipster claimed the company's collaboration with the CIA had been far more extensive. In exchange for CIA intel about foreign contracts, ITT had apparently been planting listening devices in embassies all across Europe and the Middle East.[232] Adding to the intrigue, the Chilean embassy in Washington, D.C. had been burglarized just a few weeks earlier.[233] One wondered whether the CIA had been responsible.

Levinson and Church agreed that the Subcommittee would now have to broaden its scope to include the activities of the CIA. The proposition was no small order: Until then, no congressional body had ever publicly investigated the Agency, and as soon as the idea was proposed, the CIA began aggressively lobbying the White House to have the ITT inquiry shifted to the Senate Armed Services Committee. That committee was chaired by Washington congressman Henry "Scoop" Jackson, who, although a Democrat, was a Vietnam hawk and someone the CIA felt could be "counted on not to comment further on what he learns about CIA or ITT actions in Chile."[234] With Fulbright's backing, Church preserved his control over the investigation, although it was now abundantly clear that the CIA's involvement elevated the Subcommittee's work to a new level of political volatility.

These uncharted waters prompted both Humphrey and Javits to go back to Fulbright and demand their removal from the Subcommittee. As Levinson later recalled, they believed that the Subcommittee was going to "blow itself up."[235] Let Church dig his own political grave by poking around into CIA matters; he wasn't going to drag them down with him. To ease tensions, Church decided to wait until after the 1972 election to begin the hearings into ITT. When the senators returned in November, Spong had lost his reelection bid and was replaced with Maine's Edmund Muskie, another senior Democrat. More importantly, with both Humphrey and Javits gone, Church was back in full control of the Subcommittee. If the investigation proved successful, it would lay the groundwork for increased national recognition and possibly even a bid atop the next presidential ticket.

And so it came to be that in the spring of 1973, the hearings into ITT, alongside Church's political future, began with tales of covert operations and political meddling in Chile.

The ITT Investigation: Sabotage and Subpoenas

Since publication of The Anderson Papers a year earlier, things had gone from bad to worse for ITT. For years, the company had been engaged in tense negotiations with the Chilean government around the country's attempts to nationalize ITT's local subsidiary, Compañia de Teléfonos de Chile (Chiltelco). Anderson's revelations detailing ITT's efforts to undermine Chile's 1971 democratic runoff elections had since rendered those negotiations moot, prompting President Salvador Allende to deliver a fiery speech before the U.N. General Assembly and Chile's parliament to pass legislation immediately seizing Chiltelco.

Further complicating matters was ITT's $92.6 million

insurance claim with the U.S. Overseas Private Investment Corporation (OPIC), filed by ITT to recoup its losses from Chiltelco's government takeover. Should the Church inquiry prove that ITT had indeed meddled in Chilean affairs to prevent nationalization of its corporate assets, the federal government would deny the company's claim.

One by one, each of ITT's most senior officers was subpoenaed to come to Washington to make sense of the matter. On the second day of hearings, John McCone, former head of the CIA and one of ITT's most senior directors, testified before the Subcommittee. Short, white-haired, and soft-spoken, McCone gave the impression more of a kindly grandfather than an ex-spy. But there was little doubt as to his credentials after he explained how he'd arranged a meeting between ITT's CEO, Harold Geneen, and William Broe, the head of the CIA's clandestine operations in Latin America. The rendezvous, which took place at the Sheraton Carlton Hotel in D.C. a few months prior to the Chilean election, quickly became the central focus of the hearings.

Some ITT employees claimed that Geneen had only met Broe to pledge funds to support low-cost housing in Chile; others said that Geneen had used the meeting to promise the CIA more than $1 million to sabotage Allende's election. "I don't want you to take personal offense at what I am about to say," Church told Edward Gerrity, ITT's senior vice president for corporate relations and advertising, "but it is obvious, based upon the sworn testimony that we have received to date, that somebody is lying."[236]

After weeks of building suspense, it was finally announced that William Broe himself would testify before the Subcommittee—the first time in history an active member of the CIA was called to provide public testimony. Broe confirmed he'd met with Geneen that fateful evening at the Sheraton and that he had been offered a "substantial sum" to discretely contribute to Jorge Alessandri Rodriguez, Chile's right-wing candidate. But Broe said that he refused the money, admitting instead to having advised ITT's staff in subsequent meetings on a series of steps they themselves could take to destabilize Chile's government. His instructions were right out of a CIA playbook, including proposals that ITT organize a boycott among U.S. banks of Chilean debtors while simultaneously sowing the seeds for political unrest by funding an anti-Allende propaganda campaign on Chilean radio and television.

On the last day of hearings, dozens of television crews and newspaper reporters packed room 4221 of the Senate building to watch the final showdown between Church and Geneen. Levinson glanced at Church, who was basking in the media spotlight, and caught him fighting to hide a smile. As he would later recall, it was in that moment he realized the basic truth that a congressional hearing was at its core theatrical—more inquisition than inquiry.[237]

A former accountant, Geneen looked every bit the part, dressed in a trim suit and narrow, round-frame glasses and flanked by two lawyers and a bodyguard.[238] Over the next three hours, he proved to be a tricky witness, deftly dodging a barrage of questions. No, ITT had not tried to cause economic chaos in Chile. No, of course it had never engaged in any plot to fund a military coup. Yes, the company strongly believed in aid to developing countries. But with ITT's $92 million OPIC claim on the line, the most important question yet to be answered was what had happened in that hotel room between Geenen and Broe. Had Geneen offered the money to pay for low-income housing, as some in his company claimed, or, had he made illegal campaign contributions to Allende's opponents, as Broe had said? Both, Geneen replied: Separate offers on different occasions made for dual purposes—both to aid Chile's development and to block Allende's election.

Unfortunately for ITT, Geneen's efforts to split the difference would prove too cute by half. "Paying the insurance claim would be like paying hospital costs to a would-be burglar who, after bringing his jimmy to your window, tripped and fell on your garden hose," wrote the *Washington Post*.[239] Six days later, on April 9, OPIC officially denied ITT's claim. "The recent hearings undoubtedly played a major role in this decision," extolled Church in a press release after the announcement. "At that rate of [taxpayer] savings, we could operate the Subcommittee on Multinational Corporations for nearly 350 years!"[240]

More importantly, the ITT hearings proved truly transformative in exposing the danger multinational corporations posed to global democracy. It was "disturbingly ironic," as Church noted, that U.S. troops were dying at that very moment in Vietnam to protect democratic, free elections, while ITT, a U.S. corporation, was simultaneously working to undermine the popular vote in Chile.[241] For many, Vietnam offered a stark reminder of what was at stake. The war had changed not only America's self-perception, but also its image on the global stage; America's ability to offer a viable alternative to communism had suffered a humiliating blow, calling into question the future of democracy itself. And while Allende was a leftist and certainly no ally of the United States, it was shocking to think that a U.S. company had gone to such extreme lengths to destabilize a sovereign government.

As Senator Symington noted at the end of the ITT hearings, the entire affair reinforced suspicions that "the policies pursued by some corporations are a major contributing factor to the increasing nationalism and anti-Americanism that seem to be accelerating through this hemisphere."[242] A columnist for the *Washington Post* put it this way: "[t]he most lurid of Marxist propaganda parables against the excesses of U.S. imperialism couldn't have been plotted with more heavy handed caricature than the ITT saga in Chile."[243] Suffice it to say, the hearings cast U.S. corporations in a villainous new role, something of a rogue, nonstate actor in international relations.

Corporations Without Borders

The ITT affair reflected a U.S. Congress newly skeptical of large corporations and their influence overseas. Multinational companies in the 1970s had revenues greater than the GDP of most countries and could without constraint challenge the supremacy of the American government to dictate foreign policy. That corporations now extended across national boundaries meant not only that they were beyond the reach of the American government, but that corporate interests no longer necessarily aligned with the interests of the American public.

Of course, things hadn't always been this way. As far back as the second half of the nineteenth century, the U.S. federal government had cultivated a strong, mutually beneficial alliance with industry in promoting capitalism abroad. American expansionism included the regular use of gunboat diplomacy to clear paths for U.S. businesses to set up outposts across Latin America and Asia.[244] By 1912, when President William Howard Taft declared the promotion of U.S. commerce abroad as the country's official foreign policy, the U.S. military was already involved in pacifying political leaders and quelling dissidents in places as disparate as Cuba, Puerto Rico, the Philippines, Samoa, Hawaii, and Panama.[245]

After World War II, the promotion of U.S. capitalism in foreign arenas was viewed by the U.S. government as essential, both for rebuilding the economies of Europe and Asia and for establishing spheres of influence that could halt the spread of communism. Massive tax concessions and trade agreements including the General Agreement on Tariffs and Trade (GATT) helped to usher in an era of unprecedented global growth for U.S. corporations. Between 1950 and 1970, the book value of United States foreign direct investment ballooned sevenfold, from $11.8 to $78.1 billion.[246] And while the tactics employed were often less violent than those used in the earlier half of the century, the U.S. government did not hesitate to intervene when deemed necessary—as in 1953, when the CIA helped to remove Iran's prime minister, who stood in the way of Standard Oil, and a year later, when the Agency facilitated a coup in Guatemala on behalf of the United Fruit Company.[247]

This postwar period also saw the advent of the term "multinational corporation," a new concept used to describe the phenomenon of U.S. companies establishing overseas subsidiaries. Many began as manufacturing outposts to sell directly to foreign consumers in Europe, which offered cheaper labor and lower transportation costs as well as numerous trade protections courtesy of the newly formed European Economic Community.[248] Soon, U.S. companies began using the same formula in other parts of the world, including Australia, Canada, and much of Latin America. ITT was just one example of this new global trend: By 1969, it had 331 subsidiaries and 708 affiliates across seventy countries. Of the company's 200,000 employees in Europe, the company was proud that only 100 were American.[249]

What further distinguished these new, multinational companies was the immense concentration of wealth they had amassed. By 1970, ITT's revenue was larger than the gross national product (GNP) of Ireland.[250] Similarly, Exxon generated more revenue than Austria's GNP, and General Motors boasted sales larger than the GNP of all but fourteen countries.[251] Adding to this immense wealth was a wave of corporate transactions in the 1960s in which big corporations merged with others to form what soon became known as "conglomerates."

Again, ITT exemplified this new trend, employing leveraged buyouts to take control of more than 300 companies during the decade, including the French lighting company Claude, British electronics manufacturer Kolster-Brandes, and Germany's Standard Elektrik Lorenz. Of the nation's 1.5 million corporations in 1968, the 100 biggest industrial firms owned roughly half of all total assets.[252] By 1970, only a small handful of multinational corporations—almost all from the U.S.—represented more than half of all global trade. For the average American family, this postwar industrial growth had brought about a golden age of prosperity. As the president of General Motors famously quipped before a congressional inquiry in 1953, "what's good for General Motors is good for America."[253]

Crisis of Confidence

This rosy alliance began to fray, however, in the early 1960s. Early into his presidency, John Kennedy developed an anti-business reputation, largely because of efforts taken by his administration to erode the power of lobbyists in Washington and to control inflation by pressuring industry not to raise prices.[254] These efforts continued into the spring of 1962, when Kennedy presented a "special message to Congress" in response to numerous studies showing that a wide range of common household products were harmful to the human body. Nearly fifty years earlier, progressives had responded to sensational newspaper headlines by passing the Pure Food and Drug Act of 1906; Kennedy, responding to similarly alarming articles of the early 1960s, urged Congress to pass new laws that could protect against "misleading advertisements" as well as "unsafe or worthless drugs and other products."[255]

After Kennedy's assassination, many of these efforts stalled; that is, until a few years later when a young former law professor named Ralph Nader authored a bestselling book detailing wanton disregard for human life in the auto industry.[256] In the years to follow, Nader became a household name in America, gracing the cover of *Newsweek* magazine dressed in a knight's armor with the caption "Consumer Crusader." His growing number of followers (nicknamed "Nader's Raiders") became a powerful force in Washington, and the consumer rights movement eventually influenced the passage of an impressive array of new laws.[257] For Nader, it wasn't just that corporations posed a danger to consumers, it was that they had captured the very government agencies meant to regulate them.[258] Responding to this threat, Congress created a slew of new agencies, including the Environmental Protection Agency (EPA), the Occupational Safety and Health Administration (OSHA), and the Consumer Product Safety Commission (CPSC), aimed at reasserting government oversight over corporate social conduct.

These legislative efforts mirrored shifts in popular culture during the late 1960s in which mistrust of corporations, particularly among young Americans, became a core feature of the antiwar and counterculture movements. Popular books like *The Making of a Counter Culture* depicted America as a technocratic oligopoly, and for the first time, the percentage of graduates from elite colleges choosing to enter a career in business actually declined over the decade. A poll of young adults published in *Fortune* magazine in 1969 reported that 94 percent of students agreed that business was "too profit-blinded and not concerned with public welfare."[259]

Corporations were portrayed in this new environment not merely as indifferent to the world's problems, but as the very source of them. "When machines and computers, profit motives and property rights, are considered more important than people," cautioned Martin Luther King, Jr. in his 1967 speech "Beyond Vietnam," "the giant triplets of racism, extreme materialism, and militarism are incapable of being conquered."[260] And just as activists during the civil rights movement had once employed boycotts and sit-ins to protest companies that refused to serve black Americans, antiwar protestors in the late 60s used many of these same tactics against military contractors like Dow Chemical, which made bombs used in Vietnam.[261]

By the 1970s, worsening economic conditions turned the overseas activities of U.S. corporations into an issue that crossed social, class, and political divides. Trade deficits with countries like Germany and Japan put increased pressure on U.S. multinationals to move operations to cheaper locales in other parts of the world, often at the expense of the American worker. Between 1969 and 1971, American capital increased 31.5 percent overseas, compared to only 7.4 percent domestically.[262] When combined with a decrease in real wages—which fell eighty-two cents per hour for manufacturing workers from 1965 to 1969—the overall effect was a profound stress on the working laborer.[263] At an AFL-CIO conference in 1971, the president of the steel workers union summed up the attitude toward multinationals as one in which "patriotism or concern for the American worker seldom interferes with their philosophy of 'anything for a buck.'"[264]

Economic pressures had transformed the counterculture movement of the 1960s into a broad public preoccupation with the role of big business in American society. By the 1972 election, both Democrats and Republicans were well attuned to these shifting attitudes, with Democrats promising to close tax loopholes that "encouraged the export of American jobs" and Republicans vowing to stop the "deplorable practice" of locating plants in foreign countries "solely to take advantage of low wage rates."[265]

By 1975, disdain for multinationals had become so mainstream that one Gallup poll found that just a year after Nixon's resignation, Americans had even less confidence in U.S. corporations than in the office of the president, organized labor, Congress, or the Supreme Court.[266] A Harris poll a year later showed a steep decline in Americans expressing a "great deal of confidence" in the leadership of major corporations—from 55 percent in 1966 to just 16 percent in 1976. Another poll found that big business was the least trusted of the twenty-four groups listed, with 82 percent of Americans believing that big business had "too much power."[267]

Anti-corporate sentiment extended well beyond the domestic arena, as well. The outspoken economist and intellectual John Kenneth Galbraith argued that multinationals posed existential threats to sovereign nations the world over, particularly in the Global South. "Perhaps the greatest question of social policy in our time," Galbraith wrote in 1973, "is [whether] the emancipation of the state from the control of the corporate system is possible?"[268] These ideas became exceedingly popular in South America, where intellectuals like Raúl Prebisch and Osvaldo Sunkel, along with popular leftist politicians like Salvador Allende, compared U.S. corporations to modern-day colonialists.[269] They were similarly popular in Europe, especially in France, where Jean-Jacques Servan-Schreiber's 1967 bestselling book, *The American Challenge,* warned that Europeans would soon become backwater subcontractors for American subsidiaries.

To anyone living through this moment, anti-corporatism would have been immediately recognizable in the broader popular culture as well. Entirely new genres of music—punk and new wave—rejected corporate influences in the music business as well as the more general stultifying dreariness of the workplace world.[270] "I'm mad as hell, and I'm not going to take this anymore," howls the fictionalized character Howard Beale in the 1976 Oscar-winning film *Network*. Beale, a longtime nightly news anchor, loses his job because the show is no longer generating sufficiently high ratings. The corporate executives want less journalism, more entertainment. For a brief period, Beale's call to arms would echo in the real world across schools, college campuses, and shopping centers, where groups would gather or stick their heads out of windows to scream out that they too, were mad as hell and not going to take it anymore.[271]

In response to overwhelming public criticism, many in the business world began to openly discuss what responsibility corporations bore to address social problems. Between September 1974 and September 1975, top corporate executives from firms including IBM, Exxon, Bechtel, and Hughes Tool met to discuss the future role of business in society.[272] A "Declaration of Basic Principles" issued by the Pacific Basin Economic Council, a members-only business association, stated that investors "should fully recognize the sovereign rights and responsibilities of governments and be willing to accept reasonable obligations that are placed upon business enterprises in the national interest."[273] This would not have been controversial at the time: A study found that over 90 percent of the largest American corporations had assigned formal ownership regarding corporate social responsibility to either an officer of the corporation or to a high-level committee—a sevenfold increase from just a decade earlier.[274]

That is not to say that all in the corporate world sought cultural atonement. The 1970s also witnessed the rise of a new group of conservative thinkers. These figures would doggedly embrace neoliberal economic principles and seek to realign corporate responsibility to shareholders' profits. Notable figures included Chair of the Chase Manhattan Bank David Rockefeller, Supreme Court Justice Lewis

Powell, Harvard Business School professor Michael Jensen, and Arizona Senator Barry Goldwater.

None would be as closely associated with the ascent of neoliberal thinking, however, as Chicago economist and Nobel Prize winner Milton Friedman. Friedman offered conservatives an intellectual counterweight to Kenneth Galbraith and his band of left-leaning critics, unapologetically extolling the benefits of the free enterprise system as the cure, not the cause, of societal issues.[275] Friedman viewed corporations as unsung heroes that had brought about wondrous technologies, created jobs, expanded trade across the Iron Curtain, and contributed in countless ways to progress and prosperity throughout the world.

So when the ITT hearings occurred in March 1973, it made sense that Congress would look to investigate the role corporations played in the larger global economy. The hearings garnered outsized attention precisely because they tapped into a broader social discourse, converging multiple hot-button political issues of the day into one dramatic plot line. "[W]e found a mechanism at the birth of our Republic for resolving the contest between church and state, enabling both to flourish," Frank Church told a crowd in Houston that winter. "Our challenge today is to do as well in finding the course of reconciliation between the national interests of our countrymen as a whole, and the legitimate interests of American-owned global enterprise."[276] If not for the events to soon follow, perhaps such a compromise may indeed have been possible.

On September 11, 1973, four months after ITT's CEO

Harold Geneen's testimony before the Senate, Chile's armed forces launched a surprise military coup to overthrow the Allende government. With tanks surrounding the presidential palace, President Allende took to the radio one last time to warn of "foreign capital and imperialism" that would stop at nothing "to continue defending their profits and their privileges."[277]

Within the hour, Allende was shot dead, and over the course of the following days and weeks, Augusto Pinochet and his military junta took over, banning political parties, suspending parliament, and jailing, torturing, and murdering scores of Allende's supporters and others deemed opponents of the new regime. Chile's bloody coup shocked onlookers around the globe and, to many, chillingly warned of the dangers multinational corporations posed to sovereign democracies the world over.[278]

Peril and Opportunity for Church

In the aftermath, Church and his staff felt a renewed sense of urgency in the work being done by the Subcommittee on Multinational Corporations. Soon after, the Subcommittee quickly pivoted to another pressing issue: the oil industry and the Arab embargo. Those investigations revealed that Exxon, Mobil, Standard of California, and Texaco, in exchange for more favorable purchasing terms, had all been complicit in Saudi Arabia's administration of a boycott against Israel and the United States. During one of the coldest winters on record, with many Americans forced to ration gas, the Subcommittee's findings lay bare the assumption that the U.S. government could rely on multinationals to negotiate a supply of crude oil in the interests of the American people.

Next, the Subcommittee opened an investigation into the banking industry to determine whether financial institutions were profiting on the dollar's high inflation rates by depositing cash in European subsidiaries.[279] Those hearings would be less popular, however, primarily due to the fact that they devolved into hours-long inquiries into dry banking documents. During one particularly testy closed-door session in October 1974, Senator Percy plainly told Church that he was "really fed up with coming to these meetings" and wanted to "drop the whole thing."[280] With the midterm elections only a few weeks away, Percy and Symington simply stopped attending and told Church they had better things to do with their time.

Come November, Church himself would just barely win reelection, eking out the toughest victory of his political career to that point. He returned to Washington to learn the unpleasant news that a draft funding report orchestrated by Hubert Humphrey called for the Subcommittee's termination by year-end. Humphrey, who saw the success of the Subcommittee as a threat to his own political aspirations, had been quietly undermining Church ever since the first ITT hearings. The new budget would divert funds away from the Subcommittee on Multinational Corporations into a subcommittee chaired by Humphrey to address foreign assistance and economic policy.

To make matters worse, Senator Fulbright, Church's longtime ally on the Foreign Relations Committee, had just lost his own reelection campaign. His replacement, Democratic Senator from Alabama John Sparkman, although a tenured member of the Senate, lacked the gravitas to govern the large personalities of the Foreign Relations Committee. In the end, Sparkman agreed to continue funding Church's Subcommittee for another year only after diverting over $400,000 to fund Humphrey's new subcommittee. By December 1974, Church's staff had finally moved out of their hotel offices into a federal building across the street from the Dirksen Senate Office building, but when they reconvened in January, Church learned that he had barely enough money to pay them through the summer.[281]

With the state of affairs at Church's Subcommittee at an all-time low, good news finally came early in the spring of 1975. A few days after the *Wall Street Journal* published its article linking Eli Black to bribe payments in Honduras, SEC enforcement chief Stanley Sporkin approached the Subcommittee's Chief Counsel, Jerome Levinson, to discuss both those payments as well as others he'd discovered at Gulf Oil.[282] Church jumped at the opportunity to turn the page on the interminable banking hearings, and a few days later, the Subcommittee unanimously voted to open an investigation into Gulf Oil.

Church hoped the issue of foreign bribery would return the Subcommittee to its original purpose. If ITT had given him the opportunity to expose how a multinational corporation could influence the course of history for a single country, perhaps Gulf Oil, which appeared to have made payments to various countries around the world, would grant him the chance to reveal the parameters of the problem on a global scale.[283]

But on the first day of hearings, the mood within the Subcommittee was still, on the whole, glum. As Church looked out at the half-empty room of scattered onlookers and began to hear testimony from Gulf's Chairman and CEO, Bob Dorsey, it would have been difficult to foresee just how significant an impact that testimony would have on the trajectory of the lives of both men: Eight months later, Dorsey would be ousted from Gulf amid a flurry of corruption allegations while Church would be basking in a media bonanza and once more touted as a possible presidential contender. A year that began in peril for Church would end, in many ways, as the pinnacle of his thirty-year political career. The difference in both men's fortunes lay in bribes to foreign governments made halfway across the world.

Gulf Oil in the Hot Seat

It was barely half-past ten on the morning of May 16, 1975, and Bob Dorsey's attorney announced that his client had a prepared statement that he wished to read aloud. "Very well," Church replied. Dorsey proceeded to read his remarks for over twenty minutes, and when he finished, the small assembly of senators and reporters in the room were stunned into silence.

Dorsey had just admitted that for decades, Gulf Oil had been paying off politicians—not just here in the United

States, but all over the world. The list of foreign recipients was startling: South Korea's President Park Chung-hee, Bolivia's President René Barrientos, and numerous politicians in Italy at both the local and federal levels. "The responsibility is mine," he said. "This is a sorrowful chapter in Gulf's long and otherwise productive and constructive history of achievement."[284]

Unable to contain his excitement, Frank Church gleefully turned to Chief Counsel Jerome Levinson and whispered in his ear, "can you believe this?"[285] Only days earlier, in a closed-door session, Dorsey had politely but firmly declined to answer any of Church's questions until after Gulf's court-ordered investigation was complete. In fact, for the past three months, Gulf's officers had been stonewalling just about everyone, including the SEC, the DOJ, and the press. While admitting to an off-the-books fund containing $10.3 million in a report to its investors that April, the company claimed all of it had been "used in an effort to further a corporate purpose believed at the time to be in the best interest of the company and its shareholders."[286]

So what had caused the sudden about-face? Dorsey's statement, it turned out, was a confession two years in the making. In 1973, the Watergate special prosecutor subpoenaed Gulf's head of U.S. government relations, Claude Wild, to answer questions in a televised hearing about the company's contributions to Nixon's reelection campaign. While embarrassing for Gulf, the company was ultimately refunded the $100,000 it had made to the Nixon campaign and asked to pay only a small, $5,000 fine (the maximum penalty under the then-obsolete Federal Corrupt Practices Act). Wild, for his part, paid a $1,000 fine, and a shareholders' derivative suit against Gulf Oil alleging mismanagement of funds was later dismissed. As the months passed, the company's leadership sought to put Watergate behind them. To help signal the new, more ethical direction the company was hoping to take, a nun—fifty-seven-year-old Sister Jane Scully—was selected to fill a slot on Gulf's board of directors.

Amid these rebranding efforts, Gulf's lawyers received in late 1974 a new set of subpoenas from the SEC asking to revisit the company's accounts. Sporkin's team went on to discover Gulf's $10 million off-the-books Bahamas fund, suggesting that Gulf's political machine reached well beyond Nixon and the CRP. Sporkin subpoenaed Dorsey in March 1975 to discuss the fund in private, promising the CEO that whatever he told the SEC about the foreign payments would be held in strict confidence—that he only wished to understand how it all worked.

But Dorsey was no fool; he had been coached by his legal team and knew not to take the bait. The United Brands story had not yet gone public, and the extent to which regulatory agencies could charge American companies for paying bribes abroad was still dubious at best. Perhaps the SEC could charge Gulf with making material misrepresentations to its shareholders (as indeed it later would), but Dorsey knew he was under no obligation to reveal the identity of the fund's foreign recipients.

But then, two months later—and just two weeks before

Dorsey was set to testify before the Church Subcommittee—select portions of Dorsey's SEC transcript were somehow leaked to the *Wall Street Journal*.[287] The leak contained verbatim Dorsey's refusal to Sporkin's request that he disclose the recipients of a $4 million foreign payment, including his explanation that Gulf's investments of $700 million in an undisclosed country were at stake.[288] Before long, other news outlets had taken up the story, narrowing Gulf's foreign investments of over $700 million to somewhere in Europe or Latin America and quickly setting in motion a chain reaction for Gulf's overseas investments: Peru immediately nationalized Gulf's retail outlets, Ecuador launched criminal proceedings, and Venezuela threatened a suspension of all Gulf operations unless the company exonerated its officials within 48 hours.[289]

To this day, it remains unclear who at the SEC leaked Dorsey's transcript, although Sporkin was likely in the best position to do so. Regardless, Gulf no longer had the upper hand, and the company's attempts to suppress the scandal only increased the risk it now faced of nationalization of its overseas assets. "This callous disregard of confidentiality has placed my company in an untenable situation in almost seventy countries around the world," Dorsey bitterly remarked to the Subcommittee in his opening remarks. "In fairness to them—and in order to put an end to additional destructive speculation—I requested that the foreign phase of the ongoing investigation be accelerated. I will be completely candid with you."[290]

And so began Dorsey's full, unadulterated retelling of Gulf's overseas corruption.

*

"Gentlemen, you have heard much about the Bahamas Exploration Company," Dorsey told the Subcommittee. "I will now tell you what that is about and how it worked."

The fund had been developed by Gulf's colorful former chairman and CEO, Bill Whiteford. In the late 1950s, Gulf had wanted to expand overseas, and Whiteford worried he would need cash on hand to establish "friendly relations" with foreign governments. In 1959, a small group of Gulf's senior vice presidents began to set a plan into motion. In need of an indiscrete, offshore company to help launder the funds, they landed on the dormant Bahamas Exploration Company, a subsidiary created fifteen years earlier in hopes of discovering oil on the small island nation. On rare occasions, the company had carried out exploratory surveys, but for now its value lay in the fact that it was beyond the reach of U.S. tax law.

Officially, the Bahamas company had an account with the Royal Bank of Canada, but Gulf's treasurer opened a second, off-the-books account with the Bank of Nova Scotia in Nassau. Whenever company officials needed funds to pay off governments, they would simply transfer funds from Gulf's headquarters in Pittsburgh to the Nova Scotia account, marking the payments on the parent's books as "deferred charges." At one point, Gulf was transferring so much cash to the Bahamas that the local bank branch was borrowing U.S. dollars from a nearby casino to honor the company's withdrawals. After pulling the money out of the Nova Scotia account, the company's local accountant in the Bahamas would then place it in a safety deposit box held by the Royal Bank of Canada and immediately tear up any statements of deposits or withdrawals and flush them down a toilet. The money was then carried by hand back to the United States in a suitcase and dispersed either to Wild, for domestic contributions, or directly to Whiteford, for foreign payments. On the company's books, the payments were simply written off as part of the Bahamas company's operational expenses. When Dorsey became company president in 1965, he inherited the scheme and continued, like his predecessor, to use the Bahamas account to funnel payments to foreign officials.

Most of Dorsey's testimony involved an explanation of a series of payments he'd authorized to South Korea's Democratic Republican Party, including $1 million in 1966 and $3 million in 1970. He was quick to point out, however, that he did not think at the time that he was doing anything illegal. South Korea's economy had made vast improvements during the 1960s, and the U.S. government had been putting pressure on the Korean government to hold American-style elections. President Park complained that elections were expensive and that it was only fair that foreign investors, particularly American ones, contribute toward the democratic process. At a meeting in Seoul in 1970, Dorsey met with the financial chairman of Korea's

Democratic Republican Party, who directly asked him if he would pay $10 million toward Park's reelection bid.

Dorsey initially scoffed at the request (which, in fairness, was several times greater than the amount Gulf would make to Nixon's campaign a year later), but did eventually agree to pay a more modest sum of $3 million instead. Gulf would later reveal that for years the company had also made numerous smaller payments both to Park and various local government officials. Some, such as a $2 million joint-venture deal with Park's close friend, Jung Koi Suh, were disguised as legitimate business deals.[291] Others involved routine, low-level bribes to mayors, police and fire chiefs, and economic planning boards responsible for approving Gulf's in-country expansion. As one Gulf official put it, "the wheels of progress did not turn in Korea without a little lubrication." Gulf's Korean subsidiary had even established its own off-the-books account modeled after the Bahamas fund, known locally as the "Gray Fund." [292]

In Italy, Dorsey explained, the company established a similar account known as the *Fondo Nero*—the black fund. Between 1969 and 1972, the company disguised over $600,000 to Italy's two main political parties, the Christian Democrats and Italian Socialists, through newspaper publications owned by both parties. The bribes were labeled on Gulf's books as "newspaper journalistic services," and Gulf's country head in Italy, Nicolo Pignatelli, said that he regarded the contributions "as an act of good citizenship by Gulf and other companies in supporting the existing political system in Italy."[293] Other payments were more clearly self-interested, including one instance where the company paid local officials to place traffic lights in Rome adjacent to Gulf's retail gas stations.[294]

Dorsey finished his remarks by detailing Gulf's gifting of a Fairchild Hiller helicopter to Bolivia's General René Barrientos. A former fighter pilot, Barrientos had used the helicopter during the country's 1966 presidential election to campaign in remote parts of the country. After his win, Barrientos increasingly lost favor with Bolivia's rural population who, for good reason, questioned his ties to foreign financial interests. In April 1969, while visiting a remote country village to help improve his image, Barrientos was killed when his helicopter struck high tension wires and crashed. Even after his death, however, Gulf continued making payments to other senior Bolivian government officials friendly to Gulf's interests in the country.

From Confession to Crisis

"Mr. Dorsey, this has been a dismal story you have told," Church said as Dorsey finally finished speaking. "You know it, we know it. But I think you have done the right thing in coming before this committee and making the kind of forthright disclosure that you have made this morning."[295]

Before being dismissed, Dorsey offered the Subcommittee a final parting gift. After describing Gulf's extensive corruption, he made a direct appeal to the senators: "you can help us," he pleaded, "and many other multinational companies which are confronted with this problem, by enacting legislation which would outlaw any foreign contribution by an American company."²⁹⁶ Again, Church turned to Levinson in wonderment: Was the CEO of a major, multinational company actually asking—no, *pleading*—for Congress to pass new regulations?

Dorsey's motivations—whether he believed he was doing the right thing or had more self-interested reasons at heart—remain unclear. He had been careful in his testimony to point out that his own direct involvement in Gulf's Bahamas fund had been limited to the foreign payments, and by distancing himself from Wild's domestic payments to the Nixon campaign (which were known to be illegal) and focusing instead on the need for new legislation to cover the "gap" left by overseas payments, he positioned himself as a victim to a regrettable yet technically legal practice. He had paid the bribe because he had been forced to do it; alas, no U.S. law protected him from the extortionate demand.²⁹⁷

Asked whether he believed the practice was widespread in the industry, Dorsey admitted that he did, noting that Gulf viewed its political payments in Italy as necessary to compete with bigger oil companies like Shell, Exxon, and Mobil.²⁹⁸ Within weeks, both Exxon and Mobil would admit to paying close to $50 million to Italy's political parties, and as it turned out, more than a dozen oil companies, some local though most foreign, operated a loose cartel that contributed hundreds of millions to Italy's elected officials. These revelations led a U.S. civil servant stationed in Rome at the time to describe the hearings as "political dynamite" for the country's upcoming regional elections, where, a few weeks later, Italy's Communist Party would hand the ruling Christian Democratic Party a historic defeat by not only claiming every major Italian city, but also increasing their numbers in every region of the country.[299]

Italy's elections immediately transformed overseas corporate corruption into a major foreign policy issue for the United States, laying bare deep-seated Cold War anxieties. As with ITT, the fear was that corporate misconduct played right into the hands of the worst Soviet propaganda. Not only had Gulf Oil exposed an increasingly frayed relationship between the U.S. and its key ally on Europe's southern border, but it came at a dangerous time for the rest of NATO as well. In France, the center-right government was already challenged by the "Union of the Left," a political association formed in 1972 by socialists, communists, and leftist radicals; in the Netherlands, the Socialist Party had just won power for the first time in fifteen years; and in Portugal, a radical socialist government ended a forty-year military dictatorship.

For Church and others in the Senate, however, the bribery hearings were a way for the United States to demonstrate that democracy was still capable of reckoning with its own demons. "It is important for us to determine to what extent the elected representatives of the people or a small cadre of entrenched corporate managers are establishing the economic and social policies of this country," declared New Hampshire Senator John Durkin.[300] "There is little doubt that widespread corruption serves to undermine those moderate democratic and pro-free-enterprise governments which the United States has traditionally sought to foster and support," Church later testified. "Ultimately, they create the conditions which bring to power political forces that are no friends of ours, whether a Qaddafi in Libya, or the Communists in Italy."[301]

Libya, in fact, would become a favorite cautionary tale for Church in explaining the dangers of corporate corruption abroad. There, radical anti-Western militant Muammar Qaddafi's rise to power in 1969 had stemmed from a groundswell of animosity against the corrupt regime of his predecessor, King Mohammad Idris. Under Idris, Libya had become one of the richest oil-exporting countries in the world, but as Church remarked, Idris had offered concessions to outside oil companies, many of them American, based almost exclusively on payments to his royal family. In the end, increasing disparities in wealth prompted a wave of support for Colonel Qaddaffi and his anti-imperialist agenda that would drive up OPEC's prices for years to come. At a time when the price of oil had nearly quadrupled in just two years, Church sought to make clear that overseas corporate corruption wasn't just a theoretical threat; it had a real impact on the average American's pocketbook.

There were other comparisons, too. Like ITT in Chile, corporate corruption overseas conjured up recent failures in Vietnam. "Among the many cases of tragedy in Vietnam," remarked Senator Joseph Clark on the first day of the Gulf Oil hearings, "was the corruption of the Thiệu regime and its inability to credibly articulate the wishes of the majority of the Vietnamese." Reports throughout the late 1960s had told stories of pilferers on the streets of Saigon selling American supplies on the black market—everything from cigarettes and liquor to guns and hair products. Thiệu's own officials were often the worst offenders, at times resorting to selling supplies given to them from the United States directly to pro-communist forces.[302] "South Vietnam is more likely to be defeated by corruption than communism," wrote columnist Jack Anderson in 1968.[303]

At the time of the Gulf hearings, many of those failures seemed to be repeating themselves again in neighboring Cambodia, where the U.S.-supported government had only just collapsed. There, Lon Nol, Cambodia's former prime minister, wasted much of the U.S. foreign aid sent to him to build elaborate mansions in the mountains surrounding the capital city of Phnom Penh.[304] "The brutal lesson of Vietnam and Cambodia was that a corrupt regime, no matter how great its friendship for or dependence upon the United States, does not serve our interests; no amount of armaments can save such a regime from ultimate rejection by its own people," remarked a *New York Times* editorial in 1975.[305]

Overall, then, the Gulf Oil hearings brought into stark relief many of the most pressing issues of the times: generalized anti-corporate sentiments, the country's flagging image overseas, the deterioration of America's military alliances, and existential threats posed by communism. Church made efforts to tie these issues directly to domestic life in America, including the rise in oil prices, unemployment, inflation, and the export of American jobs.

The overall result was a powerful change in mood among the American public. Gone were the days when what was good for General Motors was presumed to be good for America. Now before Congress lay the daunting task of putting the genie back in its bottle. "[M]odern corporate managements are becoming in many respects, private governments, exercising enormous control over our lives and subject to very little democratic constraint," warned Democratic Indiana Senator Vance Hartke.[306]

No congressman was more directly tied to these issues, however, than Idaho's Frank Church. A year that began with the very real danger of the Subcommittee's termination ended with Church's name and picture regularly featured in both national and international newspapers, as well as several appearances on network television. By late September, the *Boston Globe* ran a four-page spread naming Church the "dark horse candidate for the presidency."[307] Yet with the 1976 election still more than twelve months away, Church opted for a "wait and see" approach until the field of more than a dozen candidates had thinned. Many of the Democratic party's biggest players had yet to announce their intentions, including Church's adversary and colleague, Hubert Humphrey. For now, all Church needed to do was remain relevant.

As luck would have it, remaining in the public eye would not prove difficult for Church. Shortly after the conclusion of the Gulf hearings, Jerome Levinson received another telephone call from Stanley Sporkin, the SEC's top enforcement official. For months, Sporkin had been stewing, upset that his team's bribery investigation into Northrop Corporation, the California-based defense company, had been halted by the State Department. Not one to stand down simply because he had been told to do so, Sporkin leaked the secret Ernst & Ernst auditor's report detailing Northrop's bribes to the Subcommittee.[308]

On April 30, 1975, as news outlets announced the fall of the Saigon government and the retreat of the last American troops out of Vietnam, Church held a closed-door vote on whether to investigate Northrop. The vote was unanimous, and the ensuing hearings ushered in a second chapter in the Subcommittee's bribery investigations—a prolonged and utterly devastating exploration of the depths of corporate bribery abroad. Writing about those hearings years later, Levinson remarked that "it was as if the payments by the oil companies in South Korea and Italy were merely appetizers, setting the stage for the main meal: corruption on a scale and at a level previously unimaginable."[309]

Appetite whetted, Congress was now ready to feast.

CHAPTER FOUR

Bloodletting

This bloodletting, unfortunately, is continuing. It is the disgrace of our free enterprise system.

Senator William Proxmire, April 5, 1976

Northrop in the Crosshairs

In late May 1975, two weeks after the close of the Gulf Oil hearings, Jerome Levinson and Jack Blum deboarded their plane and breathed in the stale, heavy smog that blanketed Los Angeles. The investigators were in town pursuing their next lead, soon to find themselves in the back seat of a taxi headed toward the global headquarters of Northrop Corporation. The building was located in the heart of the glitzy Century City neighborhood, and once inside the air-conditioned lobby, they stopped to admire an impressive Persian rug hanging behind the receptionist's desk. They were told that it had been a gift from the Shah of Iran to the company's CEO, Tom Jones.

From the Ernst & Ernst auditor's report, Levinson and Blum had gleaned a rough picture of Northrop's international sales practices, which included relationships with some of the world's most elite global leaders. Over the next few days, that image would come into full relief as the two interviewed numerous senior Northrop employees. One manager openly bragged to Levinson about having the best job in the world, replete with international travel, intrigue, beautiful women, fine wine, and exquisite meals.[310]

Back in Washington, the rest of the Subcommittee staff was tasked with the much less glamorous work of combing through hundreds of pages of supplementary materials provided by Ernst & Ernst detailing the company's overseas financial activities. Northrop had made a name for itself during World War II through its P-61 Black Widow fighter plane, which the U.S. military had purchased to launch night raids across Europe. In the postwar years, however, the U.S. government was buying far fewer planes in favor of more advanced technology, and with the military's new emphasis on electronics and automatic control systems, old airframe makers like Northrop had begun losing out.

By the time Jones joined the company as an engineer in 1953, Northrop was in desperate need of a turnaround.[311] Jones's blunt, practical approach to sales allowed him to quickly rise up the company's ranks, and he successfully convinced others at Northrop that the company could realize larger margins by focusing on selling components and parts instead of entire airplanes. His efforts reshaped Northrop from a lagging prime contractor into a broad-based "supplier of suppliers," offering buyers fixed-fee planes that were cheaper to make and less complicated to fly.[312] In just a little over five years, Jones had singlehandedly upended the airplane industry's entire pricing model, a feat that convinced Northrop's board of directors to name him as the company's next CEO, landing the forty-one-year-old executive on the cover of *Time Magazine* as "the bright star of the aerospace industry." "At an age when most successful executives are hopefully eying a vice-presidency," wrote the magazine in 1961, "personable Tom Jones has rocketed to the top of an industry that bears the heaviest responsibilities ever imposed upon any branch of private enterprise."[313]

But Jones didn't just have a good understanding of how to sell planes; he embodied the new image Northrop presented to the world. He dressed impeccably, spoke fluent Portuguese, and lived on an impressive thirteen-acre villa in Bel Air. The home had once belonged to iconic Hollywood film director Victor Fleming, and Jones had turned it into a sprawling terraced vineyard where he hosted weekend parties for politicians, dignitaries, and military personnel alike. As one reporter noted at the time, while the house lacked a bomb shelter, it boasted an impressive wine vault. When he wasn't entertaining guests at his villa, Jones hobnobbed with movie stars and the elites of the entertainment industry aboard his seventy-foot sailboat, venturing to Catalina Island or other equally stunning locations off the coast of southern California. In Maryland, Northrop built a high-end hunting lodge, where Jones and other senior executives invited scores of D.C.-based Pentagon generals, admirals, and influential civilians for weekend getaways.[314] In just a few short years, he'd transformed the culture and image of Northrop into one that mirrored his own, defined by a lifestyle of luxury, entertainment, and finesse.

Although Jones' showmanship had helped to make inroads with the U.S. military, by the late 1950s, Northrop was still losing out to its competitors overseas. Notably, in 1959, the company lost a sizable bid in Germany to its rival, Lockheed, on a contract that Jones felt the company deserved to win.[315] Jones had even been told by Germany's top generals that they preferred Northrop's F-5 to Lockheed's Starfighter, signaling to the CEO that Northrop was simply being outplayed behind the scenes.[316] Jones responded by hiring William Savy, a former French intelligence officer who introduced Northrop to various experts in the field. Savy helped launch a new global strategy for Northrop that involved a network of well-connected consultants who could open backdoor channels with foreign governments.

The Ernst & Ernst report provided the Subcommittee's staff with a detailed description of the work being performed by each of these consultants. In Switzerland, Northrop had engaged Hubert Weisbrod, a "top European consultant" who could be relied upon to "discretely act as a 'gray eminence' to further Northrop's interests" on the continent.[317] In France, there was General Paul Marie Stehlin, the former Chief of the French Tactical Command during World War II and Chief of Staff of the Air Force under President Charles de Gaulle. Stehlin was secretly paid over $50,000 to report on policy changes within NATO as well as competitor activities. In the Netherlands, Northrop hired Johannes Gerritsen, another former intelligence officer who'd been active in the Dutch underground. Gerritsen served as a backdoor channel between Northrop and the highest levels of the Dutch government.

Closer to home, Jones commissioned Frank J. DeFrancis, a Washington, D.C. lawyer who'd represented the Italian embassy and served as legal counsel for the government of West Germany. Despite admitting he didn't know "a damned thing about an airplane except the nose and the tail," DeFrancis was paid what at the time would have been a hefty salary of $100,000 per year simply to open doors for Jones.[318] Others on Northrop's payroll included Kermit Roosevelt, Jr., former CIA operative and grandson of President Theodore Roosevelt. It was he who introduced Jones to the Shah of Iran, facilitating what would evolve into a close friendship between the two; apparently, every year, the Shah sent Jones a kilogram of caviar to commemorate their ties.[319]

Overall, the Northrop documents laid out what Senator Church described as "a cast of characters out of a novel of international intrigue."[320] Above all others was Adnan Khashoggi, the thirty-nine-year-old multimillionaire used to broker arms deals in the Kingdom of Saudi Arabia. Inside Northrop, a whole secret language had developed around Khashoggi—known internally as "wishbone"—and the Saudi ("Surf") government. Like most of Northrop's consultants, Khashoggi was hired because of his connections. His father had been the personal physician to the late King Faisal, and Adnan, who had been educated in the United States, built his career as a go-between for Western companies seeking to do business in the Kingdom. The Ernst & Ernst report detailed how he'd once made payments on the company's behalf totaling $450,000 to two Saudi generals in exchange for their help ensuring that Northrop won a lucrative contract.[321] In describing the findings, Church lamented how these payments had occurred alongside what had become "an unprincipled race to arm to the teeth the newly rich nations of the Persian Gulf."[322]

Even more troubling was the discovery that the U.S. military not only knew about Northrop's bribes, but for years had also tacitly approved them. In 1973, the company had even set up a meeting between Khashoggi and various representatives from the Air Force to explain "how business is conducted in Saudi Arabia."[323] After the meeting, a Defense Department official said that "if he had to translate to his superiors what Mr. Khashoggi had told him it would be something to the effect that Khashoggi is an 'inexpensive aid program'" to the Saudi government.[324] Later, the U.S. military would go so far as to distribute to various defense contractors a memo entitled "Agents' Fees in the Middle East" which not-so-subtly spoke of the political "influence" of agents in the region. "Obviously the agent with the greatest margin of profit or percentage has a distinct advantage over those with a lesser fee in that greater 'influence' can be applied to all personnel in the government decision-making chain," the memo explained.[325]

On June 3, Northrop's outside counsel met with Church and the rest of the members of the Subcommittee in an executive session with the aim of keeping the documents in the Ernst & Ernst report confidential. Before the meeting, State Department officials had already reached out to Senator Charles Percy, the senior-ranking Republican on the Subcommittee, to ask that the Senator do what he could to limit the report's release.[326] Beyond just the embarrassing details revealed by the Khashoggi saga, the State Department knew that other defense companies—specifically Lockheed and Raytheon—had paid Khashoggi even larger sums. "Khashoggi has provided cars, houses, girls and other services for various princes," the State Department wrote in a cable to the U.S. embassy in Cairo on June 4. "If this comes out it could mean a first-rate scandal ... [and] if members of the Royal Family are implicated, we will be in for a painful time."[327]

Ignoring these concerns, the Subcommittee voted to release more than 530 pages from the Ernst & Ernst report, although Church capitulated somewhat by agreeing to exclude the names of the two Saudi generals. For its part, Northrop did its best to limit the report's damage by quickly issuing an apology to the Saudi government the day after the report's release.[328]

Neither the State Department nor Northrop nor Church could ultimately foresee, however, all of the downstream effects once the report became public.

Fallout in Paris

In the early hours of June 6, a French reporter telephoned General Stehlin, the former vice president of the French National Assembly, to ask about a letter he'd written to Jones that was about to be printed in the *New York Times*.³²⁹ Surprised by the reporter's questions, Stehlin hung up the phone, left his sleeping wife, and briskly walked to his nearby office in Paris, where he immediately began burning all of his files on Northrop. The documents detailed years of intel that he'd secretly provided Jones while serving in the French government. Upon leaving the bureau, Stehlin entered the Avenue de l'Opera and stepped in front of a city bus.³³⁰

While Stehlin's death was a sobering reminder of the stakes of the investigation, the Subcommittee pressed forward and held its first public hearing into Northrop on June 9. In contrast to the Subcommittee's inquiry into Gulf Oil one month earlier, the hearing room inside the Dirksen Senate Building was now packed to the brim with onlookers, including a battery of TV cameras set up in the front of the room. On the second day of the hearings, the Subcommittee heard from Jones himself, who made a grand entrance, arriving to the hearing in a stretch limousine and escorted by, in Levinson's words, "what can only be described as two babes."³³¹ Both women sat in the back row of the audience, behind two Subcommittee staffers who later recounted that, throughout the hearing, they were treated to the women's running commentary on the differing levels of attractiveness of the various senators and staff on the Subcommittee.³³²

Jones, for his part, sported a slicked-backed hairstyle and fashionable, thick-framed black glasses. Reading from prepared remarks, he denied any direct knowledge of

Senator Frank Church, left, chats with Thomas V. Jones, chairman of the Northrop Corp., prior to hearings of a Senate Subcommittee on Multinational Corporations in Washington, D.C., June 10, 1975.

Credit: The Associated Press, photo by Henry Griffin

bribes paid on Northrop's behalf, a bold claim given that many within Northrop's network of consultants reported directly to him. But when the Subcommittee pressed Jones on Khashoggi, the CEO skillfully explained that he had only briefly met the man during a dinner a few years earlier. Yes, he'd been told about "a problem with a general," but denied knowing any of Khashoggi's day-to-day activities.

Sensing that any further questions as to Khashoggi would be fruitless, the Senators soon turned their attention to Northrop's European sales model, focusing on an entity called the Economic Development Corporation (EDC). EDC was the brainchild of DeFrancis and the vehicle through which Northrop secured sales of its F-5 fighter plane. The Ernst & Ernst report had shown how Northrop had secretly set up EDC as a third-party shell company in Zurich and that the shareholders of the company were hidden and paid based on a percentage of sales of the planes to government customers.

"Was this whole arrangement not patterned after the Lockheed arrangement?" Church asked Jones. The question was rhetorical: Both Jones and Church already knew the auditor's report showed that DeFrancis had used the very same agreement to create EDC—almost word for word—as the one DeFrancis had used previously with Lockheed. When Ernst & Ernst's auditors visited his office in Suite 812 of the Watergate Office Building, he had even shown them a weak, xeroxed copy of the EDC agreement with pencil changes to reflect Northrop's name instead of Lockheed's.[333]

"Yes, sir," Jones replied.

"So you knew what the Lockheed arrangement was, and it was patterned after the Lockheed arrangement," Levinson reiterated.

"That is right," Jones responded.

A crack had appeared in the facade, and soon, other Senators began peppering Jones with questions about EDC. How common was this practice in the airline industry? Who else, specifically, was involved? Jones, too, began to change in demeanor, veering from his prepared remarks into more off-the-cuff answers. Northrop and Lockheed had been fierce competitors ever since Jack Northrop, Lockheed's chief engineer, had severed ties with the Loughead brothers in 1929 to start his own airplane company. The rivalry only intensified over subsequent years, and when Jones joined Northrop in the 1950s, he'd heard rumors that Robert Gross, Lockheed's then-president, had been going around saying that Northrop made "cheap airplanes for barefoot nations."[334] Over the following decade, and to varying degrees of success, Jones had made it his mission to outsell Lockheed's Starfighter plane in any market he could. Where Northrop failed to beat Lockheed head to head, Jones had adopted their tactics, even if that meant paying bribes to do so.

Senator Percy, the Republican to whom Northrop's lawyers had once tried making their most direct appeal, found the apparent normalcy surrounding corruption in the defense industry particularly disturbing. Calling it "the dry rot of the capitalistic system,"[335] Percy lamented that "Northrop is a case study, but I'm afraid not an isolated case and should not be looked on as such."[336] Toward the end of his afternoon testimony, Percy asked Jones if he too, like Gulf's CEO Bob Dorsey, thought passage of a statute outlawing the payment of overseas bribes would be helpful for U.S. corporations operating abroad. Although Jones initially tried dodging the question, he eventually agreed: a law requiring disclosures of contributions to foreign officials would likely be "very helpful."[337]

As Jones walked out of the hearing room, his usual entourage of lawyers and assistants now included an even larger ensemble of journalists and TV reporters following closely behind. His testimony had been scintillating, bringing to life the Ernst & Ernst report through dramatic testimony that would capture newspaper headlines nationwide. What's more, Church now had two major multinational corporations on record in support of a law against foreign corruption. He also had a clear path forward for launching a third investigation into Lockheed, the largest aerospace and defense company in the world.

The next day, Northrop announced that after careful consideration, the company had decided to terminate its relationship with Ernst & Ernst.[338] A spokesman for Northrop said the decision was unrelated to the auditor's recent report regarding questionable payments overseas.

Lockheed Under Pressure

In the days that followed, Lockheed's public affairs department vehemently denied the allegations made by Jones. "We have never established or ran an EDC type operation, the type apparently operated by Northrop," Lockheed's spokesman told the *Washington Post*. "I cannot figure out why Northrop keeps comparing its foreign operations with Lockheed's."[339] But inside the company's walls, Lockheed's senior executives were scrambling to assuage concerns from the company's external auditors at Arthur Young & Company. One of the firm's partners, William Findley, had first discovered overseas bribes on Lockheed's books back in 1971, but when he'd brought them up at that time with Lockheed's CEO, Daniel Haughton, Haughton had declined to raise the issue to Lockheed's board.[340]

In the wake of Jones's testimony, the accounting firm was now refusing to sign off on Lockheed's books until senior management certified to not knowing of payments made to foreign officials. In the press, Lockheed was making similar denials on a daily basis, but in private, senior management refused to sign the papers.[341] The impasse meant that not only would the auditors not attest to the accuracy of Lockheed's financial statements, but the company would have to postpone its upcoming annual shareholders' meeting until the situation was resolved.

To add to the company's troubles, officials from the Emergency Loan Guarantee Board (ELGB) flew to Los Angeles shortly after the Northrop hearings to meet with Lockheed's executives to discuss with them the company's overseas business. The ELGB was a federal agency established by Congress a few years earlier almost exclusively to oversee Lockheed. During the 1960s, Lockheed had invested in a series of failed ventures that left it mired in debt, and by the end of the decade, the company was barely profitable. Passage of the Emergency Loan Guarantee Act in 1971 allowed Lockheed access to a taxpayer-guaranteed loan of $250 million—the largest government bailout of any company up until that time.

When the bill was first introduced, many in Washington opposed the idea, but Lockheed won the support of just enough congressmen—especially those with Lockheed manufacturing plants in their states—to secure its passage.[342] The ELGB, which was comprised of representatives from the Treasury, the Federal Reserve Board, and the Securities and Exchange Commission, had been created to oversee the loan. Now, four years later, the Northrop revelations seemed to cast the controversial decision to save Lockheed in a new light. Had the company lied to Congress regarding the viability of its overseas sales to get approval for the loan? Even worse, was it using taxpayer-backed funds to bribe foreign governments?

Again, Lockheed's officers were quick to deny any wrongdoing. They told the ELGB representatives that they knew of no overseas political payments except a mere $20,000 that had gone to foreign political parties, something they were told by their lawyers had been permissible under local law. The Lockheed executives also explained that Arthur Young & Company was in the process of conducting a more thorough report, which would be made available to the ELGB as soon as it was completed. Both statements were untrue.[343] Behind the scenes, the company's auditors and senior executives continued to engage in a bitter standoff. Lockheed's senior executives severely limited the auditor's access to company documents, causing the auditors, in turn, to continue to refuse to sign off on the company's books.

Finally, in early July, Arthur Young & Company presented its findings (such as they were) to Lockheed's board of directors. Despite obtaining only oral representations from a few Lockheed employees, the auditors had been able to cobble together several thousand dollars in off-book accounts and suspicious commissions that Lockheed had paid to a smattering of international sales agents. "There are probably additional such items that have not come to our attention," the auditors explained to the board, but even so, the mere creation and maintenance of the off-book accounts "is it itself a material fact ... which causes us considerable concern."[344]

The audit report, together with the visit from the ELGB, convinced Lockheed's board that it would have to adopt a more proactive response. Soon after, the company hired William Rogers, a tall, suave Washington insider whose credentials included serving both as Eisenhower's attorney general and Nixon's secretary of state. Rogers' first task would be to run interference between Lockheed and the growing list of U.S. government officials now knocking on the company's door. Some were familiar faces, like Church and Sporkin, while others, including Wisconsin Senator William Proxmire, presented distinctly new challenges.

Proxmire served as Chairman of the Senate Committee on Banking, Housing, and Urban Development and shared a long and storied relationship with Lockheed. In 1970, he'd led hearings investigating the Pentagon's defense budget, criticizing the ever-increasing spending on military defense companies.[345] A year later, he'd led efforts opposing extension of the ELGB loan to Lockheed, a campaign that would convert animosity between both parties into outright rancor. Referring to Lockheed, Proxmire told the National Federation of Independent Business over the summer of 1971 that "the freedom to fail may at times appear to be an overly painful solution, [but] business failures serve a higher public purpose. They are a means by which our economy discards obsolete or inefficient ways of doing business."[346] In response, Lockheed bought full-page newspaper ads–framed as an "Open Letter to the Citizens of Wisconsin"–proposing a boycott of various Wisconsin products until Proxmire was removed from office.

Much to Lockheed's dismay, however, Proxmire went on to win reelection easily that year and became chair of the Banking Committee in January 1975. His appointment, coincidentally, was occasioned by Senator John Sparkman's resignation from the post in order to chair the Foreign Relations Committee. The new role gave Proxmire full oversight of the ELGB loan, meaning the allegations now swirling around Lockheed's overseas payments fell squarely under his purview. In early August, Proxmire had announced he would be revisiting the company he'd long had in his crosshairs; by the end of the month, he would hold public hearings into Lockheed's foreign bribes.[347]

Lockheed wasn't the only one upset by that news; Frank Church, who until then had been the only senator to carve out the issue of foreign bribery, wrote Proxmire an urgent letter in an attempt to draw border lines between their two committees. "As Chairman of the Banking Committee I know you are interested in the Lockheed payments because of your Committee's involvement in the Lockheed loan guarantee," Church wrote. "The Lockheed problem is sufficiently complex to warrant work by both of our committees . . . your focus being the domestic and regulatory issues and ours the foreign payments issues . . . ."[348] But Proxmire, a former journalist who was not known for shying away from headlines, ignored Church's proposal, and a few days later announced that the Banking Committee's first bribery hearing would feature none other than Lockheed's CEO, Daniel Haughton.

Church was said to have been furious at Proxmire's intrusion, but there was little else he could do.[349] With Gulf Oil and Northrop, Church had enjoyed a singular role in uncovering corporate bribery abroad. With the addition of Lockheed, he would now have to get used to sharing the limelight.

As Congress readied itself for multiple sets of hearings, William Rogers advised Lockheed's executives that they would do well to get ahead of the problem. If the company had secrets in its closet, better to disclose them now on its own terms than have to confess them later on someone else's. Haughton agreed, but only so long as the company could keep the identities of Lockheed's foreign recipients a secret. Otherwise, he explained, full disclosure would cripple future business opportunities overseas. It was under those conditions that on August 1, Lockheed made the strategic decision to announce that it had paid $22 million to foreign officials over the last five years, plus $142 million in commissions and other payments to overseas sales agents.[350] While the company did not believe that all of those commissions represented bribe payments, it acknowledged that at least some probably were.

At the time, the disclosure seemed like the right thing to do. The payments were comparable in size to those made by Gulf Oil and Northrop; one might assume the revelations would cause momentary embarrassment but eventually blow over. And if nothing else, the disclosure served the purpose of finally convincing Arthur Young & Company to sign off on the company's financial statements. In the very same press release, Lockheed was able to put forth its quarterly earnings report, happily announcing an increase in share profit of $1.03 over the previous year.

But whatever effect the disclosure may have had in helping the firm on Wall Street, it would do little to appease the company's critics in Washington, D.C. "Lockheed refuses to answer the questions asked by this committee about the details of the payoffs and bribes to foreign government officials," Proxmire stated, admonishing Haughton during his testimony three weeks later before the Banking Committee. "It has refused to comply with a subpoena of the SEC. It is stonewalling this committee, a duly authorized body of the U.S. Senate . . . the question that remains is whether a giant corporation whose business is largely dependent on sales to the U.S. Government will be permitted to continue to act in utter contempt of the U.S. Government," Proxmire concluded.

Throughout the hours-long tongue-lashing, Haughton largely kept his cool, gamely explaining that disclosing the names of foreign recipients would jeopardize the company's future operations. The sixty-four-year-old CEO was said to be seen blushing only once, when he was told point blank by the much younger thirty-two-year-old Senator from Delaware, Joseph Biden, "I think your answers are phony, and I don't like it."[351]

Secrets and Suicides

Congress certainly had its reasons to be suspicious of what was going on at Lockheed behind closed doors. In addition to the revelations by Northrop's Tom Jones, Lockheed's Treasurer, Robert Waters, had shot himself through the temple with a hunting rifle only days before Haughton was set to testify before the Banking Committee.[352] Waters was one of the company's few senior executives aware of Lockheed's payments to foreign officials, and while the company claimed that his death was unrelated to the overseas payments, the timing of his suicide, which was blamed on "business pressures," did little to alleviate the general impression that the company was hiding a great deal more than it was letting on.

A few weeks later, in his testimony before the House Subcommittee on International Economic Policy, SEC Commissioner Philip A. Loomis told Congress that for months, Lockheed had refused to provide the SEC's staff with the names of foreign recipients. "[T]hey appear to believe … that detailed disclosures would be very harmful to the company … and that this possible injury to the company and its stockholders and employees outweighs any possible public interest," Loomis told the House subcommittee.[353] Even if the SEC could force Lockheed to produce the information before a judge, Loomis explained, it could take years for the request to work its way through the court system.

An apparent breakthrough occurred in early September when two deliverymen mistakenly dropped several cartons of documents on behalf of Arthur Young & Company at the doorstep of Church's Subcommittee. When Arthur Young's lawyers at the New York law firm of White & Case realized their error and called Jerome Levinson to demand that the documents be returned, Levinson politely refused. "Possession is nine-tenths of the law," Levinson chuckled to himself in remembering the affair years later.[354]

The victory was short-lived, however, as the documents proved of limited use. Lockheed's senior executives had carefully curated what Arthur Young & Company was allowed to see, which meant that the discovery showed payments of only about $5 million—less than one-quarter of what Lockheed had publicly disclosed—and only pertained to countries where Lockheed had no active business dealings. The Subcommittee was able to confirm their earlier suspicions that Lockheed (like Northrop) had employed Adnan Khashoggi in the Middle East, but, in Jack Blum's words, these revelations were "very low hanging fruit." "Great stuff, blah, blah, lots of fun," Blum recalled, "but who in the world gave a shit about who was bribing who [sic] in Saudi Arabia?"[355]

For now, the approach William Rogers advised—to batten down the hatches and ride out the wave—was working. Congress may have succeeded in denting Lockheed's wall of silence, but without more, the company could count on the investigations eventually fizzling out. There was already nascent backlash against the negative press companies were receiving surrounding overseas payments. "If corporate bribery abroad has offended the post-Watergate morality," complained one writer for the *New York Times*, "the companies implicated have nevertheless taken a greater share of the blame than they deserve."[356]

Even Church, who was beginning to look ahead to the

upcoming Democratic presidential primaries, worried that the investigations occupied too much of his time. On an almost daily basis, the Subcommittee was receiving phone calls with anonymous tips of corporate bribery; some tipsters even showed up in person to the Subcommittee's doorstep, dropping off thick binders of confidential corporate documents. For the most part, these proved to be nothing more than intricate conspiracy theories. In October, Church told the Subcommittee he hoped to wrap up the bribery investigations by the end of the following month.

*

Over at the SEC, Stanley Sporkin's team of investigators were also starting to lose steam. There continued to be strong disagreement among the SEC's Board of Commissioners regarding how appropriate it was for the Commission to be leading the charge into overseas corporate political payments. For Sporkin, the application of U.S. securities law to overseas bribes was relatively clear-cut. "The only people who have any difficulty interpreting what we're trying to do are the lawyers," Sporkin later explained. "Morality needs no guidelines."[357]

But Chairman Ray Garrett and Commissioner Al Sommer, Jr. worried that Sporkin's expansion of the concept of "materiality" under the securities laws could lead the Commission down a slippery slope. "We can't be suing every company," Garrett told Sporkin plainly. He worried that aggressive interpretation of the 1934 Securities Act would eventually justify requiring corporations to make almost any disclosure deemed necessary to investors after the fact.[358]

For others, however, like Commissioners Phillip Loomis and John Evans, Sporkin's chutzpah was a welcome relief. "We don't need to be apologetic or defensive about our actions," declared Evans, who prior to joining the SEC had worked with Proxmire as a staff member on the Banking Committee. "Business practice must be based on common understandings of social and ethical values, and it seems rather fundamental that the activities of corporations and those who direct their operations must comport with such standards."[359]

A compromise of sorts was reached in July 1975 when the SEC announced that it would commence what was dubbed the "voluntary disclosure program." The idea had come from the Watergate special counsel who, after bringing charges against American Airlines for violating the Federal Corrupt Practices Act, allowed other companies to voluntarily come forward and disclose political contributions made during the 1972 election.[360] In the same vein, the SEC program allowed companies that uncovered evidence of bribery overseas to come forward and receive clemency. Not long after, however, Loomis admitted to the House Subcommittee on International Economic Policy that the program had yet to achieve success.[361] Of the approximately 10,500 SEC-registered companies at the time, only one—an Oklahoma-based oil company—had thus far taken the government up on its offer.[362]

To further complicate matters, Sporkin's leads into corporate bribery overseas were beginning to dry up. The wellspring of corporate cases arising out of the Watergate investigation for failure to disclose political payments to Nixon's campaign had slowed to a trickle.[363] Without any new cases and little political leverage within the SEC to expand beyond the Watergate inquiry, Sporkin's team was uncharacteristically forced to show restraint.

Then, in early October, the White House announced that SEC Chairman Ray Garrett, whose wife had been ill for several years, was stepping down.[364] Garrett had wanted his protégé, Commissioner Al Sommer, Jr., to be named his successor, but President Ford decided instead on White House Counsel Roderick Hills.[365] Hills's wife Carla headed the Department of Housing and Urban Development, and the couple were said to be two rising stars of the Republican party. Like his predecessor, Hills came to the SEC suspicious of overregulation and heavily influenced by the notion that economic incentives within the free market were often better than the law at regulating Wall Street. It was a philosophy that was initially met with deep skepticism from Sporkin, but Hills made it clear that he had no intention of blocking the Enforcement Division's work on corporate political payments abroad.[366]

Hills stayed true to his word, giving Sporkin the green light in late November to file a motion against Lockheed and Daniel Haughton before D.C. District Court Judge John Pratt. The motion was to compel Lockheed's compliance with the SEC's earlier June subpoena; if the voluntary disclosure program had been Commissioner Loomis's attempt to motivate Lockheed with the carrot, now it was time for Sporkin to apply the stick.[367]

The Informant's Diary

That same month, Church's Subcommittee staff received an unsolicited visit from Ernest Hauser, Lockheed's former head of sales in Europe. Frustrated by what he'd been reading in the newspapers about Lockheed's stonewalling of the Subcommittee, Hauser had traveled from Phoenix to confess to personally paying bribes on Lockheed's behalf in Europe over the course of several decades. Although Levinson and Blum were unsure what to make of the fast-talking ex-Army intelligence officer, they were impressed when Hauser showed them a diary he apparently had kept of his activity during those years. The diary described meetings between himself and some of Europe's top officials, including Germany's Franz Josef Strauss, Minister of Defense and head of the Christian Social Union party, as well as Prince Bernhard of the Netherlands. Blum and Levinson showed the diary to Church, who immediately realized its potential. Any thoughts Church might have had of wrapping up the Lockheed hearings by the end of the month would have to wait, and within days, Blum was on a plane bound for Germany.

Meanwhile, in response to the SEC's order before Judge Pratt, William Rogers reached out to his former colleague, current Secretary of State Henry Kissinger, in the hope of convincing him to intervene once more.[368] Although relations between Rogers and Kissinger were frosty when Rogers was at the State Department, Kissinger agreed, and on November 28, he wrote a letter to Attorney General Edward Levi asking that he make an appeal to Judge Pratt to withhold ordering Lockheed to disclose the identity of foreign government officials. "[T]he making of any such payments and their disclosure can have grave consequences for significant foreign relations interests of the United States abroad," Kissinger warned.[369] Yet Lockheed's move to involve Kissinger ultimately backfired; his letter was leaked in the newspapers, and the ensuing bad press (the Secretary of State's popularity was nearing an all-time low due to revelations of covert operations in Angola) effaced any positive influence Lockheed hoped Kissinger's involvement might have. On December 16, Judge Pratt granted the SEC's order to enforce the subpoena.[370]

In Europe, meanwhile, Jack Blum met with Christian Steinrücke and other prominent West Germans who corroborated details from Hauser's diary. It turned out that Hauser had been the best man at Strauss' wedding and had even been asked to be the godfather to Strauss' son.[371] Strauss was said to have received over $10 million from Hauser in connection with both the sale of Lockheed's Constellation and Electra commercial airplanes to Lufthansa, as well as Lockheed's F-104 Starfighter plane to the German military. Hauser had also, apparently, paid bribes in the form of a gold Rolex watch and other luxury items to Strauss' personal secretary, Colonel Werner Repenning. When details of those gifts emerged in the German press in 1967, Repenning committed suicide, although the German government apparently suppressed the true cause of death in the press, making it seem like a heart attack.[372]

Blum learned some disturbing news about Hauser as well. According to several sources, the former intelligence officer was a known liar, and there were even rumors that he had ties to the Russian KGB. A few years prior, he was charged by a Bonn court with malfeasance and falsification of documents, and Blum soon discovered that sections of Hauser's sales diary appeared to have been forged as well.[373] Hauser may have been right about Lockheed's bribes in Germany, but Blum knew the Subcommittee would never approve of a witness as unreliable as Hauser testifying in public.

In early December, a despondent Blum flew back to the U.S. as unsure about the future of the Lockheed investigations as when he'd left. There, he found the rest of the Subcommittee staff sifting through a recent batch of documents that had just been delivered by Lockheed and Arthur Young & Company per Judge Pratt's recent ruling. Noticing that a large number of the documents appeared to be written in what looked like Japanese, Blum recalled a piece of advice a diplomat had shared during his travels: "Stop wasting your time in Europe, everyone knows that Lockheed's biggest bribes were all in Asia."[374]

Blum picked up one of the documents and observed what looked to be a receipt bearing a large red stamp in the upper lefthand corner of the page. Grabbing a handful of papers, he walked over to the Congressional Research

Mug shot of Yoshio Kodama while he was held as a war criminal in Sugamo Prison in Tokyo in 1946.

Credit: Public domain image via Wikimedia Commons

Office to seek help in making sense of the documents. Returning a few days later, Blum learned that the papers were indeed handwritten Japanese receipts, and one receipt had been signed by someone named Hiroshi Itoh. Written across the center of the page were the following words: "I received One Hundred Peanuts." Another one, signed by a Yoshio Kodama, read "Amount Ninety Million Yen Only." The Congressional Research Office had looked up the identities of these men and told Blum that Mr. Itoh was an executive director at Marubeni Corporation, a large Japanese trading firm. As for Mr. Kodama, he was listed in several published articles, including one from 1960 entitled "Nationalism and the Right Wing in Japan."

Blum did some more digging and soon discovered that Kodama had been one of twenty-eight officials designated by the post-World War II International Military Tribunal as a Japanese Class A war criminal. Officially, he'd been a covert civilian employee of the Imperial Navy during the war, setting up large business operations responsible for plundering gold and other resources across China; unofficially, he'd operated a black-market opium trade with ties to the Japanese Yakuza. After Japan's defeat, Kodama had been sent to Sugamo Prison only to emerge three years later as one of the richest men in postwar Japan. In the years since, he'd used his vast wealth and connections to Japan's underground criminal rings to become a kingmaker for the country's ruling Liberal Party.

The more Blum learned, the more Lockheed's activities in Japan seemed even stranger than the fiction in Hauser's diary. After months of frustrations and dead ends, here, finally, was proof of Lockheed's overseas payments and where they'd gone. And from the looks of it, Blum was finally beginning to understand why the company had gone to such lengths to keep them a secret.

The Black Curtain

The year was coming to a close, and on December 17, 1975, President and Mrs. Ford invited Congress and the White House staff to a black-tie Christmas ball. Church, along with the ball's other nearly 1,000 attendees, were welcomed by carolers and then ushered into the State Dining Room, where an impressive buffet and several cases of champagne awaited them. Next door, in the East Room, a pianist-led orchestra kicked off the evening's festivities with "This Could Be the Start of Something Big" as the President and Mrs. Ford took a spin around the dance floor and mingled with guests.

But anyone hoping to put politics out of mind for the evening would have been hard-pressed among the growing field of presidential contenders in attendance that night. Church himself, while not yet having officially announced his plans, had registered the "Church for President Committee, Inc." with the newly created Federal Election Committee only a few days earlier.

It would have been easy at the time for Church to look back at the remarkable reversal of fortune he had experienced over the course of the past twelve months. Only a year had elapsed since he'd fought off Hubert Humphrey's efforts to cut funding to the Subcommittee on Multinational Corporations. Since then, not only had the Subcommittee survived, but Church had spent the better part of the year both juggling high-profile investigations into Northrop and Lockheed and wrapping up another well-publicized inquiry into abuses by the CIA. By year's end, the CIA hearings—complete with the dramatic display of a poison dart gun on national television—had launched Church firmly back into the public eye and made him once more a recognizable figure on the nightly news. This could be the start of something big indeed.

But Church wasn't alone; other Democratic hopefuls in the room who had recently launched presidential campaigns included Congressman Morris Udall of Arizona, Congressman Henry "Scoop" Jackson of Washington, and

Senator Birch Bayh, Jr. of Indiana. Some newspapers were even beginning to talk of the up-and-coming Governor of Georgia, Jimmy Carter. But by and large, Minnesota Senator and former Vice President Hubert Humphrey was believed to be the presidential frontrunner. For now, Humphrey was biding his time, publicly stating that he was mulling the decision over while secretly undergoing x-ray treatment for bladder cancer—his second diagnosis in as many years. Even so, Humphrey continued to hold a place in the hearts of a generation of loyal Democrats, and he nursed ambitions of taking one last shot at the presidency. Donnie Radcliffe, a journalist for the *Washington Post*, found himself standing next to Humphrey toward the end of the evening, and as the clock struck midnight, the two watched the President and First Lady make their exit up the White House stairs. Looking about the room full of soon-to-be rivals, Humphrey described to Radcliffe "a feeling of 'high noon' in the holiday air."[375]

Among Humphrey's potential opponents, there were certainly some who posed a greater electoral challenge, but none had the potential to personally embarrass him as much as Church did. Both of Humphrey's recent presidential campaigns, in 1968 and 1972, had been tarnished by allegations of illegal corporate donations. In fact, in June 1975—around the same time that Church held his first bribery hearings into Gulf Oil—Humphrey's former campaign manager was sentenced to four months in prison for arranging unlawful donations.[376] There were even allegations that Humphrey had personally accepted a suitcase containing $50,000 in cash from the controversial business magnate Howard Hughes.[377] The whole ordeal was said to be a low point in Humphrey's political career, and there were rumors that he'd contemplated quitting public life altogether. In the months since, the former vice president had tried to put the scandal behind him, understanding that his financial house would have to be in order if he hoped to make another run at the White House.[378] In part, that meant keeping close tabs on Church and any domestic fallout that might come from his investigations into overseas corporate bribery.

One way for Humphrey to monitor the situation was through William Proxmire, his close colleague in the Senate. Besides both being senators from neighboring states, Humphrey had been a mentor to Proxmire ever since the younger congressman unexpectedly won Joe McCarthy's vacant seat in a 1957 special election. Humphrey was among the first to greet Proxmire and his wife as they deboarded their plane in Washington, D.C. after that election, advising Proxmire that very first day in office on how he should vote on three bills that were before the Senate.[379] Over the years, the two had remained close, and Humphrey had sought to mold Proxmire into a protégé, another midwestern progressive in the tradition of Wisconsin's Robert La Follette. The relationship, of course, was meant to be mutually beneficial, and insofar as Proxmire was now the ranking Democrat on both the Senate Banking and Senate Currency Committees, Humphrey trusted that he could rely on the younger senator to glean information that might prove useful for his political aspirations.

But unlike Church, Proxmire had no full-time investigative staff at his disposal, and therefore no ability to independently uncover corporate corruption on his own. When SEC Chairman Roderick Hills testified before the Banking Committee in January 1976 and Proxmire probed Hills to share any information the SEC might have on the Lockheed case, Hills deflected, stating that he hoped that "Congress would not interfere with the course of the ongoing investigation."[380] Irritated by the response, Proxmire asked Hills whose side he was really on, to which Hills confidently told him "with complete certainty" that the SEC would do "whatever has to be done" to finish the investigations properly.[381] Proxmire and Humphrey would just have to wait patiently for the investigation to run its course alongside everyone else.

Meanwhile, Church's team of investigators, who worked quite literally just down the hall from Proxmire, were putting the finishing touches on their own months-long investigation into Lockheed's overseas bribery scheme. Jack Blum was back from another trip to Europe, where he'd met with Lockheed's former sales consultants in the Netherlands and Switzerland, and the rest of the staff were combing through documents obtained as a result of Judge Pratt's recent ruling.[382]

Ernie Hauser, the original Lockheed informant, was also keeping busy; in December, he had been interviewed on German television, boldly accusing Strauss of taking bribes from Lockheed. The German government ultimately won a judgment to pull the broadcast just forty-five minutes before it was scheduled to be aired, but an unswayed Hauser was back on television just a few weeks later, this time in the U.K., where he conducted a lengthy interview broadcast to 12 million British viewers.[383]

Realizing the Subcommittee would need to act quickly if it wanted to stay ahead of the emerging story, Church invited Daniel Haughton, Lockheed's CEO, and Carl Kotchian, its president and head of sales, to a closed-door executive session before the Subcommittee on February 2. Inside the Senate's Foreign Relations Committee room, Church laid out before the two executives the substantial evidence they had collected so far: payments to highly connected intermediaries across Europe, backdoor agents in Japan, and suspicious dealings in a handful of countries across the globe.

Neither Haughton nor Kotchian bothered to deny the evidence, although they each reiterated the company's need to withhold the names of foreign officials from public hearings. Church agreed, not out of any concern for Lockheed or its future business dealings, but because he worried that disclosing the names of government officials— in particular, Prince Bernhard of the Netherlands and former Prime Minister Kakuei Tanaka of Japan—would be a political mistake. A few weeks earlier, Richard Welch, the CIA's Station Chief in Greece, was killed in Athens after his identity was leaked. Although there was no evidence Church had anything to do with the leak, the rumor was that Welch's identity had been compromised due to the carelessness of Church's investigations into the CIA.[384] The combination of both those allegations and the upcoming presidential election meant Church had little appetite for taking on whatever additional heat might come from revealing the names of foreign government officials linked to his investigation into Lockheed.[385]

And so, with the ground rules now set, the Subcommittee at long last opened its second round of hearings into Lockheed on February 4, 1976.

*

"I feel today's hearings have special relevance," Senator Percy began as the proceedings got underway before the sizable crowd in attendance. "Previous hearings of this Subcommittee have dealt with payoffs, bribes and corruption in the less developed world. Many people, including diplomats at the OECD, have scoffed at these practices as being unimportant because they constitute standard business practices in the third world. Today we shall see these 'standard business practices' come quite close to home. In today's hearings we will deal with industrialized nations, with close economic, military and political allies of the United States."[386]

As the senators took a brief recess before calling the first witness, the Subcommittee's Chief Counsel, Jerome Levinson, distributed to the news media in attendance thick packets comprising some 300 pages of documents collected from Lockheed and Arthur Young & Company.

"What we have given you is a distillation of documents which the Subcommittee obtained," Levinson explained as he passed out the materials. Inside was evidence of more than $12.5 million in bribes Lockheed had paid in Japan, $2 million spent in Italy, $1 million in the Netherlands, hundreds of thousands in "gifts" to officials in Turkey, and undisclosed amounts to officials in Germany, Sweden, and the Netherlands.[387]

Quickly skimming the materials, the room full of reporters soon erupted into a cacophony of questions.

"Mr. Levinson, I gather we are in a press conference format, more or less?"

"No."

"I add up the stuff on the sheet, and I come to $15,800,000. Now is that to be taken by us to be the total amount of the bribes that were found?"

"Those are commissions."

"One of the commissions paid was clearly to 'LSTA.' What does that mean?"

"We will explain that in the course of the hearing."

When the senators finally returned and order was restored to the hearing room, William Findley–the Arthur Young & Company accountant responsible for Lockheed's books–was sworn in as the day's first and only witness. The purpose of Findley's testimony was to explain the complicated lengths to which Lockheed had gone to hide what it was doing. In order to disguise payments in Italy, for example, Lockheed had created a fake charitable institution, the "Panamanian Temperate Zone Research Foundation," whose sole purpose was to serve as a corporate vehicle through which to funnel bribes to Italian politicians.

Elsewhere, as in Japan, Lockheed had avoided using ordinary commercial banks altogether by engaging with Deak & Company, a specialized currency exchange firm. Deak's Hong Kong office had built a reputation during the Vietnam War for funding clandestine CIA operations in Saigon. At first, Lockheed simply wired the funds to Hong Kong, where Deak put the cash into orange cardboard boxes or airline flight bags that were hand-delivered to Tokyo. Later on, Deak would develop more sophisticated methods, laundering the funds via bearer checks that were deposited into the local Japanese bank account of a Jose Gardeano, a Spanish-born former Catholic missionary who had since become a naturalized Japanese citizen. After about a week, Gardeano would withdraw the cash from his account and deliver it either directly to a Lockheed representative in Tokyo or to another Deak courier. Cash deliveries were usually documented with coded receipts, Findley explained, noting how one "peanut," signified 1 million yen. For tax purposes, Lockheed then marked the payments on its accounting books either as "prepaid commissions" or "marketing services."[388]

For most journalists in the room, however, the real story was not the accounting methods used, but the identity of those to whom the bribes had been paid. Nowhere was this truer than in Japan. Even before Findley had finished his testimony, wire services in Washington, D.C. had already begun dispatching news of the Lockheed payments to

Tokyo, and within hours, it was the number one story on Japanese television's nightly news. By the following morning, Lockheed's name was splashed across the front page of all five major Japanese newspapers.[389]

Much of the focus revolved around the company's payment of over $7 million to Yoshio Kodama, who was already a household name in Japan. Kodama was known as part of the *kuromaku,* or "black curtain." The term, which refers to the divider in kabuki theater used for hiding set changes, also denotes a person who directs the actions of others from behind the scenes—in effect, a kingmaker.

In Kodama's case, his power derived both from his enormous wealth and his connections with violent, right-wing nationalist groups. After his release from prison, he'd employed an army of thugs to help his business friends settle labor disputes, while his enormous contributions to the mainstream Liberal Party gave him unknown political leverage. But it wasn't until 1970 that Kodama gained widespread notoriety in Japan. He'd caused a stir after composing the song "Minzoku no Uta" (or "The Song of the Race"), which he first introduced at the posh Okura Hotel before a crowd of 3,000 nationalist supporters. Proposed as a new national anthem, the song resembled the Japanese rallying songs of World War II and evoked the mythology of Japan's racial superiority.

That Lockheed had hired such a controversial figure to do its dirty work was scandalous in itself, but it was made all the more intriguing by the fact that Church had omitted the identity of the officials on the receiving end of Kodama's payments. Noting that America's ambassador to Japan at the time, James Hodgson, was himself a former Lockheed employee, the Japanese press accused the U.S. government of being complicit in helping Lockheed cover up the scandal. The State Department tried its best to clarify that Hodgson had not been involved in sales activities while at Lockheed, but it did little to quiet the general belief in Japan that the company's underground political connections extended both far and wide.[390]

Japan Erupts

On the morning of Friday, February 6, the Subcommittee reconvened for its second and last full day of Lockheed hearings. By 8:00 a.m., a throng of Japanese correspondents had begun lining up outside the Dirksen Senate Building, and when the doors to the Foreign Relations Committee hearing room finally opened two hours later, the crowd rushed in to fill the reserved media tables. "We had to call in the Capitol police and have them clear the room," Levinson later recalled. And while the police tried to divide the tables equitably between the Japanese and American correspondents, some, like Jerry Landauer of the *Wall Street Journal,* took it upon themselves to apportion the room: "axis powers to the right, allies to the left," Landauer was heard shouting as the doors to the Committee room reopened.[391]

Eventually, calm was restored, and Lockheed's President and Head of International Sales, Carl Kotchian, was sworn in as witness. Kotchian began his testimony by explaining

Carl Kotchian appears before the Senate Subcommittee on Multinational Corporations on Feb. 6, 1976, in Washington, D.C.

Credit: The Associated Press, photo by John Duricka

Lockheed's overseas sales strategy. In the early 1970s, Japan's two principal airlines, Japan Airlines (JAL) and All Nippon Airways (ANA), both became interested in buying jumbo airbuses, with the most lucrative contract by far being with ANA. Competition between Lockheed's wide-bodied TriStar plane and the McDonnell Douglas DC-10 was extremely stiff, and Kotchian recounted how the Marubeni Corporation, one of Japan's largest trading companies and Lockheed's primary consultant in Japan, had told him that Lockheed would have to bribe officials both at ANA and within the Japanese government in order to secure the contract. Sensing he had no other choice, Kotchian agreed.

But if Lockheed's president was hoping for sympathy from the senators, he would receive little. As had been the case during questioning of Northrop's Tom Jones, Senator

Percy leaned on his prior experience as president of the Bell & Howell Corporation to debunk Kotchian's claim that bribery was a normal business practice in Japan.[392] Percy had certainly never seen it in his twenty-eight years of doing business there, and in any event, Lockheed seemed to have no qualms making similar payments in other parts of the developed world. In Italy, the Senator pointed out, Lockheed employees had even kept a little black code book to reference public officials, and in one of the more amusing moments during the hearing, Percy pressed Kotchian on the identity of the "Antelope Cobbler"—one of the secret code names Lockheed had used in Italy.

Senator Percy's questioning would be just one of many embarrassing moments for Kotchian during his two-and-a-half-hour-long ordeal. Whereas Northrop's Tom Jones had been confident and assured, Kotchian, a white-haired and naturally soft-spoken native of North Dakota, had trouble keeping up with the panel of senators. His responses to their questions at times barely rose above a murmur.

"Am I not speaking in the microphone?" Kotchian asked at one point.

"Just pull the microphone a little closer to you," Church answered.

"Excuse me, would you repeat the question? I've lost the trend of thought," Kotchian responded amid the glare of television cameras and reporters.

The question had been about a $1 million payment made in the Netherlands. Kotchian had just stated that Lockheed originally intended to gift "the recipient" one of its JetStars, the world's first private jet, but that the offer was turned down in favor of an outright cash payment.

"Was the payment made to a high government official in the Netherlands?" Church asked.

"Yes, sir, to the best of my information, the records indicate that, yes sir."

"In connection with the possible sale of Lockheed aircraft to the Dutch Government?" Church clarified again.

"Yes, sir."[393]

Levinson later recalled an audible collective gasp in the hearing room as it became clear from the line of questioning that the recipient of the Dutch payment could be none other than Prince Bernhard himself.[394] The next day, the *New York Times* reported that a "source in Washington" had confirmed the connection.[395] In addition to being husband to the Queen, Prince Bernhard was also the Inspector General to each of the Dutch armed services, a position he easily would have been able to leverage to influence procurement decisions by the Dutch government.[396]

The news "sent a shock wave through Holland," the U.S. embassy in the Hague reported in a telegram sent to Washington over the weekend.[397] Scrambling to formulate a response, Dutch government-run TV news services stated on the evening of Saturday, February 7 that further information would be made known "within hours," but this was followed by silence through most of Sunday, suggesting—at least to some within the U.S. State Department—that the Dutch government "had employed [the] rare step of [a] news blackout."[398] The next day, the Dutch government admitted that the "high government official" mentioned during Kotchian's testimony was indeed the Prince and that the government would be proposing an independent commission to investigate the matter fully. "Should the Prince's denial not stand up," the telegram concluded, it might "affect the position of the Queen [and] could also raise serious questions about the institution of the monarchy."[399]

Kissinger was receiving similarly worrisome telegrams from embassies around the globe. In Rome, the Italian press had begun making connections between Ovidio Lefebvre, Lockheed's local agent, and President Giovanni Leone, leading many to wonder whether Leone was in fact the famed "Antelope Cobbler" described during the hearings. In Mexico, newspapers alleged bribes to an unnamed Mexican army colonel, and likewise, in South Africa, it was rumored that Lockheed had skirted U.N. sanctions to pay bribes to officials. Similar stories were popping up in Sweden, Nigeria, Colombia, Indonesia, Venezuela, and Spain.[400]

Nowhere would Kotchian's testimony whip up more of a frenzy, however, than in Japan. For days, television networks broadcast subtitled versions of Kotchian's testimony on repeat. By the following week, the Japanese government had canceled over $1 billion in orders from Lockheed, and the Lower House of Parliament had voted to create the "Lockheed Problem Research Committee" with the purpose of immediately sending an emissary to Washington to meet with Church. Hawkers on the streets of Tokyo could be seen selling white handkerchiefs bearing the inscription "I received One Hundred Peanuts," and for a brief moment, the pop song "I Also Would Like Peanuts" topped the Japanese music charts.[401]

Not all of the attention would be light-hearted, however; two days after Kotchian's testimony, the Subcommittee received a disconcerting telegram message from Japan addressed to Senator Church:

> Lockheed problems seemed favorable for Communist bloc. /Stop/ Stop Hearings of Contributions Problems at Subcommittee On Multinational Corporations to Maintain Friendly Relations Between America and Japan in Future. /Stop/ Special Attack Corps is Alive in Japan. /Stop/ Shunzo Kiwai Chairman Kikusui Rengo United Conference[402]

At first, Church and Levinson believed the note to be someone's idea of a bad joke, but the U.S. embassy in Tokyo sent an urgent communication shortly afterward explaining that a radical Japanese group known as Chrysanthemum and Water was real, dangerous, and had even boasted of dispatching a team to Washington to kill Church. Not taking any chances, the Secret Service ordered extra protection for all senators on the Subcommittee and their staff.

Meanwhile, in Tokyo, the Japanese media had already begun connecting the dots between Lockheed and Kakuei Tanaka, a popular political figure within Japan's ruling Liberal Democratic Party (LDP). Tanaka had been prime minister when Lockheed was awarded the ANA contract, and he was forced to resign in 1974 amid accusations that he had set up a network of shell companies to profit from his public office. But those allegations had never stuck, allowing Tanaka to maintain his seat in the Japanese Diet, where he continued to control a powerful faction within the LDP. By early 1976, there was already talk of his mounting a comeback to become prime minister again.

Even so, the allegations coming out of Washington surrounding Lockheed were impossible to ignore. The Subcommittee had published documents showing how money paid to Kodama had gone to Kenji Osano, another wealthy businessman who also happened to be one of Tanaka's oldest friends.

These revelations placed Japan's then-Prime Minister, Takeo Miki, in a difficult position as well. The head of a much smaller faction within the LDP, Miki had been chosen to lead the party largely because his "squeaky clean" image had helped the LDP restore its legitimacy after Tanaka's resignation. To many observers, Miki was the feckless caretaker, a premier whose sole purpose was to maintain the post until such time as a more adequate replacement was found.

While calling for increased transparency in public, the message to Miki from the party establishment was clear: Pursuing the Lockheed story would only weaken his own political standing. On the evening of February 18, LDP Secretary General Yasuhiro Nakasone personally visited the American Embassy in Tokyo asking for the U.S. government's help in hushing up ("*momikesu*") the matter.[403]

Yet the Lockheed scandal would not be easy to dismiss. "The country has heard little else for the past two weeks and the televised Diet hearings ranked third in postwar viewership behind the Japanese Red Army Retreat Massacre and Queen Elizabeth's visit," the U.S. Embassy in Tokyo reported to Kissinger on February 20. Whether due to the remarkable public furor or to his own personal sense of conviction, Miki would forego consulting party leaders and write a letter on February 21 to President Ford urging him to help make relevant documents on Lockheed available to the Japanese government. The letter pressed for full disclosure of all names of those involved and served both as plea for judicial assistance and as a declaration of Miki's own independence from his party establishment.

Ford Moves to Contain the Scandal

The démarche marked the second time in as many weeks that President Ford was forced to address the Lockheed affair publicly. After the Church Subcommittee's bombshell revelations earlier in the month, Ford quickly announced that he, too, would be investigating overseas bribery. He assembled a cabinet-level Task Force on Questionable Corporate Payments Abroad and appointed Secretary of Commerce Elliot Richardson to head the group. The announcement came as a surprise to some at the White House who viewed Treasury Secretary William Simon as better informed on the issue, but Ford believed Richardson represented a more credible authority in the eyes of the American public given his resignation as Attorney General after being ordered by President Nixon to fire the Watergate special prosecutor.[404]

To the press, however, the Task Force was just another deft ploy.[405] "One of President Ford's motives in ordering the White House investigation simply may be to convey a public impression that he and his administration are on top of the burgeoning developments," one writer stated in the *Wall Street Journal* on February 11. "Many of the disclosures of bribes and payoffs have been coming out of Congress so far, particularly from a Senate subcommittee chaired by Idaho Democrat Frank Church, who is thinking of running for Mr. Ford's job."[406]

Miki's letter offered Ford the opportunity to change that narrative. On March 11, Ford responded to the Japanese prime minister with a proposal that the two governments "meet without delay" to work out a plan that would provide the Japanese government access to confidential findings.[407] Ford's proposal was to exchange information in an orderly manner through the Department of Justice. In the weeks since Kotchian's testimony, Secretary of State Kissinger had occasion to remind several diplomatic missions in Washington that it was against diplomatic etiquette, if not against established rules of law, for members of foreign countries to approach Congress directly in request of information. Under Ford's proposal, the Japanese government would have to go through the executive branch rather than approach the Senate directly to secure that information.

To outsiders, Ford could claim that his approach balanced

the Japanese government's desire to obtain the immediate disclosure of the names of corrupt officials with the privacy rights of foreign citizens—not to mention potential U.S. defendants. But an ulterior motive also existed: Ford's proposal took the Lockheed affair outside the realm of a congressional investigation and placed it in the hands of the executive branch. And by framing the investigation within the formalities of international legalism, Ford could buy additional time for the affair to eventually lose momentum on its own. The DOJ would need to reach an agreement on evidence exchange and cooperation with Japanese law enforcement authorities, and questions pertaining to the proper form of the agreements, constraints of international judicial assistance, and the reciprocal obligations assumed by each of the parties might take months to hash out. Ford believed that moving the matter to this level of technicality served both U.S. and Japanese interests of scaling down tensions by prolonging the investigation and removing the flow of information from the public sphere.[408]

To others, however, it was clear that the White House was simply stalling. As William Proxmire noted during a Lockheed hearing on February 19, "the greatest mistake former President Nixon and his associates made in the Watergate affair was an attempt to hide the truth … It seems to me that foreign countries, Holland and Germany and Japan and other countries … since it's been disclosed that this bribery took place—have a right to know who is guilty."[409]

Many in those countries felt similarly, including a group

comprised mostly of prominent Japanese media and religious leaders calling itself the "Ad Hoc Committee of Citizens to Uncover the Lockheed Scandal."[410] The group purchased a series of quarter-page ads in the *New York Times* appealing for America's assistance in exposing the facts surrounding Lockheed. The first ad, an open letter to President Ford, read simply: "Your Decision Kills Japanese Democracy."[411]

*

For his part, Frank Church welcomed the involvement of the Department of Justice in the Lockheed affair. For two weeks straight, he and his staff had been fielding nonstop requests to release the names of the recipients of Lockheed's foreign bribes. The requests were coming not just from the Japanese government, but also the governments of Italy, Greece, Turkey, Belgium, the Netherlands, and Spain.[412] It was only a matter of time before some name was leaked and Church would have to take the blame for the fallout. Referring requests from foreign dignitaries to the Justice Department provided him much-needed relief.

But to Church's surprise, Jacob Javits and Hubert Humphrey required an explicit vote by the Foreign Relations Committee to approve the procedures by which he was to hand over documents to the Department of Justice. It was an unusual power move designed to remind Church that the Subcommittee was beholden to the graces of its parent organization. Pat Holt, Chief of Staff to the Foreign

On the left, Senator Frank Church speaks during his presidential campaign announcement in 1976. On the right, a collection of campaign button prototypes shows Democratic nominee Jimmy Carter's potential running mates, one of whom was Church. Carter eventually chose Minnesota Senator Walter Mondale.

Credits: Left, Special Collections and Archives, Albertsons Library, Boise State University; right, public domain image via Wikimedia Commons

Relations Committee, had already begun accusing Church of using the Lockheed affair purely to chase headlines. He ultimately got the approval he was seeking, but it was, as Levinson later recalled, "a warning shot to Church that the investigations by the Multinational Subcommittee were cutting too close to the bone."[413]

Be that as it may, Frank Church had little time for Committee backbiting. He had other, more pressing matters to attend.

The '76 Democratic Nomination

Only a few days later, on March 18, Frank Church stood on the steps of the historic red brick courthouse in Idaho City to formally announce his campaign for the presidency. Convinced to throw his hat into the ring by the soft support for Jimmy Carter in the Northeast—Carter had lost primaries in both Massachusetts and New York—Church became only the second Idahoan in history to run for president; the first had been Church's boyhood hero, Senator William Borah.

Adopting what he called the "late, late strategy," Church's plan was to gain enough momentum in the Western states to send the convention into a second-round ballot where anti-Carter, non-Carter, and doubting-Carter delegates would look for a place to coalesce.[414] If he were to pull it off, Church knew he would need to go on a frenetic, ten-week campaign blitz. It would require mortgaging his home to pay for additional airtime on television and radio, as well as being on the road seven days a week for the next two months and flying back to D.C. at night if he needed to be on the Senate floor the following morning for a vote.[415]

With Church spending so much of his time on the campaign trail, the Subcommittee's work investigating Lockheed largely ground to a halt. Even so, the attention surrounding Lockheed had recast foreign bribery as a matter of public urgency that extended well beyond the activities of the Church Subcommittee. The constant stream of media attention had led boards of directors across America to question their corporate executives on overseas payment practices, prompting many companies to come forward to the SEC under its voluntary disclosure program.

In late February, Grumman Corporation, a rival to Lockheed, admitted to paying $28 million in bribes in Iran. McDonnell Douglas, Lockheed's top competitor in

Japan, would itself admit to $2.5 million in bribes paid to undisclosed foreign officials.[416] Other multinationals to come forward in the weeks and months to come included Castle & Cooke, Ford, General Motors, Phillips Petroleum, Rockwell International, G.D. Searle, and Whittaker Corporation.[417] By midyear, over 100 American firms, including 10 percent of the Fortune 500, had voluntarily disclosed to the SEC more than $100 million in questionable payments abroad.[418]

The cumulative result was what Humphrey had likely always feared: a revisiting of corporate corruption not only abroad, but at home as well. When it was revealed that Ashland Oil had used a foreign subsidiary, Ashland Petroleum Gabon Corp., to make payments to foreign officials in Gabon, Nigeria, Libya, and the Dominican Republic, previously undisclosed payments to politicians here in the U.S. were also brought to light—including to the former vice president.[419] On March 22, newspapers announced that Humphrey had collected, all told, an additional $30,000 in illegal payments both from Ashland Oil and Gulf Oil.[420] The timing of yet another corruption headline, together with the senator's continuing health problems, would strike a final blow to any future presidential aspirations. On April 30, Humphrey announced he was officially withdrawing his name from the contest.[421]

Church, meanwhile, continued to stake his bet on the Western states, and in late May, he won primaries in Oregon, Nebraska, and Idaho, giving him the momentum needed to make his case as the liberal alternative to Carter.

His campaign was blindsided, however, when California Governor Jerry Brown made the announcement that he, too, was entering the race. Soon after, Church suffered the one-two punch of losing badly in both California and Ohio. "On television tonight, Frank Church looks exhausted," one reporter wrote on the night of the California and Ohio losses. "Ordinarily an articulate man, he talks hesitantly and confuses some of his words."[422]

The next day, it was officially announced that Jimmy Carter had earned enough delegates to secure the nomination. In the weeks that followed, several TV networks continued to say that Church was a "top pick" for the vice presidency, but internally within the Democratic party, Hubert Humphrey lobbied vigorously against the man who had helped derail his last shot at the presidency. Carter would eventually pick Humphrey's old portage, Walter Mondale, to serve as his running mate.[423] In the end, the rivalry between Church and Humphrey had proven mutually destructive, preventing either one from realizing their dream of reaching the White House.

*

As media attention in the U.S. began to turn toward the upcoming presidential election, the Lockheed affair continued unabated, though much of the action now occurred overseas. In Italy, there were rumors that President Leone would have to resign, while stories surrounding Prince Bernhard continued to dominate headlines in the Netherlands.[424] There, in a matter of just a few short weeks, the scandal had rewritten many long-standing rules on what could be said or printed about the Royal House of Orange. It was revealed, for example, that the Prince apparently owned an apartment in Paris where he maintained a relationship with a French woman nicknamed "Poupette," said to be the sister of French tennis champion Jean Noel Grinda.[425]

Tabloid headlines aside, the Lockheed scandal opened the door to serious questions about the Dutch monarchy. Labor party advocates began to discuss what steps could be taken to convert the Netherlands into a parliamentary republic, while others believed the political pressure would simply force Queen Juliana to abdicate the throne. Supporters of the monarchy soon launched a counteroffensive, with one group of Dutch veterans seen passing out decals in the streets of Holland with the dull (if straightforward) slogan "We Maintain the Fullest Confidence in Prince Bernhard" printed on them.[426]

Meanwhile, in Japan, Prime Minister Miki and the Japanese Ministry of Justice, bolstered by the local media's unrelenting attention to Lockheed, continued to press forward with their own investigations. On March 3, Hiro Hiyama, President and Chairman of the Marubeni Corporation, resigned. A week later, Japanese authorities formally indicted Yoshio Kodama, Lockheed's shadowy middleman, on charges of tax evasion.

Having suffered a stroke some years earlier, Kodama was permitted by Japanese police to conduct the usual in-person questioning from the comforts of his mansion located in one of Tokyo's high-end residential districts. Outside the compound's gates, a group of journalists set up a daily presence, and on March 23, they found themselves with front-row seats to a surreal scene. At around midday, a single-engine airplane plunged into Kodama's home, sending flames and billows of smoke pouring from the second-floor veranda. Moments before crashing, the plane's pilot had been heard by air traffic controllers shouting "Tenno Heika Banzai" over the radio, the traditional kamikaze war cry made infamous during World War II.

Tokyo police eventually learned that the plane had been piloted by a Japanese pornographic film actor named Mitsuyasu Maeno. Five years earlier, Maeno had been among the select band of ultranationalists gathered inside the Okura Hotel to hear the premiere performance of Kodama's "Song of the Race."[427] The right-wing dissident apparently targeted Kodama out of a sense that the nationalist figure had betrayed his home country by taking bribes from a company so closely tied to America's World War II efforts. And though Kodama was uninjured during the attack, the incident elevated the Lockheed affair to a whole new level of public ignominy in Japan.[428]

For Prime Minister Miki, however, these events only hardened his resolve to pursue the investigation to its bitter end. Lawyers from the Japanese prosecutor's office flew to Los Angeles soon thereafter to meet with Kotchian in person. By then, the Lockheed president had been let go by company's board of directors, and in a highly unusual move under Japanese law, the prosecutors offered him legal immunity if he cooperated in revealing the details of Lockheed's bribery scheme.[429] No longer muzzled by Lockheed's corporate lawyers, Kotchian agreed, believing that he could finally tell his side of the story. Over the course of the next several days, he gave the Japanese prosecutors an unabridged recounting of the company's maneuverings in Japan to secure the TriStar deal.

Shockwaves in Tokyo

Kotchian began his story in August 1972 inside none other than the lobby of the Okura Hotel. He and his wife checked in and were soon booked into a suite that had just recently been vacated by U.S. Secretary of State Henry Kissinger. The couple came to call the hotel their home for the next two months while Kotchian worked to secure the TriStar deal.

The first matter of business was to meet with Toshiharu Okubo, Marubeni's primary point of contact for Lockheed. "Good news," Okubo told him during their first meeting a few days later. "Tomorrow at 7:30 a.m., we are seeing Prime Minister Tanaka."[430] It had not been an easy appointment to arrange, but Marubeni told Kotchian that they would absolutely have to meet with the prime minister soon before his summit meeting in Hawaii with President Nixon the following week. Any later, and Tanaka might not reach ANA before a decision was made.

To guarantee Tanaka's support, Kotchian was also told that Lockheed would need to make a "pledge" to the Prime

Minister. The suggested price was 500 million Japanese yen, (roughly $10 million in 2025). Kotchian had no time to hesitate; he would, of course, make the pledge.

Later that evening, Kotchian met with Lockheed's second agent in Japan, Yoshio Kodama. To avoid drawing attention to his visits, Kotchian would see Kodama only at night, entering his office through a side entrance inside Tokyo's Sony Building. "So Byzantine were the TriStar maneuverings," Kotchian later recalled, "that Marubeni, our 'above ground' agents and consultants, had no idea that Kodama was on Lockheed's payroll."[431]

Before meeting for the first time, Kotchian had read *Sugamo Diary*, Kodama's memoir published after his release from prison. When they eventually met in person, Kotchian was surprised that the former war criminal was somewhat shorter in height than he had expected and had a disarmingly soft voice.[432] But whatever his appearance might belie, Kotchian had little doubt that the man before him wielded untold power in Japan.

Kodama explained that if Lockheed truly wanted to guarantee Tanaka's backing, the company would need to commit at least another 500 million yen. This time, the money would not to be paid to Tanaka directly, but to Kenji Osano, a major shareholder of ANA and lifelong friend of Tanaka. "It was the second time that day that I had been asked for 500 million yen," Kotchian remarked, wondering if the number held special significance to the Japanese.[433] Again, he obliged.

Early the next morning, Okubo, accompanied by

Marubeni's President, Hiro Hiyama, met with the prime minister. Since taking office, Tanaka had restructured his two-acre private estate in downtown Tokyo into a multi-building complex, adding offices to the main living quarters so as to better receive guests. He called the compound Mejiro-Dai, and it was there that he hosted upward of 100 visitors per day. Each group was allowed a brief audience with Tanaka in which to secure a favor or give thanks of one sort or another.[434]

When Marubeni's time came, Hiyama introduced himself and explained that Marubeni's client, Lockheed, was having trouble selling the TriStar planes to All Nippon Airways. He wondered if the prime minister might use his influence to help cement the deal. "*Yoshiyoshi*," meaning "okay, okay," Tanaka responded roughly. But that was all that was needed, and a few hours later, Kotchian was called into Marubeni's office where he was told by a jubilant Okubo that "the pledge had been made."[435]

Tanaka stayed true to his promise, calling ANA's President Tokuji Wakasa to press him on the TriStar bid before leaving for Hawaii only a few days later. Yet even with the backing of the prime minister, the deal was not assured. Lockheed still faced tough competition from both Boeing and McDonnell Douglas. The Boeing 747 and McDonnell DC-10 each performed better in noise tests in Tokyo and Nagasaki, a key factor according to ANA officials. Industry-wide comparisons had also shown that Lockheed's TriStar engines required both more fuel and more maintenance than the DC-10.

Come October, Kotchian learned the disconcerting news that ANA had made the decision to select the DC-10 over the TriStar and that Lockheed would get the much less lucrative JAL contract. By his own account, Kotchian nearly "jumped out of [his] skin," precipitating another series of frantic meetings with Kodama and Marubeni.[436] Hadn't he paid enough? What had gone wrong?

A few days later, Okubo called Kotchian in his hotel room and informed him that there was still a chance for Lockheed to win the ANA contract but that Kotchian would have to come up with another 120 million yen (roughly $2.5 million dollars) within the next twelve hours. Three-fourths of the money would go directly to Wakasa, Kotchian was told, with the remainder to be distributed by ANA to six politicians whose names Kotchian jotted down on a hotel notepad.

Kotchian showed the Japanese prosecutors the piece of paper, which included the secretary general of the LDP, the minister of transportation, and the LDP chief cabinet secretary. Thanks to Deak & Company, Kotchian was able to arrange for the money to be delivered to Okubo the next morning. Later that evening, Kotchian, accompanied by Lockheed sales executive Peter Mingrone, were summoned to ANA's offices and finally heard the news they'd been waiting for: ANA had chosen the Lockheed TriStar. After months of heartache, he'd done what he had come to Tokyo to do. The next day, Kotchian and his wife held an impromptu party in their room at the Okura. "Everybody's face looked so happy and bright," Kotchian would recall. "Champagne was opened, one bottle after another, [and] when I poured a glass of champagne on top of Mr. Mingrone's head, the party became even happier."[437]

*

The Japanese prosecutors, too, had reason to celebrate. Kotchian's sworn testimony, together with the documents they had obtained through the U.S. Department of Justice, gave them enough hard evidence to finally go after the highest echelons of Japan's political hierarchy.

On May 10, 1976, Kodama was again indicted, this time for violation of Japan's more severe Foreign Exchange and Foreign Trade Control laws. In the coming weeks, Marubeni's Hiyama, Okubo, and Itoh, as well as Wakasa and a variety of other ANA officials would also be arrested. Remaining defiant throughout, Tanaka publicly declared his innocence while working behind the scenes to organize various LDP factions to join in a final effort to oust Miki. "Either he would have to prosecute Mr. Tanaka," wrote one newspaper, "or Mr. Tanaka would devour him."[438] Buoyed by an outraged public, Miki pressed on.

On the morning of July 27, at around 6:30 a.m., two agents from the Tokyo district prosecutor's office arrived at the Mejiro-Dai to bring Tanaka in for questioning. After waiting about thirty minutes, the agents were eventually greeted by the Japanese prime minister, dressed in a sharp, navy suit. They escorted Tanaka to the prosecutor's office, where he was formally placed under arrest for suspicion of violating the Foreign Exchange Law, and after receiving a routine physical and having his necktie and belt confiscated, was placed in a small holding cell inside the Tokyo House of Detention. All told, Tanaka would spend twenty days in jail, the maximum allowed under the law, after which he was released on a $690,000 bail—said to be the second-largest bail ever set in Japan at that time.

Unsurprisingly, Tanaka's arrest and the ensuing revelations received wall-to-wall coverage in the Japanese press. One Japanese government official told a counterpart at the U.S. embassy that it had generated the biggest headlines he'd seen in Japan since the declaration of war thirty-five years earlier.[439] "The Tanaka arrest is quite obviously the biggest shock the LDP has ever received," wrote an embassy official in an electronic telegram to Henry Kissinger. "If a Tanaka can be arrested, the possibility of arresting other politicians is wide open."[440]

The detention of the prime minister, though temporary, provided the Tokyo prosecutors sufficient time to detain Tanaka's personal chauffeur, Masanori Kasahara. On the second day of his interrogation, the chauffeur broke down, recounting between sobs his handling of Tanaka's illicit winnings over the years. He even provided the Japanese prosecutors with hand-drawn diagrams of where in Tanaka's home he'd hidden the money. After his release, a distraught Kasahara drove his car to a wooded area in the suburbs of Tokyo and—in either desperation or a final act of loyalty—committed suicide by connecting a hose from the car's exhaust pipe to its interior.[441]

The headlines continued for months until finally, in December, the country held a general election. Dubbed "the Lockheed Election" by the local press, it was widely seen as a referendum on the LDP. The final result was a loss of twenty-two seats, marking the first time in its twenty-five-year reign that the LDP had lost its overall majority in the House of Representatives.

The Global Reckoning

"Well, we did it in Japan," a frustrated Kissinger told President Ford in a meeting at the Oval Office the next day. "Frank Church should be proud of himself."[442] Yet Church saw things quite differently, and in his mind, the Lockheed investigations had done more good than harm. As Church put it before a crowd gathered at the Harvard East Asian Society that winter, there is "no reason to tread lightly in cleaning up the corrupt practices of multinational corporations.... There is every indication that instead of incurring the animosity of other peoples, our investigation, disclosure and enactment of remedial legislation engendered admiration abroad."[443]

Indeed, many jaded observers of Japanese politics had expected the Lockheed affair, like other Japanese corruption scandals before it, to simply be swept under the rug. Instead, there was both surprise and appreciation for Miki who, supported by ongoing public fervor, had proven so tenacious in seeing the investigation through to the end. Robert Shaplen, the *New Yorker's* Far East correspondent, described the mood in Japan at the time by noting

Prince Bernhard of the Netherlands at a 1961 NATO Air Force shooting competition in Leeuwarden in his medal-adorned military uniform and right in 1976, shortly after being stripped of his military positions after a bribery investigation.

Credits: Nationaal Archief (Dutch National Archives)

a "degree of pride that the democratic judicial process has worked so well—much the same feeling produced by the resolution of Watergate in America."[444] "[T]here is widespread gratitude for American exposure of the scandal," wrote another reporter at the *New York Times*, "as well as recognition that if foreigners had not been involved, the corruption would probably have been smoothed over."[445]

Back in Washington, Senator Proxmire aptly compared the Lockheed affair to the ancient practice of bloodletting, the painful medieval treatment once believed to have medicinal properties. Outside of Japan, other countries would undergo their own treatments. Come late August 1976, the Netherlands' three-man independent commission published its report on Prince Bernhard, concluding that over the years, the Prince had both solicited and received illicit payments from Lockheed in exchange for influencing the purchase of aircraft in the Netherlands.[446] The lengthy report itself became an immediate local sensation; the first print run of 5,000 copies sold out on day one, prompting the Dutch government printing office to run several more editions, all of which sold out in advance.

Ultimately, Queen Juliana was permitted to keep her title, although Prince Bernhard was stripped of his military positions and forced to resign from his business functions. In Italy, Lockheed prompted both the resignation of President Giovanni Leone and further gains by the Italian Communist Party in the June general election. When all was said and done, the scandal resulted in investigations in more than thirty countries across four continents. In the process, it heavily impacted three elections, causing the resignation of a president, the arrest and trial of a former prime minister, and the near toppling of one of Europe's oldest monarchies.

The affair prompted a fair amount of soul searching here in the U.S. as well, revealing an unspoken complicity between the executive branch and big business. "American embassies around the world have long known of these practices but voiced no protests to host governments and offered no protection to honest American businessmen," complained one witness during his testimony before Congress. "Those U.S. exporters who thought they were serving their country's foreign policy interests by making under-the-table payments to friendly foreign officials and political parties were never told otherwise."[447] Defense Department officials were found on occasion to have counseled American businesses on exactly how and when to pay bribes to foreign governments.[448] Other times, CIA officials simply used U.S. multinational corporations as fronts to make payments to foreign officials themselves.[449]

It is unsurprising, then, that calls for legislative reform would naturally emerge. Washington's first recourse was to go after the defense industry, with the Northrop hearings prompting the State Department to amend the 1975 International Traffic in Arms Regulations (ITAR) to require companies to identify their agents and commission payments to foreign governments. A year later, in the wake of the Lockheed scandal, Congress passed the Arms Export Control Act, demanding that defense companies report political contributions, fees, and commissions in connection with sales of arms abroad.

But the breadth of misconduct made evident that these incidents were not isolated to any one industry. By January 1977, a whopping 225 corporations had revealed "questionable" or illegal overseas payments under the SEC's voluntary disclosure program; by April, that number swelled to over 350.[450] The IRS separately identified the use of slush funds or illegal activity in over 270 companies.[451]

Numbers alone told only part of the story. Tales of corporate coverups, suicides, and the dramatic unmasking of high-level government officials had created quite a public spectacle. In the words of one writer at *Newsweek*, the frenzied discoveries poured forth "week by week, name by name, country by country, like some neatly plotted thriller of international intrigue."[452] With each new scandal, the calls to Congress mounted—not just for a legislative answer to the illegality, but as a kind of moral counterweight to the corporate vice so nakedly on display. Yet what form such a law might take, who would spearhead its passage, and whether it would prove more salve than cure were all still very much unknowns. Only this much was clear: Washington would have to do *something* before the bloodletting stopped.

CHAPTER FIVE

Legislating Morality

We cannot legislate morality. We have tried many times, and have always failed.

Senator Mike Gravel, October 6, 1975

Few criminal justice laws have passed with as much outward bipartisan accord in U.S. legislative history as the FCPA. The bill was adopted in the Senate by a unanimous voice vote and in the House of Representatives by a vote of 349–0. Appearances, however, can be deceiving. In speaking of the statute's passage a few years later, Representative Bob Eckhardt (D-TX), who introduced the bill in the House, told a different story: "While most everyone testifying at the hearing and speaking publicly supported the legislation," Eckhardt recounted, "there was a strong sub rosa effort to scuttle the bill."[453] Those efforts occurred at all levels of government, both in Congress and in the White House, buttressed by an active contingent of business lobbyists and other Washington insiders. In the end, these interests succumbed to mounting public outrage prompted by corporate scandals—Northrop and Lockheed chiefly among them—although they would remain potent enough to defang the statute's final version of its most anti-business components. This chapter explores the series of negotiations and compromises—that potent "witch's brew," as Jerome Levinson once described it—that eventually led to the enactment of the Foreign Corrupt Practices Act in December 1977.

H.R. 7539: A Freshman's Ambitious Start

It is a curious truth that the first legislative impulse to outlaw the bribery of foreign government officials came from the unlikeliest of sources. In May 1975, Bob Dorsey, CEO of the seventh richest company in the world, told the Church Subcommittee something it never expected to hear: "[A] statute on our books would make it easier to resist the very intense pressures which are placed upon us from time to time."[454] Dorsey's motivations in making the statement mattered little; if the business community was asking—no, *pleading*—for legislation, then surely, thought Church, Congress could oblige it.

Two weeks later, junior Congressman Stephen Solarz (D-NY) would be the first to put pen to paper. The bill he introduced, H.R. 7539, sought to criminalize bribery of foreign officials and directed the Secretary of State to monitor the overseas activities of American companies.[455] It was an ambitious piece of legislation, especially coming from a legislator who had been elected only a few months earlier. Solarz had beaten Bert Podell, a longtime New York Democrat who, incidentally, was himself under federal indictment for taking bribes. But it was also reflective of the makeup of the 94th Congress. Solarz was one of seventy-three other freshman Democrats entering Congress as a result of the 1974 midterm elections. Nicknamed the "Watergate babies," the group represented the largest infusion of new faces in the House of Representatives in modern political history and was comprised of young, ambitious men who had come of age during Vietnam and Watergate and viewed it as their mission to reform Washington.

But passing legislation aimed at tackling corporate bribery overseas would take more than a CEO's attempts to deflect bad press and a novice congressman with lofty aspirations. Youthful exuberance and newspaper headlines aside, the prevailing opinion in Washington was that any unilateral effort by the U.S. government to stop foreign bribery was either quixotic or built on fundamentally flawed assumptions about how international business was conducted. Two days after Solarz introduced H.R. 7539, Michael Butler, a senior Ford administration official, flatly told Congress that he had his "doubts whether we in this country can police the morality of the world," and that passage of such a law would create "very serious foreign relations problems ... which could be easily regarded as outrageous interference in the governmental affairs of a foreign country."[456] Another Ford official, Mark Feldman, Deputy Legal Advisor at the Department of State, similarly told Congress that passage of a statute outlawing bribery in other countries would plainly violate concepts of international law.[457]

Other arguments against passing legislation were less policy oriented, relying simply on long-standing cultural prejudices. As the Republican Senator from Texas John Tower told his colleagues at the time, "most countries in this world are governed by autocracy or oligarchy [such that] their ethical standards of conduct are vastly different from our own."[458] Mark Feldman likewise told a House committee that "it would be not only presumptuous but counterproductive to seek to impose our specific standards in countries with differing histories and cultures."[459] Both men borrowed from the same playbook used four decades earlier when Felix Du Pont of the DuPont chemical company testified before the Senate Munitions Inquiry that graft was simply "an old Chinese custom," and that bribes were "looked upon differently from the way they are in this country."[460]

Against the still-unfolding recession of the early 1970s and a first-ever trade deficit, this "when in Rome" approach had certain appeal. Employing the rhetorical straw man of "post-Watergate morality," conservatives argued that worrying about corruption in overseas markets was a luxury that the U.S. economy simply could not afford. Cold War hawks, for their part, claimed that corporate bribery was a necessary evil to "protect democracy" on the world stage and extend American influence and prestige around the world.[461] After all, the Pentagon had not only acquiesced to arms companies paying bribes to ply their wares abroad, but in many instances had helped them do so. "Multinational companies, like government agencies, are instruments of our nation's global power," wrote one columnist for the *New York Times*. "They should not be hobbled by home-bred notions of business morality."[462]

By late 1975, however, tales of foreign corruption had become so widespread that even those on the right had mostly abandoned trying to defend the practice and instead began to argue against the need for new laws to regulate against it. "The criminalization of questionable overseas business payments would contribute little to deterring such payments beyond that which is already accomplished by existing securities, tax, and criminal law," explained a representative of the U.S. Chamber of Commerce to Congress.[463] Some pointed out that the Internal Revenue Code already prohibited companies from deducting illegal payments made to a foreign official, while others looked to the applicability of antitrust law.[464] "Are there good reasons for any of the new laws now suggested in Congress or elsewhere?" SEC Chairman Roderick Hills asked an audience at the New York Bar Association in March 1976. "I doubt it," he replied. "If my assumptions as to what is happening now are correct, we can correct the deplorable practices we have seen with the tools we now have."[465]

Democrats remained skeptical, however. The legal grounds to prosecute overseas corporate bribery under existing securities laws were tenuous at best, and within the SEC, at least one commissioner had already publicly expressed doubts regarding the materiality standard's applicability to foreign bribes.[466] As for the tax code, most companies did not claim overseas bribes as a deduction on their tax returns, either because those payments were considered solely foreign transactions with no domestic tax consequences, or simply because they refrained from doing so.[467] Regarding antitrust law, reform advocates pointed out that in order to bring charges, the DOJ would not only have to prove a conspiracy of multiple firms to bribe a foreign government, but also show that the bribery scheme somehow negatively impacted U.S. trade. This meant that in most instances of transnational bribery, antitrust law had no practical application.[468]

By late 1975, then, it had become increasingly clear to the Democratic party that new legislation addressing overseas bribery was needed. Both younger members of the party, like Solarz, and more tenured lawmakers, like Pennsylvania Congressman Robert Nix, were supportive of the idea.

Given that Democrats controlled Congress, President Ford sensed that he too would soon have to propose a solution or else deal with the unflattering optics of having to veto an anticorruption law he did not support. To buy himself some time, the White House recommitted to finding a diplomatic resolution, a tactic formally put in place in September 1975 when Secretary of State Henry Kissinger pledged before a Special Session of the United Nations that the United States would seek to codify ethical guidelines for international business practices. Meanwhile, Treasury Secretary William Simon opened channels within the OECD to form a working party on restrictive business practices.[469]

If proffered earlier, perhaps these efforts would have successfully staved off further inquiry. But by the winter of 1975, Congress was already becoming aware of widespread corruption at both Northrop and Lockheed, and as those allegations grew in pitch, promises of a multilateral solution were increasingly viewed as palliative. "When has the OECD ever accomplished anything?" questioned Senator Abraham Ribicoff (D-CT), Chair of the Senate Subcommittee on International Trade.[470] "An international treaty on the subject is really a prescription for doing nothing," echoed Senator Proxmire. "[W]hile high sounding in purpose [it] would be devoid of practical effect."[471] The Senate consequently passed Resolution 265, which conceded congressional support for the development of a multinational code of conduct on illegal payments but reiterated the legislative branch's ability to reject any international treaty negotiated by the White House that it deemed too soft or otherwise unsatisfactory.[472]

Work on drafting a legislative solution, therefore, continued into the spring of 1976, just as the Lockheed investigation began ratcheting up into a truly global scandal. And the more things began to spiral out of control at Lockheed, the more divided Ford's cabinet became as to how to respond. Secretary of Commerce Elliot Richardson, Attorney General Edward Levi, and Ed Schmults, Deputy Counsel to the President, all favored a legislative solution. "In my view, the incalculable harm being done domestically to American business and our free enterprise system far outweighs the disadvantages involved in any legislative initiative," wrote Schmults in a June 4 memo.[473] Others in Ford's cabinet, including Secretary of State Henry Kissinger, Treasury Secretary William Simon, Senior National Security Advisor Brent Scowcroft, and top economic advisor William Seidman all remained stalwart opponents. "We are not yet prepared for a legislative initiative, and we must not let a perceived tactical need to 'do something' push us into a course of action which we have not thought through carefully," warned Scowcroft in a memo addressed to the president.[474]

It was ultimately Richardson, Ford's pick to lead his anticorruption task force, whose opinion would win out. A legislative solution, Richardson explained, was the most politically expedient course of action. "The issue is one of symbols as well as substance," he wrote to the president.[475] In an election year, Ford was apt to agree: What form a new anticorruption law might take was still up for debate, but by midsummer in 1976, the White House had signed off on backing some kind of legislative solution "to allay skepticism as to the seriousness of the Administration in its quest for remedies."[476] With the president's support, the issue of legislating transnational corruption had crossed an important threshold. And with Democrats controlling both the House and the Senate, it seemed no longer a question of if, but when, such a law would be passed.

Senator William Proxmire chats with reporters prior
to his appearance on CBS' "Face the Nation"
on Feb. 15, 1976, in Washington, D.C.

Credit: The Associated Press, photo uncredited

S. 3133: The First Comprehensive Bill

Over a mere two-year period—between the summer of 1975 and the summer of 1977—an impressive thirty-two bills were introduced in Congress aimed at addressing overseas corporate corruption.[477] Some sought to close existing loopholes, including one proposal to change the tax code so as to prevent corporations from claiming deductions for bribes paid abroad.[478] Others sought to address the problem head on. Bills in this latter category fell into one of two strains: The first proposed criminalizing overseas bribery outright, while the second would require mandatory disclosure of foreign political payments.

Senate Bill 3133, introduced by Senator Proxmire on March 11, 1976, combined both approaches. Adopting a "more is better" philosophy and aided by Proxmire's overall popularity at the time, S. 3133 was the first comprehensive piece of legislation aimed at stopping overseas bribery with serious political backing. Appearing on TV's *Face the Nation*, Proxmire explained how the statute would work. First, it would amend the Securities Exchange Act of 1934 to prohibit issuers of U.S. securities from making improper payments to foreign officials.[479] The language of the bill borrowed heavily from existing domestic bribery statutes, including the frequently used 1872 Federal Mail Fraud Statute, and relied on the company's "use of the mails or any means or instrumentality of interstate commerce" to assert jurisdiction over payments to foreign officials.[480] Second, the bill included a disclosure provision requiring issuers to file periodic reports with the Commission of foreign political payments in excess of $1,000.[481] "Disclosure is at the heart of S. 3133," Proxmire explained, a requirement that he saw as necessary to go beyond the SEC's materiality standard in order to "require systematic disclosure of all such payments, *per se*, whether or not materiality were asserted."[482]

Finally, a third provision required issuers to maintain "accurate" books and records, something that had been proposed directly by the SEC. In fact, Proxmire had called Sporkin personally and offered him the opportunity to insert his own language into the bill. "Bringing to bear both my legal and accounting training," Sporkin later recalled, "I analyzed the various cases the SEC had brought and came to the conclusion that in no instance was an illicit payment recorded in the corporation's books for what it was."[483] Such a requirement for publicly traded companies would make it "virtually untenable" for someone to admit in writing that the corporation was paying bribes overseas, Sporkin told Proxmire.[484]

Not everyone at the SEC was supportive of the bill, however—least of all Chairman Roderick Hills. It was no secret in Washington that Proxmire and Hills disliked one another. Not only had Proxmire voted against Hills' confirmation as chairman of the SEC, but he'd also voted against his wife's confirmation as secretary of the Department of Housing and Urban Development.[485] Interactions between the two were frosty, and within just days of Proxmire introducing S. 3133, Hills penned a six-page open letter voicing his objections.

According to Hills, the bill was unnecessary and would prove both "ineffective and undesirable."[486] But Hills also realized that if Congress was truly set on passing a statute, the SEC would need to offer a more palatable alternative. He offered his public support to Sporkin's proposal regarding the need for companies to keep accurate corporate records while promising to submit a more expansive draft legislation to Congress in the months to come.[487]

Senator Church, too, was displeased with Proxmire's proposal, albeit for different reasons. Having been at the center of investigations into Gulf, Northrop, and Lockheed, he felt snubbed at not even having been consulted on the bill. Church would later discover, however, that it was Humphrey, not Proxmire, who had connived to introduce S. 3133 into Congress without his involvement. Humphrey still held a senior role in the Foreign Relations Committee and had recruited Richard "Dick" Moose, a member of the permanent staff of the Committee to draft the bill's antibribery section. The draft language was then referred by Senate Majority Leader Mike Mansfield directly to Proxmire, bypassing the normal Foreign Relations Committee approval process.[488]

The backhanded maneuver typified the rancor within the Committee at the time. When Fulbright left the Foreign Relations Committee in 1975 after a fifteen-year tenure, leadership transferred to Senator John Sparkman, a Democrat from Alabama who many considered aging and fundamentally uninterested in foreign affairs. Without a strong leader, the Committee had begun to splinter into various factions. Subcommittees whose staff and budgets had grown under Fulbright became the new seats of power, and distrust and rivalry between them grew, fed by rumors that Sparkman would soon have to step down. The question became whether Humphrey, who represented the old guard, or Church, who represented the new one, was the heir apparent.[489] It was within this context that Humphrey deliberately arranged for the antibribery bill to go through the Banking Committee. According to Levinson, it was Humphrey's way of demonstrating that while Church may have been the "show horse" of the Foreign Relations Committee, Humphrey was still, in fact, the "workhorse" who did the more mundane but more important work of drafting legislation.[490]

S. 3379: Sunlight is the Best Disinfectant

In response, Levinson quickly helped Church put together his own proposal, which Church introduced on May 5, 1976. Like Proxmire's bill, Church's S. 3379, titled the International Contributions, Payments, and Gifts Disclosure Act, required issuers to submit yearly reports of their payments to foreign officials to the SEC. It also included a few expanded requirements, like covering payments between private parties, allowing shareholders or competitors who had suffered damages to sue companies that paid bribes, and requiring SEC-regulated companies to establish audit committees to investigate payments to foreign officials and report them to their boards of directors. But unlike Proxmire's bill, S. 3379 did not actually criminalize the overseas bribes themselves.[491]

For Church, the omission was purposeful and avoided involving the American judicial system in what he and Levinson perceived as the diplomatic complexities of investigating foreign officials. How, for example, would U.S. prosecutors compel testimony from foreign witnesses? By requiring corporations to report their payments publicly, Church believed that his proposal gave the foreign country involved the best chance of pursuing the matter on their own terms. It was an approach based on the truism voiced by Supreme Court Justice Louis Brandeis that sunlight is said to be the best disinfectant. "At first glance, the disclosure rule may seem weak," wrote one columnist for the *Washington Post*, "but it promises to work more effectively in practice than Sen. Proxmire's criminal sanctions."[492]

On a more pragmatic level, Church likely believed that his approach had the best chance of passing the Senate. A few months earlier, Church and Republican Senator Charles Percy had coauthored an amendment to the Foreign Military Sales Act requiring U.S. companies selling military equipment overseas to disclose their commissions, fees, and other forms of payment to foreign agents.[493] That bill had won wide bipartisan support and was signed by the president into law in June. In introducing S. 3379, Church hoped to build off that bipartisan success by effectively broadening those same disclosure requirements to other sectors of the economy.

Yet Church faced more difficulty in gaining support for the proposal than he likely imagined. Percy, who had initially been in favor of S. 3379, surprised Church by refusing at the last minute to cosponsor the bill, voicing concerns that public disclosure in the U.S. should be contingent on other countries requiring their companies to do the same.[494] To further complicate matters, Church's hectic schedule in the middle of the 1976 presidential primaries made it nearly impossible for him to hold the necessary public hearings to gain additional support. Eventually, he secured the aid of Senator Clifford Case, his old Republican ally, to cosponsor the bill in the Senate, but after initially failing to win over Congressman Henry Reuss (D-WI), the Chair of the House Banking Committee, Church was forced to settle on the succor of freshman Democrat Stephen Solarz to introduce a counterpart version of the bill in the House.

Even so, both proposals by Church and Proxmire were viewed as the most likely bills to pass through Congress. Both also largely conformed to a hoary tradition of anticorruption jurisprudence in the United States. As legal scholar Zephyr Teachout writes in *Corruption in America*, U.S. anticorruption laws have generally come in two forms.[495] Proxmire's bill seeking to criminalize overseas corruption exemplified the first type, known as a "corrupt intent" laws. These share in common five key elements for a payment to be considered illegal: (1) the giving of a thing of value or a benefit (2) to a public official or candidate (3) corruptly (4) with intent to influence (5) an official action.[496] Such laws trace their lineage in American history as far back as the 1853 Act to Prevent Frauds upon the Treasury and through more contemporary applications, like the Hobbs Act.[497] They can be difficult to enforce but are rhetorically quite straightforward. Bribery is illegal, so long as you can prove that the offeror intended to give the benefit in order to corruptly influence the recipient.

In contrast, the emphasis in Church's bill requiring the disclosure of payments to foreign officials (but not their outright criminalization) fits squarely within Teachout's second category, laws that are "prophylactic or structural," meaning they shy away from defining corruption or trying to determine a person's intent and instead seek to regulate specific behavior already deemed inherently corruptive by its very nature. In effect, they eschew moral considerations in favor of bright-line rules wherein the intent of the person to cause some specific outcome is irrelevant. Existing examples at the time ranged from the 1910 Federal Corrupt Practices Act, which required the reporting of all political contributions in national elections, to the

1970 Bank Secrecy Act, which sought to curb illegally transferred funds by requiring the reporting of all wire transfers of more than $5,000 in and out of the country.[498]

It comes as little surprise, then, that both criminalization and disclosure would emerge as the two primary approaches for addressing the problem of overseas corruption. Why Proxmire was drawn to one approach and Church the other, however, requires consideration of each person's overall political worldview. For Church, bribery wasn't a moral question *per se;* it was wrong because it eroded democratic political systems, which, in turn, threatened U.S. security interests. In a memoir published years later, Church's son wrote that his father was "very sensitive to being mislabeled an idealist or naïve," and Church himself, in fact, made clear at the outset of his investigations that he consciously wished to avoid judgment as to whether corporations were "good or evil, rather what role they played in the world and particularly vis-a-vis America's national interests."[499]

Church's views had been shaped by his experiences in China during World War II and his rejection of America's militarism in Vietnam. His beliefs were rooted in a respect for the sovereignty of nations, their interdependency, and their ability to work in concert despite their differences.[500] A disclosure regime permitted the U.S. to play a leading role while simultaneously giving other countries the freedom to enforce their own laws as they saw fit. If the Netherlands, Italy, and Japan had each been capable of launching investigations into Lockheed, then there was no reason to think that this approach could not be borne out successfully in other countries around the world.

For Proxmire, on the other hand, corruption was fundamentally a moral issue. It was a question of corporate greed, something "he just thought … was wrong" recalled Ken McLean, Proxmire's chief of staff on the Banking Committee. "He looked at it really in moral terms—you should not get ahead by bribing somebody. It just rubbed him the wrong way that bribery even existed."[501] Proxmire's staunch beliefs toward international corruption not only grew out of his interest in the increasingly popular idea at the time of "human rights," but also stretched further back to his early days as an investigative journalist uncovering local corruption in Madison, Wisconsin. Over the years, he had carried with him a muckraker's sensibilities and an innate distrust of the large and powerful. Once in the Senate, he'd built a reputation scrutinizing government ties to corporations, garnering attention through his "Golden Fleece Award"—a tongue-in-cheek recognition of government-funded projects that enriched contractors and "fleeced" taxpayer money. By 1971, he'd been on the cover of *Time Magazine* with the tagline, "Proxmire, the Giant Killer."[502]

Proxmire's dogmatism also meant that at times his principled stance on issues caused friction with his Senate colleagues. When Boeing sought government funding in the 1960s to finance the development of a supersonic transport plane, for example, it was Proxmire who single-handedly led the campaign to cut federal subsidies to the program, angering his fellow Democrats who relied on support from labor unions that had been promised jobs by Boeing. Critics said that his pious rhetoric tended toward a flattening oversimplification and that his reputation as a gadfly stemmed from his constant need for attention. When Proxmire appeared at a 1972 hearing wearing dark sunglasses and bandages over his head, his opponents smirked, surmising what the Senator later admitted to a staffer was the result of a facelift and hair transplant surgery in hopes of improving his appearance on television.[503]

Whatever his personal vanities, Proxmire's commitment to reform was undeniable, and once he took to an issue, he hung on to it with an indefatigable spirit. In one prolonged effort to ratify the UN Genocide Convention, he carried out what amounted to a one-man crusade, speaking on the topic more than 3,200 times over the course of nineteen years, until finally, in 1986, the Senate voted to ratify the treaty.[504] Ellen Proxmire, his ex-wife, said it was a trait he had carried with him ever since his days in prep school, where he had been voted by his peers not "most likely to succeed," but rather "biggest grind."[505]

What meaning, then, can we draw in comparing these two central figures? Both Church and Proxmire were independent, midwestern Democrats whose politics leaned firmly to the left of the states they represented. Church was the only Democrat ever to win reelection to the U.S. Senate from Idaho, and Proxmire was the first to do so in Wisconsin since 1851. Neither relied on corporate campaign contributions, instead cultivating a national media presence to reach a broader audience. For Church, this meant following in the footsteps of his childhood idol, Idaho Senator William Borah; like Borah, Church sought to project the image of a gifted orator and statesman who could weigh in on complex issues of foreign policy. Proxmire, for his part, saw himself in the image of his Wisconsin predecessor, Robert La Follette, or "Fighting Bob" as he was known to his constituents—someone who fought for social justice in the name of the common man.

These personas heavily colored how each man approached the issue of international corruption. To Church, corruption was intrinsically a foreign policy matter, a threat to Western democracy that made the world more susceptible to communism. His solution lay within the traditional postwar college of independent nation states. Once properly informed, S. 3379 enabled those countries to pursue corruption by multinational corporations each on their own terms. Proxmire, in contrast, saw himself as part of a new movement that elevated the human rights of the individual above the large, stultifying grip of nations. For him, corruption was an inherently borderless problem, one that plagued humanity; Proxmire's S. 3133 allowed the U.S. government to proactively intervene in these matters simply as a matter of right and wrong.

And so, as the 94th Congress readied itself to vote on these two divergent bills, both senators' larger-than-life personalities would prove decisive in the outcome.

S. 3418: The SEC Weighs In

Meanwhile, across town, SEC Chairman Roderick Hills had convened his staff to decide whether the SEC should put forth its own legislative proposal. Although Hills personally disfavored any new legislation, Proxmire had effectively forced his hand by proposing in S. 3133 that the SEC alone would be responsible for policing overseas corporate bribery. If the Commission were to succeed in convincing Congress to vote against Proxmire's plan, Hills would need to offer an alternative solution. Perhaps the best way to solve a problem that he didn't think existed was simply to offer an answer to a different one altogether. After all, Hills thought, the SEC had been offered an opportunity to write legislation—an opportunity he could leverage to address other long-standing gaps in the area of corporate governance.

Hills began by taking a hard look at corporate accounting standards. Beginning in the 1960s, a number of lawsuits had found that investors were being misled by some of the country's largest accounting firms due to material misstatements and omissions in corporate financial statements.[506] Much of the problem, as the SEC saw it, stemmed from the fact that the accounting industry had no common set of principles as to what corporations were required to disclose to their shareholders. In fact, competing standards known as the Generally Accepted Accounting Principles (GAAP) and the Generally Accepted Auditing Standards (GAAS) both existed at the same time. As a result, companies were tabulating even the most basic figures on their balance sheets differently from one another, and the SEC had found that variations only seemed to increase as companies moved their operations overseas. In the words of Abe Briloff, an accounting professor at the time, the cumulative effect was that multinationals were marrying disparate accounting methods and using accountants as "hired miracle workers" to create "a tidy world for investors, regulatory agencies and tax collectors."[507]

In response, many lawmakers began floating the idea that the SEC should have direct oversight over the accounting industry. Inside the SEC, however, the proposal was widely unpopular, although the Commission did begin working behind the scenes with the American Institute of Certified Public Accountants (AICPA) to develop more workable standards.

The revelations involving corporate bribery therefore provided another avenue to address what was seen within the SEC as a long-standing problem. And it's not as if the two issues were completely unrelated. After all, in at least one case, Sporkin and his team had discovered that accounting and internal audit departments were themselves colluding with their business colleagues to conceal illegal payments on the company's books.[508] Further complicating matters was the fact that in March 1976, the Supreme Court issued a ruling in *Ernst & Ernst v. Hochfelder* rendering it harder to hold professional accounting firms responsible for accounting fraud committed by their clients.[509] So when Hills turned to the SEC's Chief Accountant, Sandy Burton, and gave him carte blanche to draft a set of provisions to put into law, the moment seemed ripe to address standards in the accounting industry once and for all.

Working with Lloyd Feller, David Boyd, and others in the chairman's office, Burton proposed a set of three recommendations. The first required issuers to "devise and maintain an adequate system of internal accounting controls."[510] Borrowing almost word for word from the AICPA's own guidelines, Burton stipulated that the controls needed to be sufficient to provide "reasonable assurances" that the company's financial statements were in conformity with Generally Accepted Accounting Principles. All told, it was a modest proposal that largely codified existing SEC rules and regulations, but it at least gave the SEC further recourse to ensure that publicly traded companies met basic, minimum requirements.[511] Next, Burton proposed making it a crime for a company to falsify its books and records and added a second provision prohibiting employees from making materially false or misleading statements to their accountants—or omitting any material fact. These last two provisions were based directly on what the SEC had observed as a result of the bribery cases.

Hills adopted all three provisions, as well as Sporkin's original proposal, and delivered them to Proxmire on May 12, 1976. As chair of the Banking Committee, Proxmire introduced the proposal into the Senate as numbered bill S. 3418, but in doing so, did not hold back from criticizing what he viewed as a woefully inadequate solution. He bluntly stated that "of the three bills before the Committee, the SEC measure is the weakest." It would "merely codify the requirement that a corporation keep honest records, a requirement that is at least implicit in the entire system of corporate accountability."[512]

While perhaps an oversimplification, Proxmire was correct to point out that the SEC sought to address overseas corruption only indirectly. According to Hills, identifying bribe payers was not the government's responsibility, nor did the SEC have the resources or capabilities to do so. Instead, if given the proper tools, accountants were best positioned to ferret out bribery. "It is important, Mr. Chairman, to indicate that we continue to have faith in the system of self-regulation," Hills replied during his testimony. "We think that adoption of our proposals will give both the business community and our Commission the capacity to restore the damage done to the integrity of the system."[513]

In retrospect, it is difficult to imagine how Hills could have thought that the SEC's proposal would satisfy the needs of the moment. After months of painfully embarrassing revelations implicating heads of state from some of America's closest allies, was Congress really expected to believe that everything was due to accountants not doing their job correctly? But neither could Congress afford to dismiss the SEC's proposal out of hand. After all, Sporkin and his team had been instrumental in shining a light on overseas corporate bribery before the American public.

Yet for those who knew where to look, S. 3418 represented a more substantive change to how the SEC approached securities law. For decades, the guiding principle as to what information companies were required to disclose to their shareholders had been determined by the stock market. In other words, companies needed only to have disclosed information that would "materially" change the company's stock price. But from now on, "materiality" would be decided, at least in part, by objective industry standards of corporate accounting, and moreover, companies would have to put in place internal controls to meet those standards. To the SEC's critics, Hill's proposal may have seemed all too obvious, but by tying corporate disclosures to external considerations, the SEC had quietly opened the door to concepts of corporate stewardship that bucked years of traditional thinking. At the time, it meant requiring corporations to meet minimum accounting standards, but in the years to come, it could mean other kinds of generally accepted standards, be they environmental, social, or otherwise.

S. 3741: Ford Responds

Now that Church, Proxmire, and the SEC each had bills before Congress, pressure inside the White House was building for the president to put forth his own recommendations. For weeks, the press had derided the president's Task Force on Questionable Corporate Payments Abroad, for both its lack of independent, full-time staff and its uninspired mandate to report out "before the end of the current calendar year."[514] Facing reelection in November, the White House was sensitive to any issue that might impact Ford's polling numbers, and already, Jimmy Carter, the *de facto*

Democratic nominee, had accused Ford of "stonewalling" the release of information regarding Lockheed's payoffs in Japan—a term deliberately intended to evoke memories of Watergate. In response, Ford had countered with the tepid claim that Carter had no problem accepting free flights from Lockheed while governor of Georgia.[515] But by late spring of 1976, it was evident that a more forceful response was required, and turning to his cabinet, the president asked that a set of legislative proposals be drafted and brought to his attention immediately.

The directive prompted a flurry of memos, proposals, and counterproposals across the Ford administration. Attorney General Edward Levi was the first to write the president to voice his support for criminalizing overseas bribery, recommending that the U.S. outlaw the practice anywhere it was prohibited under another country's own laws (so long as that country also had a bilateral enforcement agreement with the United States).[516] Arthur Burns, Chairman of the Federal Reserve Board, similarly called for criminal penalties, going so far as to say so publicly (and without first clearing it with the White House) while appearing before a congressional hearing.[517] Commerce Secretary Elliot Richardson took a more middle-of-the-road approach, rejecting direct criminalization in favor of some less onerous form of disclosure requirement.[518] Secretary of State Henry Kissinger and Treasury Secretary William Simon, meanwhile, continued to reject any form of U.S. legislation until a multilateral solution was reached first.

On the morning of June 10, Ford called a meeting of

the Task Force inside the White House Cabinet Room. Seated around the large mahogany table, Ford and some of his closest advisers spent the better part of the morning debating the merits of each approach.[519] Senior National Security Advisor Brent Scowcroft advocated that the administration wait for an international treaty, pointing out that an OECD Ministerial Conference was planned for later in the month to vote on a code of conduct for multinational corporations. If that didn't suffice, then the UN Economic and Social Council (ECOSOC) was meeting in Geneva in July to pass a resolution on drafting an international treaty. Richardson countered that it would likely take years before an international treaty was signed—time Ford agreed he hadn't the luxury to spare.

Yet between the criminalization and disclosure approaches, Ford was unclear which was the better path. Proxmire's bill, which adopted both, seemed untenable, as it was clear that the existence of criminal penalties for overseas payments would only deter their disclosure.[520] Putting forth a bill criminalizing foreign corruption seemed like the strongest possible rhetorical assertion, but multiple advisors, including Richardson, cautioned the president against it. How would it be enforced? Could U.S. prosecutors be expected to know the difference under foreign laws between criminal payments and legitimate political contributions? The State Department further cautioned that calling overseas witnesses to testify against their own elected officials seemed like a surefire recipe for damaging relations with other nations. It was therefore decided that the president would support mandatory disclosure of foreign political payments.

The next question was whether to endorse one of the existing disclosure bills already introduced, like the one suggested by the SEC, or whether Ford should offer his own proposal. For Richardson, the Hills bill was insufficient insofar as it failed to reach non-SEC-regulated firms; of the 30,000-odd companies doing business overseas, less than one-third were traded on a securities exchange. Richardson was also leery that the SEC's proposal had already been incorporated into Proxmire's statute, meaning any endorsement might lend credibility to Proxmire's other, more radical provisions while also preventing the president from staking a victory of his own. The State Department agreed, and in any event, if the president was determined to adopt corporate disclosure requirements, then Kissinger would ensure that the State Department vetted them first.[521]

The following Monday, Ford held a televised press conference to announce his plan. Beginning with prepared remarks, Ford was then followed by Richardson, who took to the lectern to answer questions. In his remarks, the president announced that the Task Force would soon be introducing legislation meant "to renew and to restore public faith in free enterprise," a promise that would be acted upon a few weeks later when Richardson introduced to Congress S. 3741, The Foreign Payments Disclosure Act. The bill required U.S. multinational companies to disclose "significant" payments made to foreign officials to the Department of Commerce, which would share that information with other relevant government agencies, including the Department of State, DOJ, IRS, and SEC. Disclosures would be opened to the general public after a twelve-month grace period unless doing so was deemed inadvisable by the Secretary of State or the Attorney General.

To the administration's chagrin, however, reaction to his proposal was overwhelmingly negative. The *New York Times* deemed it nothing more than "pious evasions," and the *Washington Post* called the bill's one-year delay to make disclosures public a "gaping defect."[522] Jimmy Carter told reporters that it effectively legalized overseas bribery, Church accused the president of trying to "paper over the problem," and Proxmire dubbed the bill a "bureaucratic cop-out."[523] Much of the criticism had to do with the bill's subordination of the role of the SEC to the Department of State and Department of Commerce, the two government bureaus seen as least invested in combatting foreign bribery. Even within his own party, Ford had difficulty finding allies, and although the bill was ultimately referred by Democratic Senator Warren Magnuson from Washington to the Senate Committee on Commerce, it was never voted on.

In the end, despite his best intentions, Ford's foray into combatting overseas corruption had been hugely counterproductive. Every successive attempt to control the narrative—from forming a task force to holding televised press conferences and putting forth a legislative proposal—served only to reinforce the general public's impression that he did not have a handle on the issue. In part, this was due to the president's own circle of advisors, including Kissinger and Simon, who shared deep misgivings about the entire venture and often stymied the president's efforts behind closed doors. Philosophically, they believed that the United States shouldn't seek to police the internal affairs of foreign states, and, in the context of the Cold War, that the unbridled spread of capitalism by U.S. corporations overseas was more important than left-leaning ideas of corporate morality. Eventually, domestic political realities would compel Ford to adopt a more pragmatic approach—one that recognized the optics: U.S. corporations bribing foreign governments was a problem. That he was motivated primarily from a need to battle public perception rather than some overarching principles, however, resulted in a bill that was so full of compromise and so bereft of substance that it could please no one.

Overall, these lackluster efforts also made it clear that responsibility to stop corporate corruption overseas would now fall to Congress. But like Ford, many in the House and Senate were already beginning to turn their attention away from lawmaking and toward the upcoming election. In July, Congress would adjourn for the Democratic National Convention, and in August, they would do so again for the Republican National Convention. The reality was that by midyear, the window to pass legislation was quickly narrowing. If there was a moment to act, it seemed it had arrived.

S. 3664: The Composite Compromise

On June 14, Proxmire called a meeting of the members of the Committee on Banking, Housing, and Urban Development to discuss the three bills pending before them: S. 3133 (the bill he had introduced), S. 3379 (the bill introduced by Senator Church), and S. 3418 (the bill drafted by the SEC). The path ahead was clear: If a simple majority of members on the Committee could agree to report out a single bill, it would go before the full Senate and be put on the calendar to be motioned up by the party leadership.

Making that happen, however, proved no easy task, and it was made more difficult by Proxmire's efforts to forge a composite bill incorporating all three approaches. In theory, Proxmire believed that the bills were additive, not mutually exclusive. His own bill envisioned the SEC as overseeing both the disclosure of foreign payments by publicly traded companies and the enforcement of a criminalization provision against companies that had actually paid bribes. Church's bill expanded these requirements, lowering the dollar threshold for disclosures while expanding civil liability to allow both shareholders and competitors to sue corporations for harm resulting from illegal payments. It also strengthened corporations' internal governance by requiring that at least one-third of a company's board of directors be independent. The SEC's bill made governance its central concern, seeking to enhance the independence and stature of corporate auditors to ensure greater compliance with securities laws.

Although compelling testimony had been heard in support of all three approaches, their combination proved controversial.[524] Among the most vocal critics on the Committee was the Republican Senator from Texas John Tower. Tower had emerged as one of the fiercest Senate Cold War hawks of the era, and he and Proxmire had vehemently clashed on numerous issues over the years. Previous dustups included Proxmire's efforts to curb spending at the Pentagon, as well as his attempts to cut aid to Chile after the rise of Pinochet. Tower had once said that he supported continued funding to the Pinochet regime on the basis that "nations like Chile lacked the sophisticated political systems of Western Countries and therefore had not yet reached a point in their history to concern themselves with human rights."[525] In approaching bribery, Tower took a similarly dim view and complained that how companies "ought to act" in "developed" countries simply did not apply to how business needed to be done in less developed areas of the world. Proxmire responded by pointing out that the issue was not really about exporting U.S. values, but rather applying those values consistently to Americans when they went overseas; "we outlaw murder, armed robbery and certain activities by American citizens even though they may take place abroad," Proxmire reminded the Committee.[526]

Even so, Proxmire knew that he would have to appease Tower and some of his Republican colleagues, resulting in an exception to the criminalization provision for low-level facilitation payments. These small gratuities or "grease" payments to help expedite a ship through customs or to secure required permits, even if technically illegal, would not be covered by the statute. "[I]t does not appear feasible for the United States to attempt unilaterally to eradicate all such payments," the Committee conceded.[527]

It was more challenging, however, to get a majority to accept the disclosure provisions. At first, Proxmire offered a reciprocity clause, meaning companies could forgo disclosing foreign political contributions if disclosure was not required by the country where the contributions had been made.[528] But concerns remained that even in those jurisdictions, having multinational companies disclose all political payments, including those that were legal, would be overly broad and serve to place an unknown administrative burden on the U.S. government to process those disclosures. Neither Church's nor Proxmire's staff had calculated in their proposed bills the added costs to the U.S. government that would result from reviewing public disclosures. Ultimately, in a vote of 11–3, the Committee decided to "postpone action on the disclosure provisions of S. 3133 and S. 3379 until more information could be obtained as to their costs and benefits."[529]

For Proxmire, the decision to eliminate the disclosure requirement was disappointing but not fatal. He still believed that outright criminalization sent the strongest possible message that overseas bribery was wrong. For Church, however, the move effectively gutted the statute of its entire purpose. And without Church being present to argue on his own behalf, the Committee rejected his other proposals as well, including the creation of a private right of action for competitors, which they found "created ambiguities" in the law, and his one-third rule for independent directors.[530] On the other hand, the Committee wholly accepted the SEC's proposal, noting that Secretary Richardson, Hills, and Church had all advised the Committee favorably on those provisions.

In the end, S. 3664–the cleaned-up bill to emerge out of the Banking Committee–was reported out to the Senate unanimously by both Democrats and Republicans on June 22.[531] Section 1 incorporated the SEC's proposals to require issuers to keep accurate books and records, develop adequate systems of internal accounting, prohibit falsifying books and records, and prohibit false or misleading statements to an accountant in connection with an audit. Section 2 made it unlawful for issuers to corruptly give anything of value to a foreign official or instrumentality of a foreign government in order to obtain business. The word "corruptly" had been imported directly from domestic bribery statutes and meant that a person had to *intend* to wrongfully influence a recipient–a notion of bribery based on *quid pro quo* that had become a tenet of the criminalization approach in American jurisprudence.[532] Section 3 extended criminalization beyond SEC-regulated companies to any "domestic concern," meaning any citizen, national, or corporation of the United States. In order to reach "domestic concerns," the bill vested enforcement authority with both the SEC and DOJ. And while some raised the point that authorizing both agencies to enforce the law was duplicative, Proxmire and others made clear that they wanted the SEC's involvement given both its considerable experience in matters of foreign bribery and the perception that the SEC would act more independently than the DOJ on sensitive political questions.[533]

On returning from their August recess, Congress quickly went to work on passing the bill. On September 8, Congressman John Murphy (D-NY) introduced an identical companion measure in the House, which was referred to the Committee on Interstate and Foreign Commerce. Six days later, S. 3664 was motioned up by Senate Majority Leader Mike Mansfield for a floor vote. In addressing his colleagues, Proxmire methodically laid out his arguments for its passage: Corporate corruption overseas was creating a race to the bottom; businesses were under increasing pressure to lower their ethical standards, or risk losing business. This was damaging America's reputation abroad, lending credence to the worst suspicions sown by communists that American multinationals had a corrupting influence on other countries' political systems. "More importantly, bribery is simply unethical," Proxmire concluded. "It is counter to the moral expectations and values of the American public."[534]

To subdue critics, Proxmire stressed that the approach taken in S. 3664 was both pragmatic and enforceable. Under the legal nexus principle, it had long been settled that the U.S. government had the power to regulate the conduct of its citizens abroad. Other legal concepts of aiding and abetting and parent-subsidiary liability would prevent companies from relying on foreign agents to do their dirty work for them. In using their power to subpoena corporate records and, when necessary, to enter into mutual legal assistance agreements with foreign governments, the SEC and DOJ could obtain evidence to prove bribery occurred—wherever in the world that might be. The bottom line was that the government was capable of both outlawing bribery overseas and bringing successful cases in U.S. courts to enforce such a law.

Amendment 2292: The Last Stand for Disclosure

Then, in a surprise move, after Proxmire introduced S. 3664, Church introduced Amendment 2292, which reincorporated the bill's original disclosure requirements. Although Proxmire both knew of the amendment and indeed encouraged it, it had been unprinted and unannounced, a deliberate tactic meant to take advantage of the fact that more often during open discussions, senators were on and off the floor between roll calls, allowing an amendment such as this one to be disposed of by quick, almost unobtrusive action. Church, who enjoyed a hideaway office only a few steps from the Senate floor, formally introduced the amendment himself. In so doing, he assured his colleagues that "the package complements and strengthens Senator Proxmire's anti-bribery bill." "It provides the reporting necessary to identify those payments, many of which may not be necessarily illegal but could have serious consequences for our foreign policy, while establishing mechanisms that allow the private sector to police itself."[535]

Yet hopes of getting a quick vote on the amendment were quickly dashed by Senator Tower, who asked for a delay until the Senate had a chance to hear from the SEC on the ramifications of the added provisions. Overnight, the SEC's lawyers drafted a rush letter from Chairman Hills, which was delivered to Senator Tower just in time for the floor debate on the amendment the following day. Hills reiterated his disapproval of the disclosure requirement and said that he would recommend to Ford that he veto the bill if the Church amendment was incorporated. Among the concerns raised in the letter was the fact that requiring firms to disclose all overseas payments, regardless of value, took away discretion from the SEC as to what kinds of disclosures it believed to be "material" for shareholders. "Now is no time for us to impose inhibitions on the ability of the United States to do business abroad," said Tower, invoking the law's impact on the ability of U.S. companies to compete overseas. "We have a balance-of-payments problem and we must remain competitive in the international marketplace."[536]

Church's response was to point out that these arguments were only further proof of the effectiveness of his proposal. "I know that the reporting requirement is objectionable to these big companies precisely because it would be effective," he remarked. Without the disclosure provision, Congress would be "engaging in pure tokenism," avoiding the hard work to address the root causes of the problem in favor of rhetorical breast-beating.[537] "[I]f this bill were really sufficient to provide a remedy for this immense amount of corruption that we have uncovered abroad in connection with the sale of arms and the sale of oil and the sale of other commodities by large companies, we could be sure that this place would be buzzing with lobbyists," he declared. "They are not concerned with this bill. They have no reason to be concerned about it. That is why these corridors are not filled with the lobbyists of any companies coming here to tell us that we must not pass this bill."[538]

In the end, however, Church's forceful pleadings were not enough. Amendment 2292 was voted down by a margin of 58–29, and although he won the support of Proxmire, Mansfield, and other senior Democrats who either believed in his arguments or with whom he had developed lasting ties over the years, he failed to convince several newer Democratic senators, including Joe Biden (D-DE), John Glenn (D-OH), and Wendell Ford (D-KY). Virtually all Senate Republicans voted against the measure as well. "Perhaps Senator Church is surprised that I would oppose his amendment," Senator Percy told his colleagues. "I say that Senator Church has done a noble job in getting this whole trend going, I just tend to think it is a question of overkill now."[539] Church even failed to secure the vote of Republican Senator Clifford Case, a cosponsor of his original bill and someone Church had once viewed as a key ally on the Subcommittee of Multinational Corporations.

Decades later, Jerome Levinson struck a fatalistic tone about the failed amendment: "simply put, we had exhausted our political capital."[540] The national spotlight in which Church had been basking for months had become glaring, and the Subcommittee on Multinational Corporations—long the envy of many in his own party—had fallen into disfavor. In fact, a mere week after the vote on Amendment 2292, Church received a letter from John Sparkman notifying him that the Subcommittee was formally being wound down in lieu of a new Foreign Economic Policy Committee.[541] For Levinson, the news was a sort of welcome release. "We trampled on a lot of conventions, and frankly, I had become toxic," he remarked, noting that internal disputes earlier that summer had led Jack Blum to leave the Subcommittee's staff to serve as a consultant for the United Nations. Levinson himself went on to work for the Inter-American Development Bank.

But for Church, the vote and demise of the Subcommittee were severe blows to his morale, compounded by the fact that he had failed to do well in the Democratic presidential primaries and had just been passed over by Carter as a vice-presidential candidate.[542] The rapid-fire series of disappointments began a brief period of malaise for Church in what until then had been a career marked by extraordinary success. As Church's Press Secretary Bill Hall coyly remarked at the time, "Church tended to pout a bit when things didn't go his way."[543]

Be that as it may, Church's attempts to expand the bill played an important—if unintended—role in lending Proxmire's bill broader appeal. If Amendment 2292 had been a bridge too far, it blunted criticism of Proxmire's more modest proposal, paving the way for the Senate to pass S. 3664 by a unanimous vote of 86–0. Knowing that the

House would adjourn in two weeks ahead of the 1976 elections and would likely not have time to discuss the bill as a stand-alone measure, Proxmire sought to attach S. 3664 as an amendment to a minor House-Senate conference group. Those efforts were again thwarted by Senator Tower, however, who claimed that he was "certain" that the House would pass the bill before going into recess—a certainty which, unsurprisingly, did not come to fruition.

Even so, the strong bipartisan support for S. 3664 was a testament to how mainstream the discourse around curbing overseas corruption had become to both political parties. On October 4, two days after the House adjourned, Ford signed into law a tax reform statute that officially ended the deductibility of foreign bribes. At the time, it seemed there was sufficient political will to pass a far more expansive law banning overseas bribes altogether. Of course, in politics, momentum is everything, and any question as to whether such a comprehensive law would pass was moot for now, at least until after November.

Enter Jimmy Carter

Of the many peculiarities of the presidential race of 1976, one of the most interesting is that it remains the only contest in which neither candidate had ever been involved in a national election. Although Ford had represented Michigan's 5th Congressional District for close to twenty-five years, his inexperience in national races made him an odd incumbent, a fact made all the more pronounced by the indignity of having to withstand a challenge within his own party by California Governor Ronald Reagan.

By mid-August, Ford had secured the Republican nomination, but polls indicated that he was down against Democratic newcomer Jimmy Carter by a whopping thirty points.[544] A September jobs report showing rising unemployment for a third straight month added to his woes. In hopes of turning the campaign around, Ford challenged Carter to a series of three televised debates, the first since the decisive Kennedy-Nixon debates sixteen years prior. Post-debate surveys indicated that Ford had won the first and third encounters, but an embarrassing gaffe during the second debate in which he refused to acknowledge the Soviet Union's sphere of influence over Eastern Europe cost him dearly. Even so, Carter's lead slipped going into November, and polls on the eve of the election showed a statistical dead heat between both candidates. In the final tally, Carter's popularity in the South tipped the scales ever so slightly in his favor. The victory was reportedly so slim that a shift of a mere 10,000 votes in two states—Ohio and Hawaii—would have changed the overall outcome.[545]

Narrow as it was, Carter's victory was welcome news for a Democratic party that had been unsuccessful in sending their candidate to the White House in two consecutive elections. And with a solid majority control of Congress (62-38 in the Senate and 293-143 in the House), there was plenty of optimism within the party to accomplish many of its most ambitious goals.

What those goals actually entailed, however, was still unclear. The official 1976 Democratic party platform, which Carter's team had been instrumental in putting together, mentioned the need to "eliminate bribery and corrupt practices abroad," but made no promises beyond Ford's existing stance to give "priority attention to the establishment of an international code of conduct for multinational corporations." Passing a unilateral, domestic law was one option, but only "if such a code cannot be negotiated or proves unenforceable."[546]

The simple truth was that few believed that the one-term southern governor had any particular knowledge or interest in the subject of overseas corruption. Foreign policy had been one of Carter's clear weaknesses during the campaign, and some years earlier, he'd displayed his ignorance on issues of economic diplomacy by making the misguided statement that Pearl Harbor could have been avoided had there been better cooperation between American and Japanese corporations before the war.[547]

Yet Senator Proxmire had reason to see in the new president a like-minded ally. Both he and Carter were outsiders to Washington who had campaigned on a message of government transparency and ethics. Both men embraced the relatively new concept of human rights and believed that promoting these rights would allow America to once again serve as a moral leader for the rest of the world. And so, in an effort to ingratiate himself with the president-elect, Proxmire wrote to Carter and proposed that he walk the mile-and-a-half from the Capitol building to the White House during his inauguration. It was an idea that Proxmire hoped would promote physical fitness, a personal hobby that had attracted the senator media attention when he was seen commuting to the Capitol by bicycle every day. Carter's team originally scoffed at the idea, but Carter himself warmed up to it, although not for the reasons proposed; he believed that the gesture would send a broader message of openness to the American people after Watergate.[548] As it turned out, he was right, and the sight of the newly sworn-in president and his wife Rosalyn walking hand in hand down Pennsylvania Avenue—which no president in recent memory had ever done—shocked and thrilled onlookers and those watching on television.

S. 305: The Foreign Corrupt Practices Act Emerges

When the Senate reconvened on January 18, Proxmire immediately reintroduced his anticorruption legislation. S. 305, Title I, this time named the "Foreign Corrupt Practices Act," was otherwise identical to S. 3664, the antibribery bill that had unanimously passed the Senate floor four months earlier. Also new was the fact that it had been bundled with another piece of legislation: Title II, entitled the "Domestic and Foreign Investment Improved Disclosure Act of 1977," required increased transparency for those owning more than 5 percent ownership of U.S. equity securities. The two halves of the statute were seen as complementary, each seeking to amend the Securities Exchange Act of 1934 in order to enhance corporate monitoring and oversight. All outward indicators pointed to S. 305 quickly making its way through Congress and being signed by the president within his first 100 days in office.

Yet despite early overtures, Proxmire found that Carter's attention was largely elsewhere. The administration was wholly focused on addressing countrywide oil and natural gas shortages amid one of the most brutally cold winters on record.[549] Aside from the weather, lingering voices in Washington continued to quietly disapprove of Proxmire's bill behind closed doors. Interagency memos at the State Department indicated that even though Kissinger no longer headed the agency, many career officers continued to oppose the idea of criminalizing overseas corruption.[550] And in a parting memorandum written before leaving the Department of Commerce, Secretary Richardson wondered whether, now that it was no longer an election year, the Ford administration's disclosure approach might have improved prospects over the "superficial appeal" of Proxmire's criminalization statute.[551] "Let's not kid ourselves," Proxmire accurately surmised at the outset of the Banking Committee hearings on S. 305, "this bill is not home free."[552]

Those efforts received a boost when *Washington Post* journalist Bob Woodward penned an article in late February detailing the CIA's routine use of clandestine payments to various world leaders. The list of recipients on the CIA's payroll included such notable names as Joseph Mobutu of Zaire, King Hussein of Jordan, and Jomo Kenyatta of Kenya.[553] For a candidate who had made morality a central pillar of his campaign, the revelations were hard to dismiss, prompting Carter to order the CIA to immediately halt the payments and to put Treasury Secretary Michael

Senator Frank Church speaks with President Jimmy Carter in the White House in 1977.

Credit: Jimmy Carter Library via National Archives

Blumenthal in charge of the administration's broader anticorruption efforts.

Proxmire now had the White House's attention, but he soon learned that Blumenthal was no ally to the cause. During his testimony before the Banking Committee in March, the Treasury Secretary told Proxmire point blank that he was "seriously concerned about the enforcement problems arising from the broad and sometimes vague reach of S. 305."[554] Stopping short of outright rejecting the legislation, he told Proxmire that the Carter administration was continuing to explore whether an alternative disclosure approach might be preferable.

Others on Carter's staff to favor the disclosure approach included Lloyd Cutler, a prominent Washington lawyer who'd represented both Common Cause in its first suits under the Federal Corrupt Practices Act and later, Northrop, during its bribery hearings. Cutler was brought on as White House counsel and believed, like Church, that a disclosure bill was the more practical solution, proposing that the president simply require that every U.S. export consigned to a foreign state contain a bill of lading identifying any payments or commissions made as part of the sale. "When bribes have to be disclosed the day they are paid, they will be too foolhardy for the giver or taker to risk," wrote Cutler in the spring of 1976.[555]

More generally, the administration's attitudes toward Proxmire's anticorruption legislation reflected Carter's broader ambivalence toward regulatory oversight of the private sector. The rapid growth of regulations in the late 1960s and early 1970s had caused considerable backlash. Economic uncertainty led to claims that overregulation was contributing to increased inflation, budget deficits, and a slowdown in economic productivity. Carter himself had made similar claims during his campaign, touting his background as a naval engineer to vow that he would reorganize and modernize the federal government to make it less wasteful. Once in office, he appointed economic and domestic policy advisors like Charles Schultze, chair of the Council of Economic Advisers (CEA), to fulfill those promises.[556] Schultze, Blumenthal, and others on Carter's team would stray from traditional Keynesian economic policies and push for regulatory reform as a means of spurring innovation and growth. These advisors would have to contend with many of the party's core constituents, who continued to believe in the need for federal oversight to steer the private sector in areas like workplace safety, the environment, and labor relations. One of the major challenges of Carter's presidency would be finding a middle ground between these two opposing blocs.

Then, in late January, the SEC independently announced a series of proposed rules implementing new books and records and internal accounting control requirements—the same provisions that had been included in Proxmire's antibribery bill. The move demonstrated the SEC's belief that it already possessed sufficient authority under Section 13 of the Securities Exchange Act to enact the recommendations it had made to Congress previously. In a press release announcing the rule change, the SEC even noted that while it acknowledged that legislative action would be the most "desirable means of demonstrating a national commitment to ending [these] types of corporate misconduct," the SEC had never taken the position that legislation was "the sole means by which the substantive goals of its proposals could be effected."[557] In other words, the SEC needn't wait on the slow and plodding work of Congress to get things done; through its administrative powers, it could quickly and effectively implement rules to prevent the use of off-the-books slush funds all on its own.

Hoping that the SEC's initiative might lend momentum to his broader legislative pursuits, Proxmire again called Roderick Hills before the Banking Committee, this time to answer questions about the new rules and The Foreign Corrupt Practices Act's broader criminal sanctions. The hearing turned out to be Hills' last official congressional appearance; with the change from a Republican to Democratic administration, he would depart the SEC a few weeks later to serve as chairman of Peabody Coal Company. Hills continued to stress that the SEC should avoid entangling itself in enforcing foreign bribery laws but conceded that the Commission would "not oppose" S. 305's enactment of regulatory sanctions if Congress required it. By no means a rousing endorsement, it nonetheless marked a notable departure from his comments a year earlier. In his remarks, Hills even proposed that the law allow for private plaintiffs to sue their competitors for damages suffered as a result of overseas bribes—an idea that had been a feature of Church's original bill. "I disagreed often with your wife as you may know," Proxmire remarked as he thanked Hills and wished him well on his future endeavors, adding, "I agree much more with you."[558]

A few weeks later, Proxmire received more good news in a follow-up response from Secretary Blumenthal indicating that the White House was also now in favor of the bill's criminalization provision. There was one caveat, however: The administration asked to revisit whether responsibility for enforcing the statute should properly rest solely with the Department of Justice. Proxmire bristled at the idea at an April 6 meeting of the Banking Committee: "I don't mean to demean the Justice Department in any way, although I don't think they have been quite as vigorous in the past as they might be," Proxmire said.[559] Since Watergate, the criminal conviction of former Attorney General John Mitchell, and Nixon's attempts to fire Special Prosecutor Archibald Cox, Congress had plenty of reasons not to trust the DOJ's neutral enforcement of politically sensitive areas of the law. In contrast, the SEC (largely thanks to Sporkin) had shown considerable independence and perseverance in this area. "They understand corporate finance and corporate operations thoroughly. That's their job and expertise and that's the reason why I think it's so important to keep them in as much as we can," Proxmire told his colleagues. Those views ultimately prevailed, with the Committee voting 9-3 to maintain the SEC's jurisdiction, although the final markup conceded that the SEC's responsibilities would only extend to bringing civil actions, while criminal charges would be referred to the DOJ.[560]

Otherwise, many of Blumenthal's other suggestions were roundly approved. These included clarifying the statute's application to both individuals and resident aliens, not just corporations, and expanding the maximum fine for penalties from $10,000 per violation to $500,000. The Carter administration also recommended making explicit that the bill should cover payments to third-party agents if the company making those payments knew or had reason to know that they would be passed on to a foreign government official. Lastly, in response to concerns from the accounting industry, the Committee agreed to insert the word "knowingly" to the internal audit provisions to clarify that the mere inaccuracy of a company's books and records would be insufficient without showing that the employee had intended to falsify those records.[561]

At long last, with all parties on the Banking Committee now finally in agreement, the bill was motioned up for larger Senate approval. On May 5, the amended Foreign

Corrupt Practices Act of 1977 and the accompanying Banking Committee report summarizing the bill were officially entered into the congressional record and, after a quick and inconspicuous voice vote by unanimous consent, referred to the House Committee on Interstate and Foreign Commerce.

*

As it so happened, on the very same day the Senate voted to pass the FCPA, Carter was attending an economic summit in London, marking the president's first overseas excursion since the election. On the first day of the summit, leaders from Japan and several European countries issued a joint statement denouncing bribery by multinational corporations and publicly committing to finding a multilateral solution to address the problem of corporate bribery. The timing was rich with irony, as earlier in the week, a meeting in New York of the UN Commission on Transnational Corporations had in fact failed to draft a multilateral bribery treaty.[562] Behind closed doors and away from cameras, several major European countries, including France, the United Kingdom, West Germany, and Italy, opposed any requirements to criminalize corporate bribery abroad. A few so-called "developing" countries were also against the notion, largely because they believed that a specific treaty on bribery would detract from efforts to put in place a broader code of conduct for multinationals.[563] All told, prospects of reaching an international consensus were far-fetched, even if business-friendly lobbying organizations in Washington would rely on the pageantry of the London summit to renew calls for delaying action in Congress until a multilateral treaty was signed.[564]

H.R. 3815: The Unlawful Corporate Payments Act

Nevertheless, work in the lower chamber to pass the FCPA continued, falling to Democrat Bob Eckhardt of Texas, Chair of the Subcommittee on Consumer Protection and Finance. One of the last remaining "Dixiecrats" in Congress, Eckhardt was tasked with reporting out the House's companion bill, H.R. 3815, known as the Unlawful Corporate Payments Act of 1977. Although modeled after the Foreign Corrupt Practices Act, the House version differed from the Senate bill in several important respects. For one, the House version omitted all of the language that had been proposed by the SEC, including the books and records requirements—purportedly so that the SEC would have more flexibility to adopt their own rules on the matter. It also narrowed the jurisdictional scope of the statute, requiring that use of the interstate mails be directly linked to the overseas bribery scheme. The practical effect was to render it more difficult to bring cases under the statute where a majority of the bribery activity occurred overseas.[565]

In other respects, however, the House bill was more expansive; for instance, it broadened the definition of foreign officials to include candidates for office, not just elected officials.[566] Democratic Congressman from Massachusetts Michael Harrington, a well-known critic of the CIA's overseas covert activities, advocated strenuously on this last point, drawing from the Church Subcommittee's revelations of both ITT's $350,000 contribution to Chile's Conservative Party candidate Jorge Alessandri and Exxon's multimillion-dollar payments in Italy to various political parties.[567] The House also explicitly recognized the right of private parties to sue under the statute, an idea that had already been endorsed by both Church and Hills.[568] Existing laws, such as the Clayton antitrust statute, RICO, and the False Claims Act, all successfully demonstrated that enlisting private plaintiffs against corporate wrongdoers created a multiplier effect in the public interest.[569]

On September 28, 1977, the Unlawful Corporate Payments Act was unanimously reported out of committee and referred to the House clerk for calendaring. A month later, Eckhardt motioned the bill up for a vote before the full House chamber. Even at this late juncture, however, the bill remained controversial, and several minority Republicans, led by North Carolina's Jim Broyhill, mounted one last-ditch effort against it. Likely sensing how far along the bill already was, Broyhill claimed not to be against the idea of prohibiting foreign bribery in any general sense, but rather made the more modest proposal that Congress should adopt a disclosure-based statute in lieu of the statute's criminalization language, which he said would prove too difficult to enforce. Broyhill's argument was brazenly contrived given that Republicans had roundly voted against

Church's same proposal in the Senate only a year earlier, and with Republicans in the minority, it was also a losing one. On November 1, H.R. 3815 received the two-thirds necessary votes to pass the House.

Because the House and Senate versions differed slightly, however, the bill still required a conference committee between both chambers to be formally enacted. Convened by Proxmire a few days later, the conference committee served as a final opportunity for those seeking to soften any controversial provisions in the bill. The main outcome was to remove sections 102(3) and 102(4)—the SEC's prohibitions on employees knowingly falsifying a company's books and records and making false statements to a company's accountants. Their removal stemmed directly from lobbying by the accounting industry around concerns about accounting firms' liability under the statute.

Months earlier, lobbyists had requested that the draft bill include the word "knowingly" so as to make clear that the statute would not overrule the Supreme Court's recent decision in *Ernst & Ernst v. Hochfelder.* That ruling protected audit firms from liability for the fraudulent misrepresentations of their clients in the absence of any actual fraud or intentional misconduct on the part of the firm itself. Yet the industry feared that even with the qualifying language, judges would still misapply the statute's provisions and extend liability to accounting firms that had not engaged themselves in any fraudulent activity.[570] The sections were therefore removed, even though, of the SEC's four proposals for an antibribery statute, only these two stemmed directly from the agency's investigations into overseas bribery.[571]

Notwithstanding, the conferees retained the bill's other accounting provisions, including the requirement that issuers keep and maintain accurate books and records as well as devise and maintain adequate systems of internal accounting controls to ensure the reasonable accuracy of those records. Congress created a narrow exemption to the accounting provisions that applied when a company had been instructed by a federal agency not to disclose sensitive classified information with national security implications.[572] On its face, the exception was primarily to protect properly classified CIA procurement decisions, although others viewed it as a "convenient loophole" for aerospace and defense companies to continue overseas undercover dealings so long as they were orchestrated with the consent of the Agency.[573]

Otherwise, the conferees generally conformed the language of the bill to its broadest interpretation, adopting the Senate's "in furtherance of" language related to the use of the interstate mails, its increased monetary penalties, and the House's expanded definition of a foreign "government official." Senator Tower made a point of limiting the statute's direct applicability to foreign subsidiaries of U.S. companies where those involved were not actually citizens of the United States, a concern shared by the Carter administration, which had unsuccessfully tried to limit the statute's application to foreign issuers as a matter of basic comity.[574] The conference report made clear, however, that the statute would apply both to foreign issuers and to U.S.-based parent companies that participated either directly or indirectly in the conduct of their subsidiaries. Lastly, the markup excluded the House bill's allowance for a private right of action because it was not considered during the committee conference.[575]

When taken together, then, the final version of the bill to emerge reflected significant compromises by a wide array of interested parties. It made clear that foreign bribery by U.S. corporations was outlawed but stopped short of deploying the full arsenal of tools considered by some as necessary to root out the problem. Proxmire, Eckhardt, and other supporters of the FCPA had nonetheless appeased enough of the bill's early detractors to move toward the final stage of ratification.

Public Law 95-213: The FCPA Becomes Law

On December 6, the Senate confirmed the conference report, and the House unanimously did the same the following day by a vote of 349–0.[576] The statute was then sent to the Government Printing Office to be published as Public Law 95-213 and delivered to the White House for final signature.

Passage of the Foreign Corrupt Practices Act in late 1977 marked a stunning confluence of events up until then—from the *Wall Street Journal*'s uncovering of the secrets behind Eli Black's death two years earlier, to Sporkin's aggressive investigations into corporate slush funds and subsequent leaks to the Senate Subcommittee on Multinational Corporations, to the tawdry revelations of Lockheed's massive global bribery scheme. These events had played out against a backdrop of large-scale shifts in American society that included both the gradual rise of a corporate, antibribery ethic and a growing bipartisan apprehension about the power of multinational companies. Together, these forces had not only manifested a new moral norm, but also weathered the political process to enact a statute reflecting that norm.

The signing of the FCPA into law represented less the climactic culmination of these efforts, however, than their last gasp, and final ratification of the statute was marked not with joyful, ceremonial ebullience, but with tamped, administrative solemnity. Carter, who had delegated all FCPA-related matters to his Treasury Secretary, planned no formalities to mark the signing of the bill into law, and on the day the bill reached his desk—December 19, 1977— the president spent most of the morning and afternoon meeting with his economic policy group to discuss inflation, fiscal austerity, and business deregulation.[577]

In truth, Carter likely had mixed feelings at the time about the FCPA. Putting additional restrictions on how companies did business abroad was at odds with the administration's early promises to "free the American people from the burden of overregulation."[578] Almost a full year into his first term, Carter's economic team had proposed a slew of initiatives aimed at making good on those promises, including cuts to the corporate tax rate and regulatory reforms in the transportation, banking, and communication sectors. Overall, his presidency had ushered in a profound sea change: The Democratic party was no longer defined by the generation of New Deal, Great Society liberals that had steered its leadership for decades. In many ways, the FCPA sat at the crossroads of that transformation.

Hubert Humphrey, the most prominent remaining New Deal acolyte in the Senate, died a month after the FCPA's signing, finally succumbing to his years-long battle with cancer. Passage of the FCPA turned out to be one of Humphrey's final attributable legacies, though perhaps his least well-known. Frank Church, who had also grown up in the activist traditions of the New Deal, equally saw his influence in the Democratic party wane. While Church was finally named Chairman of the Committee on Foreign Relations in 1979, his tenure was short-lived, and he lost his Senate reelection bid the following year. Like Humphrey, Church died of cancer a few years later. It was all a sign of what was to come.

The late 1970s bore witness to the ascendency of the conservative New Right movement that was quickly coalescing around its charismatic leader, Ronald Reagan. The movement embraced the economic philosophy of Milton Friedman and his flavor of neoliberalism, which would become hugely popular with mainstream America in the coming years.[579] In fact, between 1973 and 1979, the percentage of Americans agreeing with the statement that "[g]overnment regulation is a good way of making business more responsive to people's needs"—an uncontroversial assumption for decades—actually fell from 60 to 49 percent.[580] For scores of Americans, fixing the economy now meant fixing the federal government. It also meant liberating American business from regulation and focusing instead on the trade imbalance of imported manufactured goods.[581] How else to explain the fact that American automakers were now losing out to Japanese ones or that the U.S. dollar was now worth less than the German mark?

Carter sensed these concerns and, in fact, shared in many of them.[582] After passage of the FCPA, one lawyer recalled that the "ink was hardly dry before a steady drumbeat of attack on the statute began."[583] Within just a few months of its enactment, a White House task force created by President Carter regularly submitted recommendations calling for immediate weakening and eventual abandonment of key provisions of the statute.[584] By 1980, Reagan had called for the statute's outright repeal.[585]

In this changing political climate, corporate influence in Washington also began to morph.[586] Emboldened corporations began to enter the political fray once more, funneling campaign funds through newly established political action committees (PACs), which were designed to circumvent finance restrictions imposed by FECA.[587] By making "independent expenditures" (spending not directly coordinated with a campaign), corporate PACs could pour potentially endless amounts of money into political advocacy issues—and they soon would.[588] Whereas in 1974 there were only about 100 registered corporate PACs, by 1976 there were 450, and by 1979 there were over 1,350.[589] These independent groups played a significant role in the 1978 congressional elections, outspending political parties by a margin of three to one, as well as the 1980 presidential election, contributing to Ronald Reagan over Jimmy Carter at rates of almost nine to one.[590]

These changing attitudes were punctuated in 1978 when an FBI-led sting operation codenamed "Abscam" created nationwide backlash toward the federal government's anticorruption efforts. The FBI had employed the services of an ex-convict named Melvin Weinberg to pose as an Arab sheik looking to engage in crooked deals. Backed by large amounts of taxpayer money, Weinberg offered "bribes" to local officials in New Jersey, eventually going on to ensnare both state and federal politicians, including Pete Williams, the fifth-ranking Democrat in the Senate.[591] But the FBI's bare-knuckled tactics proved too much in the end, leading to widespread claims of overreaching, entrapment, and violations of due process. Both in Congress and in the public eye, Abscam symbolized how the pursuit of absolute integrity had reached dangerous extremes, reflecting the anticorruption ethic's ideological exhaustion by decade's end and serving more as cork than capstone.[592] "A moral government will not resort to foul means to enforce the ethic," wrote Ninth Circuit Court Judge John Noonan. "Abscam went too far: the government that touches pitch is also stained."[593]

*

For now, though, the month was still December and the year was still 1977. The FCPA sat at the crossroads of what had transpired and what was to come, between the Watergate babies and the Reagan revolution. So it happened that on the afternoon of December 19, between a packed schedule that included a luncheon with various members of Congress, Carter sat down with a small stack of paperwork before getting ready for an early evening Christmas party for members of the White House staff. The pile included such mundane matters as an appropriations bill for the SEC's next fiscal year as well as one that would reapportion four acres of national land in the state of Wyoming.[594] Also included was Public Law 95-213, the Foreign Corrupt Practices Act.

The following day, Carter's team released a brief, 220-word statement announcing that the president was pleased to have signed the FCPA into law and that he shared Congress's belief that bribery was ethically repugnant. "These efforts, however, can only be fully successful," Carter remarked, "if other countries and business itself take comparable action."[595] As no journalists had been invited to witness the signing, the events were reported only in syndicated form by the Associated Press and then reprinted in a few national newspapers the following day. In the middle of page seventy-nine of the *New York Times*, squeezed between stock tickers and an advertisement for cosmetic products, the headline read simply, "Carter Approves Bill on Corporate Bribes."[596] If not for what was to come many years later, it would have been an ignoble end to a remarkable story.

Epilogue

The FCPA: From Dormant Law to Global Blueprint

In the years immediately following its passage, the FCPA seemed destined to languish in the annals of criminal law. The Reagan administration rarely enforced the statute, while outside the United States, proponents of a multilateral anticorruption treaty were met with fierce opposition.[597] "A bunch of pip-squeak moralists running around trying to apply U.S. puritanical standards to other countries," one businessman and early FCPA critic complained.[598] As the U.S. trade deficit peaked in the mid-1980s and the U.S. dollar sharply appreciated during that same period, there were mounting calls in Congress to amend the statute.[599] In the summer of 1988, the Reagan administration eventually succeeded in passing new corporate-friendly amendments to the FCPA as part of the Omnibus Trade and Competitiveness Act—both broadening the definition of so-called "facilitating payments" and increasing the degree of knowledge required to hold U.S. businesses accountable for bribes paid by third-party agents.[600]

But then, as is wont to happen, the world changed again. The fall of the Berlin Wall in 1989 and the subsequent dissolution of the Soviet Union a few years later marked an important turning point in the history of anticorruption. Seemingly overnight, hopes for a new political order swept over Eastern Europe and Central Asia, with lawyers and political experts from the West enthusiastically engaging now formerly communist countries to provide technical assistance to implement democratic reforms.[601] The demise of the Soviet Union meant the ideological triumph of capitalism and the widespread acceptance of principles of free trade and globalization. Among both Democrats and Republicans, Milton Friedman's brand of neoliberalism influenced a broad post-Cold War consensus known as the "Washington Consensus." Accordingly, the proper role of governments and institutions became to assist in ordering the global economic marketplace. The fight against corruption, which was viewed as a threat to these open and orderly markets, was a key component of this new paradigm shift and fit neatly within the rhetoric of "structural adjustments" and "good governance" that became popular at the time.[602]

By the mid-1990s, then, focus on anticorruption had firmly become part of the overall strategy of the United States to promote economic globalization and geopolitical stability. Yet the United States government still faced the problem that among Western allies, it alone banned foreign corruption. While perhaps frowned upon at diplomatic cocktail parties, paying bribes to win business abroad was still commonplace among many European countries, including in Germany and France, where companies were even allowed to write off overseas bribes as tax deductions. To address this gap, the Clinton administration soon sought to standardize the FCPA in other parts of the world. Secretary of State Warren Christopher and Assistant Secretary of State Dan Tarullo began in 1994 by targeting the Paris-based Organization for Economic Co-operation and Development (OECD), an exclusive assembly of the world's largest trading partners. Those efforts coincided with a burgeoning anticorruption movement already taking shape in Europe, where human rights activists and development experts began campaigning against corruption as a political and economic imperative to address the needs of developing countries.

Two years later, in October 1996, World Bank President James Wolfensohn would directly link global investments to good governance and accountability in what would later be hailed as a "watershed" moment by anticorruption advocates. "Let's not mince words," Wolfensohn declared in a speech before the Bank's board of governors, "we need to deal with the cancer of corruption."[603] Until then, the Bank had assiduously avoided the topic—so much so that just a few years earlier, a program manager at the Bank, Peter Eigen, quit to found the nonprofit Transparency International (TI) after witnessing firsthand several Bank-funded projects in Kenya waste away due to corruption.[604] Wolfensohn's "cancer of corruption" speech addressed the issue head-on, eliminating any remaining taboo surrounding the topic in economic development circles and formally integrating integrity and governance reform into the formal programming of large, intergovernmental institutions.

Around the same time, U.S. lobbying efforts in the international arena equally began to pay off. In March 1996, the Organization of American States (OAS) passed the Inter-American Convention Against Corruption, the first-ever multilateral treaty on the issue. Then, the following year, in November 1997, the OECD's twenty-nine member countries signed the landmark Convention on Combating Bribery of Foreign Public Officials in International Business Transactions, often referred to in anticorruption circles simply as "the OECD Convention."[605]

It was an exciting time, as the anticorruption movement seemed to finally be taking off. Awareness-raising by the World Bank, the OECD, TI, and other nonprofits caught the attention of the global media, with coverage of anticorruption efforts appearing regularly in the *New York Times*, the *Financial Times*, and the *Guardian*. In addition to Peter Eigen, other important figures to emerge included Mark Pieth, Chair of the OECD Working Group on Bribery. It was not long before the G20, the UN Office on Drugs and Crimes, and other global organizations soon joined in what was being called "the global fight against corruption."

The crown jewel at the center of these efforts was the OECD Convention. Not only did the treaty bring together the largest assembly of global trading partners, but it also accomplished two related aims. First were its economic goals, as the United States made clear in a statement released upon ratifying the Convention by tying implementation directly to "the promotion of stronger, more reliable, and transparent foreign legal regimes that, in turn, make for more reliable and attractive investment climates."[606] The view was that tackling corruption and promoting globalization were one and the same. Second, the OECD Convention successfully internationalized the FCPA, providing the U.S. government a mechanism through which it could at long last ensure a single set of standards. Borrowing almost word for word from the language of the FCPA, the Convention required signatory countries to both criminalize bribery of foreign public officials and require their companies to keep accurate books and records.[607] Soon, other intergovernmental organizations, including the Council of Europe, the African Union, and the United Nations, would enact similar multilateral anticorruption treaties—each one incorporating the FCPA's two primary provisions almost whole cloth.[608]

The importance of the FCPA in the modern anticorruption era is, therefore, difficult to overstate. Unlike most domestic laws with international application, the FCPA has become a kind of international law unto itself, effectively serving as the blueprint for an entire international legal framework. As NYU law professor Kevin Davis notes, "since the enactment of the FCPA, U.S. transnational bribery law has grown from an idiosyncratic but weakly enforced branch of U.S. law into the lynchpin of a prominent and potent global regime."[609]

The Rise of "FCPA Inc."

It should come as little surprise, then, that the United States played a leading role in establishing this new regime, promoting best practices across enforcement agencies and regularly hosting senior officials from other nations to promote dialogue and information sharing.[610] "Nothing is more critical, both to our country and to other nations, than establishing true rule of law," declared former Assistant Attorney General Lanny Breuer in a 2010 speech on corruption before the Council on Foreign Relations.[611] At the time, DOJ resident legal advisors and senior law enforcement advisors were stationed in thirty-seven countries around the world, from Colombia and Afghanistan to Kenya and Indonesia.[612]

But it was in its aggressive enforcement of the FCPA that the United States truly set the pace. By the early 2000s, the FBI allocated a squad dedicated solely to investigating potential violations of the FCPA, around the same time as the DOJ and SEC began precipitously increasing enforcement of the statute. Within the span of just five years, the number of FCPA settlements quadrupled, from fourteen in 2005 to fifty-six in 2010—the same year the SEC created its own stand-alone FCPA enforcement unit.[613] The DOJ even began to adopt bold new tactics, employing wiretaps, informants, and sting operations to catch would-be bribe payers, strategies once relegated to prosecuting drug dealers and organized criminal gangs. The result was impressive in both breadth and depth: In the decade spanning the 2010s, the DOJ and SEC collectively concluded over 400 FCPA-related actions, leading to more than $25 billion in monetary penalties.[614]

Due to heightened enforcement, a corresponding crop of lawyers, auditors, IT professionals, and compliance organizations soon emerged to assist multinationals in avoiding sanctions—a billion-dollar industry that some have derisively dubbed "FCPA Inc."[615] This consulting class grew alongside an extensive community of nonprofit and academic institutions and a widening body of intergovernmental organizations to transform the anticorruption movement of the 1990s into a multifaceted discipline.[616]

Thus, by the mid-2010s, two decades of reform and development had resulted in a sea change in behaviors. Multinational companies engaging in bribery were more likely to be punished than at any earlier time, and abhorrence for corruption in transnational business had obtained the status of an international norm, on par with combatting human trafficking or ending the illegal wildlife trade.

"In the beginning of this process, there'll be some outlier nations," U.S. Secretary of State John Kerry noted during his opening remarks at the London Anti-Corruption Summit of 2016, but "the minute people begin to feel enforcement and a broad standard of application, watch how rapidly the standards change."[617] On stage with Kerry were leaders who reflected the united face of this vision of a globalized, anticorruption regime, including British Prime Minister David Cameron, Nigerian President Muhammadu Buhari, and World Bank President Jim Yong Kim. It seemed the "global fight against corruption," a social and political construct made in the United States of America, had successfully been exported around the world.

Leveling the Playing Field

But like all constructs, there is always a gap between

expectations and reality. Below the surface, beyond the OECD plenary sessions, the DOJ press releases, and the law firm client alerts, a different picture began to emerge by the end of the 2010s. Global indicators showed that few if any countries outside the United States were actually implementing their anticorruption obligations. In fact, twenty-five years after adoption of the OECD Convention, the United States had carried out nearly 80 percent of all successful prosecutions under the treaty.[618] A 2022 report published by Transparency International similarly concluded that of the forty-seven signatory countries, only two—the United States and Switzerland—could even be categorized as "active" enforcers.[619]

Among non-OECD countries, the record was even worse.[620] Between 2018 and 2021, Singapore, India, and China, collectively representing roughly 20 percent of global exports, failed to open or close even a single cross-border corruption case pursuant to the United Nations Convention Against Corruption.[621] As U.S.-based anticorruption scholars Michael Johnston and Scott Fritzen accurately summarized in their 2021 book *The Conundrum of Corruption*, "most countries have made little or no progress against corruption over the past 20 years."[622]

Explanations as to what has accounted for such wide disparities in enforcement between the United States and the rest of the world have varied. NYU and Duke law professors Jennifer Arlen and Samuel Buell offer one possible solution, writing in 2020 that fundamental differences in the legal doctrines governing investigations of corporate crime have made it nearly impossible to transpose U.S.-style FCPA enforcement onto other legal systems.[623] In the U.S., for example, prosecutors have used deferred prosecution agreements (DPAs) to motivate companies to collect evidence of corruption and share that information with law enforcement.[624] Arlen and Buell argue that attempts to adopt the DPA-style model in European countries have been largely unsuccessful due to local laws in other parts of the world governing attorney-client privilege and employee testimonial rights, as well as the tendency of data protection and document collection regimes to disincentivize companies from investigating and self-reporting misconduct.

Whatever the reasons for unequal enforcement globally, the net effect has been an asymmetry in the regulatory landscape which has not gone unnoticed by the United States. By the mid-2000s, the U.S. Chamber of Commerce began calling for further amendments to the FCPA to alleviate trade disparities for American companies seeking to do business overseas.[625] Lobbying from these groups, in turn, compelled the DOJ and SEC to seek to narrow the enforcement gap through more aggressive extraterritorial enforcement of the FCPA.[626] In 2010, for example, 94 percent of FCPA penalties imposed on companies involved non-U.S.-based entities.[627] This trend largely continued over the next decade, effectively turning the United States into a global police force. It is "a fact that the United States is already—if unilaterally—acting as a kind of supranational prosecutor on transnational bribery," Mark

Pieth, the onetime Chair of the OECD Working Group conceded in his 2018 book, *Confronting Corruption*.[628] By the end of 2024, nine out of the ten largest FCPA-related settlements ever—representing more than $12.8 trillion in penalties—were against foreign firms.[629]

As one might imagine, the extraterritorial nature of the United States' enforcement of the FCPA became the subject of intense debate in the anticorruption field. For some, the U.S. government's leadership in driving forward the anticorruption agenda and holding corrupt actors accountable has been exceedingly praiseworthy. The DOJ and SEC, for their part, have claimed in speech after speech to be acting as benevolent forces intent on "leveling the playing field" for international business.[630] Others, however, have pointed out that FCPA enforcement trends against non-U.S. companies reveal prosecutorial biases against foreign companies.[631] Overseas, many critics have wondered whether the United States, in taking on the role of world police, has sought not just to level the playing field, but rather to tilt it in its own favor.

In 2010, for example, German newspapers questioned why the SEC and DOJ devoted so many resources to prosecuting Daimler AG, while Daimler's U.S. competitors, General Motors and Ford, were left unscathed despite operating largely through the same distribution networks across Asia, Africa, and Eastern Europe.[632] In France, there was even greater backlash when, in 2014, the DOJ resolved a $770 million FCPA action against French power and transportation company Alstom S.A. at the same time as

Alstom's takeover by its American competitor, General Electric. The arrest of several of Alstom's top executives suggested a coordinated effort by the U.S. government to blackmail Alstom's CEO, Patrick Kron, to agree to the sale in exchange for securing his own personal freedom.[633]

Many in the United States, however, have shrugged off these accusations as nothing more than conspiracy theories.[634] It is said, if foreign companies have been the outsized targets of FCPA enforcement actions, then that is because they have been the outsized perpetrators of foreign bribery schemes. The DOJ and SEC have brought actions against foreign companies only in the absence of local actions taken by their home countries. "Today's historic resolution is an important reminder that our moral and legal mandate to stamp out corruption does not stop at any border, whether city, state or national," declared the U.S. Attorney prosecuting the Alstom case at the time.[635]

The Brazilian Crucible

Nowhere have these claims of political meddling been more damaging, however, than in Brazil. There, in 2014, the DOJ and FBI began working with local prosecutors in what became known as Operation Car Wash, a vast investigation centered around Brazil's state-owned energy company, Petróleo Brasileiro S.A. (Petrobras). The investigation, which initially focused on millions in bribes and kickbacks to Brazilian politicians and political parties, eventually led to related findings involving several other large Brazilian companies. In coordination with authorities in Brazil and Switzerland, the U.S. Department of Justice negotiated the largest FCPA resolution ever, a $4.5 billion settlement against Brazilian construction company Odebrecht. Locally, dozens of Brazilian executives and politicians connected to the scandal were eventually imprisoned, including, most famously, the former President of Brazil, Luiz Inácio Lula da Silva.

For years, Operation Car Wash was hailed by U.S. authorities as a huge success, representing the exportation of U.S. anticorruption tactics that the DOJ had long hoped to see. "It is hard to imagine a better cooperative relationship in recent history than that of the United States Department of Justice and the Brazilian prosecutors," declared Assistant Attorney General Kenneth Blanco in 2017.[636]

The judge overseeing most of the Car Wash trials, a young magistrate named Sérgio Moro, was touted as a protégé of the American model: He'd studied at Harvard Law School, participated in a three-week course for future leaders sponsored by the U.S. Department of State, and was said to be an admirer of the rigor and efficiency of the U.S. judicial system.[637] In adjudicating the Petrobras cases, Moro employed U.S.-style plea agreements to get defendants to quickly fold and turn against one another.[638] And as the trials unfolded, Moro became both a local and international celebrity.[639] In 2016, in recognition of his success, he, along with the prosecutors involved in Operation Car Wash, jointly received an award from Transparency International marking their achievements.

In the years since, however, Operation Car Wash has

been marred by claims of prosecutorial abuse and judicial impropriety, evidencing the political power struggle underpinning much of the investigation. Hacked phone messages showed that Moro and Brazilian prosecutors intentionally disregarded federal protocols by sharing evidence with the U.S. government and sought the DOJ's assistance in part because they hoped to reap the proceeds of a big, U.S.-dollar settlement.[640] Leaked texts showed that Moro, who had presided over the trial against former President Lula, even colluded with Car Wash prosecutors to build their case on weak evidence that the prosecutors themselves believed insufficient for a conviction.

After these revelations came to light, Brazil's Supreme Court suspended the landmark fines against Odebrecht and reversed Lula's conviction. Today, many Brazilians now view Operation Car Wash not as an application of the rule of law, but as a political hit job.[641] That Lula's conviction kept him off the 2018 ballot and led to the victory of his far-right opponent, Jair Bolsonaro (who, in turn, appointed Moro as his Minster of Justice), only seemed to confirm the investigation's political bent. Even within the United States, Congressman Hank Johnson (D-GA) opened an inquiry into whether the DOJ and FBI deliberately used the FCPA to weaken a leftist political figure viewed as a threat to U.S. interests in Latin America.[642]

Whether the DOJ's motives in spearheading Operation Car Wash were well intentioned or not, the political fallout in Brazil highlights the challenges the United States has faced in galvanizing support for what had become by decade's end a mostly one-sided anticorruption regime. Even for the most powerful country in the world, imposing foreign standards of rule of law onto other countries proved to be both an unwelcome and thankless task. "America has much to be proud of as a corruption-fighter," wrote a contributor to the *Economist* in 2019. "But, for its own good as well as that of others, it needs to find an approach that is more transparent, more proportionate and more respectful of borders."[643]

Fractures in the Global Order

When taken together, then, the state of affairs within the global anticorruption regime by the early 2020s could best be described as one of cognitive dissonance. On the one hand, the spread of FCPA-like laws had become nearly universal, with virtually all countries passing statutes prohibiting cross-border corruption. The United States had become a leader in the enforcement of these laws, but it did so often in coordination with foreign counterparts. The jurisdictional reach of the DOJ and the size of the FCPA penalties imposed were equally impressive, with some settlements reaching into the billions. The fruits of this labor were easily observable: Most multinationals had implemented compliance programs designed to prevent corruption, an active community of nonprofits and intergovernmental organizations regularly met to share best practices, and, in a broader sense, corruption in international business had generally become accepted as a normative wrong.

On the other hand, by almost all objective criteria, the global anticorruption regime had failed to bring about the enforcement landscape it set out to create. While successful in its role as world police in increasing the number of prosecutions, the DOJ garnered criticism both at home, from domestic business interests, and abroad, from foreign governments. And despite decades of laudable efforts by the United States to prop up a global regime, the undeniable trend line showed that cross-border enforcement was decreasing across the board while corresponding measures of corruption were on the rise.[644] At the same time, the very structures, institutions, and treaties meant to organize this new regime were increasingly viewed as both ineffective and morally suspect.[645]

As time went on, these problems became increasingly intractable. The more aggressive the United States' efforts to narrow the enforcement gap, the more politicized anticorruption enforcement appeared to the rest of the world, and the less appealing it became as a global regime. Meanwhile, disparities in global enforcement created mounting pressures inside the United States to overcompensate in the global arena in order to restore the obvious imbalance.

This dynamic played out in late 2023 when President Biden signed into law the Foreign Extortion Prevention Act (FEPA), further expanding the U.S. government's jurisdictional reach by granting the DOJ authority to prosecute foreign officials themselves for overseas corruption.[646] Most within the anticorruption community hailed FEPA as a positive development: "With the Foreign Extortion Prevention Act," read the title of one blog post coauthored by the former Chair of the OECD Working Group, "America puts the world on notice."[647] The statute even won support from business-friendly advocates by shifting the enforcement focus away from the "supply side" of the bribery equation, comprised of multinational companies, to the "demand side," comprised of corrupt public officials.

At its core, however, the statute reflected a remarkable assertion of American prosecutorial power in the domain of foreign diplomacy, allowing the United States to seek the extradition and imprisonment of elected officials of sovereign nations. Writ large, it is not difficult to imagine how prosecuting foreign elected officials could open the door to backlash against America's go-it-alone efforts and further devolve the rule-of-law aims of the anticorruption agenda into politics by another name.[648]

End of the Road

Tectonic shifts in the international economic landscape over the last decade threaten to further weaken many of the fundamental assumptions of the FCPA-based, global anticorruption regime. Growing populist revolt in both the Global North and South against neoliberal policies for failing to deliver on earlier promises have shaken the foundations of the postwar, liberal international order. Globalization, once accepted as an unstoppable force, has become widely seen as the cause for a range of social and economic ills, and many international institutions, like the OECD, that have traditionally been used to promote globalization and the rule-of-law agenda have seen their influence dwindle dramatically of late.

At the same time, geopolitical changes have resulted in the return of a great power division, reshaped long-standing allegiances, and led China to supplant the Soviet Union as the United States' new principal rival. China not only represents an economic threat to the United States—becoming in the last twenty years the Global South's new favorite investment and trading partner—but also an ideological alternative to racial and cultural issues that have long strained relations between the West and countries in Africa, Asia, and Latin America. As a result, perennial conflicts such as the Palestinian cause serve to sow deeper divisions today between the U.S. and the Global South and to reinforce growing mistrust regarding the impartiality of Western liberalism.[649]

All of these developments have had a direct impact on the global anticorruption agenda because they've undermined the narrative themes of progress and moral clarity that have long girded anticorruption discourse.[650] "The Western hegemony regarding anticorruption work no longer holds, having gone the way of many other assumptions that underlaid the post-Cold War order," writes John Githongo, a longtime anticorruption activist in Kenya.[651] Githongo's perspective, which he penned in a recent thirty-year retrospective published online, is especially helpful given his lengthy involvement in the anticorruption movement over that period of time. A journalist by background, his father was one of the original founders of Transparency

International and he, in turn, became head of TI's Kenya branch in 1999 before being appointed by Kenya's president as anticorruption tzar in 2002.[652] He has, therefore, had a front-seat view of anticorruption efforts since the start of the modern anticorruption era. He describes this era as, initially, "a package defined using Western norms of liberal democracy, human rights, and an open economy," which since has become mired in a crisis of legitimacy in the face of "Western hypocrisy and double standards in the export of those values."[653]

The reelection of U.S. President Donald Trump in 2024 hastened this crisis by forcing a resolution that no one wanted. Within his first thirty days in office, Trump issued an executive order directing the DOJ to pause all enforcement of the FCPA and began dismantling resources within the Department aimed at tackling global corruption. His rationale for doing so—that the FCPA put U.S. businesses at a competitive disadvantage in the global marketplace—was a familiar one that harkened back to some of the earliest criticisms against the statute. But it was also a revisionist interpretation of FCPA enforcement over the last several decades, one in which foreign companies, not American ones, have actually borne the brunt of that regulatory burden. This reality may not be entirely lost on the Trump administration, and by aligning enforcement of the FCPA more closely with Trump's "America First" policies, the DOJ may very well seek to double down on the weaponization of the FCPA to pursue short-term competitive gains.

More broadly, Trump's efforts to reassert American

primacy by putting up trade restrictions, pulling out of multilateral obligations, and retreating from global aid commitments all signal a new era of American isolationism. The resulting disruption in global supply chains, the uncertainty surrounding long-standing international legal norms, and the creation of new trading blocs have only made it more difficult for U.S.-based multinational companies to operate overseas. Investment in low-income, developing countries has become especially fraught with peril, driving a wedge between U.S. capital and large swaths of the developing world.

All told, America's retreat from the world stage has upended a global anticorruption movement that was under considerable strain already. The OECD Convention lives on, but its implementation outside the United States remains to be seen. The organizing principles of globalization and rule of law that have long framed anticorruption discourse are no longer driving forces. Without clear justifications rooted in an existing global economic and political world order, the anticorruption movement is left trying to appeal to universal, moral principles. All of this is a stark reminder that the fate of anticorruption depends far less on what the anticorruption movement does than on the incentives and structures of the international order upon which it depends. The current challenge, therefore, is to articulate new justifications for curbing corruption at a time when these power structures are so rapidly changing.

Reimagining the Fight Against Corruption

Some of the difficulty in adapting to the current environment will be to jettison past ways of thinking. The existing literature around the FCPA and the anticorruption movement grew almost entirely out of the end of the Cold War and the triumph of democratic capitalism. Political scientist Francis Fukuyama appropriately summed up the mood in the 1990s as a period marking "the end of history," with capitalism and Western liberal democracy as its ideological endpoint.[654] The FCPA, alongside more general anticorruption efforts, became entwined in larger "development" goals and that complex of processes sometimes referred to as "Westernization." The fact that corruption was universally recognized as harmful lent these efforts a moral justification that approached a kind of missionary zeal.

In practice, this meant that experts over the last thirty years have tended to address corruption through top-down, technocratic solutions. The FCPA, with the United States as its global champion, became a blueprint to be grafted onto legal systems across the globe. Doing so meant close coordination between legal experts of both countries, which could be facilitated through the OECD and other intergovernmental organizations.

This top-down approach belies the FCPA's own endogenous beginnings, however. The statute undoubtedly owes its existence to the whistleblowers and investigative journalists who fought to expose truth to power in the United States.[655] It was the *Wall Street Journal*'s exposé into the death of Eli Black, after all, that convinced the SEC to bring its first charges. Subsequent leaks by the SEC to the Subcommittee on Multinational Corporations helped sustain focus on the topic. The history of anticorruption efforts in America is replete with similar examples, from the *Harper's Weekly* and *New York Times* takedowns of William "Boss" Tweed and Tammany Hall in the 1870s to the *Wall Street Journal*'s inquiry into Teapot Dome in the 1920s and the *Washington Post*'s exposure of Nixon's involvement in Watergate in the 1970s. That these efforts resulted in actual changes—not only to the black-letter law, but also to existing political power structures—is due in no small part to the authenticity of the struggles that birthed them.

The ahistorical approach of the modern anticorruption regime has also meant that its proponents tend to be blind to their own implicit historical biases. Fukuyama's future is one that can only be linear; the rest of the world must shed its anachronisms to "catch up" with the West. Corruption has been viewed as one of the most venal of anachronisms precisely because it impedes two of the primary goals of Western society: the spread of democracy and an orderly global economy. It is also seen as an exotic menace, existing apart from affluent societies—something that must be navigated and overcome.[656] This has been evidenced consistently over the past thirty years in efforts to translate the language of bribery in other countries (*"baksheesh"* in Egypt, *"morditas"* in Mexico) for Western audiences. In a globalized economy, the noble burden of the West has been to carry this lawlessness into the light.

This justification for addressing corruption in the global economy differs considerably from the way it was perceived in America in the 1970s. People at that time on both sides of the aisle worried that the excesses of capitalism and the greed of multinational companies was driving a worldwide corruption epidemic.[657] This is why, after the Gulf Oil hearings, Republican Senator Charles Percy called corruption the "dry rot of capitalism." It is also why Stanley Sporkin, (also a registered Republican at the time), saw his mission at the SEC to rein in corporate power, not out of disdain for business, but as a conservative, capitalist value to help preserve the free enterprise system.[658]

This explanation is helpful in understanding how corruption persists today, especially as the last three decades have shown that despite best efforts and considerable resources, corruption is an enduring presence in our modern society. Its longevity may have less to do with some external, primordial evil, however, than with the very animating forces of our global economy and contemporary power structures.

One need not look far to find examples of how this plays out in the real world. Large surveys in thirty-four African countries have found that as global trade has increased, most feel that corruption has worsened.[659] Political scientists have shown that China's recent economic boom occurred in part *due to* its high degree of corruption, not despite it.[660] Watchdog groups have shown how international financing of debt in less affluent countries has in fact entrenched existing kleptocracies.[661] And investigative reports have shown how humanitarian aid and money spent on nation building is, more often than not, either lost or stolen.[662]

These examples are not simply instances of waste or poor leadership; they speak to the origins of some of the grandest forms of corruption and the ways in which they spread. Corruption is less a foreign danger and more akin to a pollutant emanating from the global financial system and permeating the poorest parts of the world. Yet as any contemporary corruption index would imply, it is in these countries where the problem most lies.

*

As the world enters a new, multipolar era, then, the existing anticorruption movement must face a daunting new reality. Justifications that it once took for granted—the moral worthiness of its cause, the integrity of its institutions, and the universality of its rules—can no longer be assumed.

It should come as some comfort, however, that the conditions of this reality are not altogether different from those of another era in which the current global regime first took root. The FCPA was conceived at a time of deep moral ambiguity and self-reflection for the United States. Then, like now, the world was split into geopolitical divides, and people worried about how to win the ideological battle for global influence. America may no longer be fighting a Cold War against the Soviet Union, but its interests nonetheless remain threatened by the spread of authoritarianism and extreme, antidemocratic beliefs. And just as multinationals were once vilified as antagonistic to democracy and U.S. foreign policy, there is a growing sense in America that a select few wealthy individuals have formed an oligarchic class that wields too much power in Washington. To survive, the U.S.-based anti-corruption community can learn from the FCPA's origins by reframing the statute to meet these contemporary challenges. As historian David Lowenthal wrote, "the prime function of memory is not to preserve the past, but to adopt it so as to enrich and manipulate the present."[663]

Lawyers, political thinkers, and policymakers must therefore refrain from trying to return the statute to its glory days and instead summon a compelling narrative that positions the FCPA, and the United States' enforcement of it, within the emerging world order. Global corruption must not only be exposed anew, but contextualized and made sense of in relation to our most pressing political and social problems: extreme inequalities in wealth, preferential policies that reward close business allies while punishing others, the politicization of legal institutions, and the undoing of America's soft power in the world. Much like it always has, the future success of the FCPA will depend on the work of investigative journalists, courageous whistleblowers, imaginative politicians, and the regard of the general public. The good news is that insofar as the FCPA has always been about defending American ideals of democracy against private greed, our present-day political environment seems as primed as it ever has been to rearticulate this urgent need. The makings of the next chapter in the story of the FCPA, whatever form that might take, are all close at hand.

The Way Forward

Of course, reviving the FCPA is only part of the battle that lies ahead. In the wake of President Trump's "America First" approach to international law, anticorruption experts must also reevaluate the FCPA's place in the larger global regulatory landscape. Because the FCPA has served as the foundation of the modern anticorruption regime, anticorruption advocates now rightly worry whether the United States' hard turn away from combatting global corruption will usher in a new era of impunity. So far, authorities in the United Kingdom, France, and Switzerland have promised to help fill this void, jointly announcing the creation of an International Anti-Corruption Prosecutorial Taskforce shortly after the Trump administration declared a pause on enforcement of the FCPA.[664]

European countries' efforts to step up and continue prosecuting corruption in international business is both laudable and long overdue. It also signals the potential for a more sustainable regulatory environment in which countries are able to address transnational corruption outside of a single, FCPA-based legal framework. Here again, history shows us an alternative path forward. The successful proliferation of antitrust law around the world over the last century serves as a model legal experts should heed when thinking about the next era of the anticorruption movement.

Modern antitrust law was first conceived in the United States in 1890 through passage of the Sherman Act, and the landmark 1945 *Alcoa* case established the principle that America could pursue anticompetitive agreements made abroad as well.[665] The United States subsequently led the charge in applying antitrust laws extraterritorially to prevent restrictive business practices in international trade, often against the wishes of other countries who viewed the United States' jurisdictional assertions as an encroachment on domestic sovereignty. Many countries even introduced so-called blocking statutes aimed at obstructing the long reach of U.S. antitrust laws, leading the United States to a dawning realization by the mid-1960s that unilateral enforcement of antitrust law was both difficult to implement and beginning to alienate its closest trading partners, including Canada, Britain, and the Netherlands.[666]

By the 1970s, the U.S. largely abandoned international antitrust enforcement, and conservative legal scholars including Robert Bork and Richard Posner put forth new economic theories that called into question its domestic enforcement as well.[667] Without the United States as its global leader, antitrust law receded from the international agenda, although it did not disappear altogether. Other countries gradually came to develop their own antitrust laws (called "competition laws" outside the United States), which today flourish in over 120 jurisdictions. What is most notable is that the variability of these laws reflects the differences in cultures, economic circumstances, political systems, and histories of the countries they represent.

Emerging economies, for example, are more likely to take into account considerations such as the protection of jobs or heightened protections of domestic industry against foreign competition.[668] But even between large economies such as the United States and the European Union, principles differ, including on matters such as vertical price fixing, territorial restraints, and Most Favored Nation contractual provisions.

Overall, this diversity has been a net benefit to the development of antitrust law. Because the onus of enforcement has not fallen unilaterally to any one country, ideological shifts in the international political environment have had less impact on the welfare of global consumers. And because competition laws have proliferated in other countries largely on their own terms, the need for the use of blocking statutes has correspondingly diminished. As it turns out, when countries are able to enforce extraterritorial laws in ways that more closely align with their own domestic interests, they tend to be more aggressive in doing so. Take the European Union, which for decades rejected extraterritorial applications of competition law, but has since emerged as a vanguard in the effort to apply antitrust law extraterritorially.[669] It is not a stretch to imagine that federal regulators here in the United States may soon borrow from their European counterparts to advance novel legal theories of antitrust law.

The development of antitrust law over the last several decades is a reminder of the potential benefits of resisting the allure of a one-size-fits-all approach to combatting corruption. For starters, accepting a more pluralistic legal framework would reduce the perceived need for the United States to play the role of world police. This in turn, would permit the DOJ and SEC to recenter FCPA enforcement priorities on the Hippocratic precept that the United States should seek first and foremost to do no harm. "Morality in the international business community is not our responsibility, nor is enforcing the law in other lands," Senator Frank Church solemnly told his colleagues in the fall of 1975. "What this Government and this Congress must concern itself with are the very real and serious political and economic consequences that spreading corruption can have for U.S. interests both at home and abroad."[670] Church's words are a reminder that the United States can still embrace aggressive enforcement of the FCPA without feeling obligated to ensure its universal adoption.

A more pluralistic legal regime would also open the door to differing approaches to combatting corruption. One could easily envision, for example, a disclosure-based legal framework wherein countries require more transparency in corporate, cross-border dealings. In fact, one of the most exciting developments in the fight against corruption over the last decade has been the number of offshore leaks (the Panama Papers and Pandora Papers, among others) that have exposed (albeit involuntarily) corruption among the world's top business and political leaders. In the wake of these reports, there has been a growing movement for governments to require more visibility of beneficial ownership in corporate registries and transparency into what corporations pay to foreign governments. Although there has been resistance to this idea in the United States, it is not without precedent in our country's history and is reminiscent of the approach taken by Church and others at the outset of the bribery hearings in the 1970s.

Changing mindsets will certainly not be easy. The FCPA doctrine has become an engrained part of the American legal imagination, shaping how a generation of lawyers has approached international corruption. Yet its inherent limitations have become only more apparent with time. Even at home, the Supreme Court, in cases like *McDonnell v. United States* and *Snyder v. United States*, has steadily narrowed the definition of *quid pro quo* corruption in U.S. jurisprudence, demonstrating how the FCPA's reliance on criminalization is vulnerable to interpretation and poorly designed to capture the unbounded nature of how corruption works in the real world.[671] Reaction against these rulings, as well as others, such as *Citizens United v. Federal Election Commission*, have laid bare deep suspicions of corruption in our political system, much like how corruption continues to threaten democracy in other parts of the world.

Fortunately, we have faced moments like this one before, and it is when we have been most honest with ourselves that we have been able to innovate and succeed. The story of the FCPA is one of struggle and determination in the face of seemingly unbeatable odds. It accomplished something that had never been done before. Let it be a lesson for us as we brave a world that requires us to do so once more.

ACKNOWLEDGMENTS

I have often described this book, which took me thirteen years to complete, as a labor of love. But it is equally true that whatever attention I devoted to it over those years was amply matched by the love of those who supported me along the way.

I wish first to thank the team at CCI Press, who made this dream a reality. Thank you most of all to my publisher, Sarah Hadden, who took a chance on me and whose belief in this project from day one was such a source of strength. Thank you also to Emily Ellis, who was a fantastic copyeditor, and to Jennifer L. Gaskin and Jacqueline Fleming for their superb production and marketing efforts. Nor can I express enough gratitude for the assistance I received from Tal Nechmad, who although only a second-year law student when I met her, punched well above her weight on this project.

A great deal of debt is also owed to the people who inhabit this story and who generously gave their time in allowing me to interview (and reinterview) them for this book. Thank you to Mary Bralove, Steve Sansweet, Jack Blum, Jerome Levinson, Ken Mclean, Ralph Ferrara, Stanley Sporkin, Lloyd Feller, and Roderick Hills. My only regret is that I was unable to finish it sooner such that all of them could have a chance to read it. Thanks also to Fred Taylor, Karen Lissakers, and Geoffrey Shields, who helped me to fill in the blanks.

Much of this book was written either inside a library or with the assistance of one. Special thanks to all the librarians at the Brooklyn Public Library, New York Public Library, Columbia Law School Library, San Francisco Public Library, and the Mechanics' Institute Library. I also wish to thank everyone at the Frank Church Institute who provided assistance, especially Kent Randell, Gwyn Hervochon, and Cheryl Oestreicher. I am equally grateful to the folks at the Gerald R. Ford Presidential Library, including Elizabeth Druga and Timothy Holts, who were so eager to find hard-to-locate documents and papers.

My heartfelt thanks to Jason Kaune, Ronald Goldstock, and Susan Rose-Ackerman, whom I spoke to, sought guidance from, and who otherwise humored me by reading early drafts of this book. Thank you also to the bosses and mentors over the years who supported me along this journey, including Alexandra Wrage, Michael Ward, Sue DiLandro, and Anthony Moshirnia. I am grateful as well to Homer Moyer, John Coogan, Frank Brown, Gemma Aiolfi, Shruti Shah, and the countless other anticorruption professionals I have met across the FCPA bar over the last decade who shared with me their passion about this subject and from whom I drew inspiration in writing this book.

Among family and friends, I have been equally blessed. Thank you to my parents, Sharon and Pascal, for showing me the value of hard work. Thank you to my sister, Colette, for sharing her artistic sensibilities, and to my brother-in-law, John, for his kindness and support. Thank you to my brother, Benoit, for encouraging me to take risks, and to longtime friends Lee Kowitz and Russel Klopfer, who shared with me in the ups and downs along the way. Thank you to Sharon Pitts for never doubting that it would happen, and to the entire Pitts family for their support over the years. Thank you also to Yvonne Shirley and Paul Gittleman, who reentered my life just as this project was beginning and reminded me of the importance of staying true to what truly matters.

None of this could have been possible, however, without the life afforded to me by my brilliant wife, Sarah, who early on recognized this as an adventure worth taking. To our two incredible children, Jude and Soren, from whom this project took too much of their father's attention, I hope that it will now provide some measure of return.

NOTES

CHAPTER ONE: THE GHOST OF ELI BLACK

1. Mary Bralove, "Giving Up: Was Eli Black's Suicide Caused by the Tensions of Conflicting Worlds?," *Wall Street Journal*, Feb. 14, 1975.
2. Chiquita Brands Intl. in Data for 1974, Fortune 500, CNN Money, https://money.cnn.com/magazines/fortune/fortune500_archive/full/1974/1.html.
3. For a description of Eli Black's death, see Peter Kihss, "44-Story Plunge Kills Head of United Brands," *New York Times*, Feb. 4, 1975; Peter T. Kilborn, "Suicide of Big Executive: Stress of Corporate Life," *New York Times*, Feb. 14, 1975; and Bralove, "Giving Up."
4. For sources on Eli Black's life and accomplishments, see Peter Chapman, *Bananas: How The United Fruit Company Shaped the World*, (Canongate 2007); Kilborn, "Suicide of Big Executive;" Bralove, "Giving Up;" Kihss, "44-Story Plunge;" and George Wheeler and Tom Demoretcky, "Why Did Eli Black Kill Himself?," *Newsday*, Feb. 4, 1975.
5. Mary Bralove, "Giving Up."
6. Ralph Ferrara, interview by Kenneth Durr, Securities and Exchange Commission Historical Society, May 8, 2008, https://www.sechistorical.org/collection/oral-histories/ferrara080508Transcript.pdf.
7. Sporkin and Pollack were joined in going after Wall Street by Robert Morgenthau, the famed U.S. attorney of New York's Southern District from 1961 to 1977. Staff Reporter, "Nixon Appoints SEC's Enforcement Chief to Agency Seat Despite Industry Opposition," *Wall Street Journal*, Jan. 31, 1974.
8. Robert M. Smith, "S.E.C.'s Tough Guy," *New York Times*, Oct. 5, 1975.
9. Jesse Eisinger, *The Chickenshit Club: Why the Justice Department Fails to Prosecute Executives* (Simon & Schuster, 2017), 76.
10. Smith, "S.E.C.'s Tough Guy."
11. Ralph Ferrara, interview by Kenneth Durr.
12. Staff Reporter, "Eli Black's Rites Attended by 500," *New York Times*, Feb. 6, 1975.
13. Mary Bralove, "Power Struggle," *Wall Street Journal*, May 7, 1975.
14. Staff Reporter, "United Brands Officials Create Dual Leadership," *Boston Globe*, Feb. 11, 1975.
15. Bralove, "Power Struggle."
16. Marcelo Bucheli, *Bananas and Business: The United Fruit Company in Colombia, 1899-2000* (New York University Press, 2005).
17. Neil H. Jacoby et al., *Bribery and Extortion in World Business* (Macmillan, 1977), 105-106.
18. Marshall B. Clinard and Peter C. Yeager, *Corporate Crime* (Free Press, 1980), 179-180.
19. Jacoby et al., *Bribery and Extortion*, 105-106.
20. Bralove, "Power Struggle."

21 Stanley Sporkin, interview by the author, on file with the author; Stanley Sporkin, "The Worldwide Banning of Schmiergeld: A Look at the Foreign Corrupt Practices Act on its Twentieth Birthday," *Northwestern Journal of International Law and Business* 18, no. 2 (1997): 269; Stanley Sporkin, "The Foreign Corrupt Practices Act—Then and Now" (speech, 12th National Foreign Corrupt Practices Act Conference, Washington, D.C., Nov. 15, 2004); Stanley Sporkin, "Origins of the FCPA" (speech, ABA National Institute on the Foreign Corrupt Practices Act, Oct. 16, 2006); and Stanley Sporkin, interviewed by Irving Pollack, Securities and Exchange Commission Historical Society, conducted Sept. 23, 2003.

22 Corporation Finance Division; Views on Disclosure of Illegal Campaign Contributions, Securities Act Release No. 5466, Exchange Act Release No. 10,673, Investment Company Release No. 8,265, 39 Fed. Reg. 10237 (Mar. 8, 1974).

23 David Doherty, "The SEC's Management Fraud Program," *Business Lawyer* 31, no. 5 (1976): 1279; John R. Evans, "Truth or Consequences" (speech, Securities Cooperative Enforcement Conference, Denver, CO, May 15, 1975).

24 Wallace Timmeny, "An Overview of the FCPA," *Syracuse Journal of International Law and Commerce* 9, no. 2 (1982): 235; and Stanley Sporkin to Leon Jaworski, letter, Oct. 4, 1974, Securities and Exchange Commission Historical Society.

25 *Securities and Exchange Commission v. American Ship Building Co.* (D.D.C.), SEC Litigation Release No. 6534 (Oct. 4, 1974).

26 SEC Litigation Release No. 6534.

27 For example, see *Securities and Exchange Commission v. American Ship Building Co.* (D.D.C.), SEC Litigation Release No. 6711 (Jan. 31, 1975).

28 A.A. Sommer Jr., "The Slippery Slope of Materiality" (address, Practicing Law Institute, New York, NY, Dec. 8, 1975); Frank Vogl, "SEC Under Fire for Excessive Zeal in Investigating Illegal Practices," *The Times*, Apr. 9, 1976; and "SEC to Push Bribes Probe Despite Internal Opposition," *Hartford Courant*, May 18, 1975.

29 Stanley Sporkin, interview by the author.

30 Irving Pollack, interview by David Silver, Securities and Exchange Commission Historical Society, Jan. 16, 2002, https://www.sechistorical.org/collection/oral-histories/20020116_Pollack_Irving_T.pdf.

31 Anthony Sampson, *The Arms Bazaar: From Lebanon to Lockheed* (Viking Press, 1977), 273; and David Boulton, *The Grease Machine: The Inside Story of Lockheed's Dollar Diplomacy* (Harper & Rowe, 1978).

32 Chapman, *Bananas*, 2.

33 Richard Severo, "United Fruit Lives Down a 'Colonialist' Past," *New York Times*, Apr. 24, 1972.

34 Raul Romero, "United Brands Polishes Its Image in Latin America," *Management Review* 64, no. 3 (1975): 25-30.

35 Douglas C. Lyons, "CAB Official Shot Dead in Va. Home," *Washington Post*, Feb. 19, 1975.

36 Staff Reporter, "C.A.B. Aide Faults Airlines on Election Laws," *New York Times*, Mar. 3, 1975.

37 Several airline companies had pleaded guilty to charges involving unlawful campaign contributions to the CRP, and in the wake of those initial revelations, the Aviation Consumer Action Project, a group tied to consumer advocate Ralph Nader, pressured CAB to investigate the entire industry for possible further violations of the Federal Aviation Act. William H. Jones, "2 Airlines Accused of Illegal Gifts," *Washington Post*, Mar. 13, 1974.

38 Leonard Curry, "Bribes by the Millions," *The Nation*, May 24, 1975, 619.

39 Braniff was a Texas company and one of the most profitable airlines in the industry. Both Braniff and Harding Lawrence, Braniff's CEO, had been found guilty in 1973 of illegally paying $40,000 to Nixon's reelection campaign, but CAB's suit two years later alleged that the Nixon payment had only been the tip of a much larger iceberg involving an off-the-books account that the company kept secret. Jones, "2 Airlines Accused of Illegal Gifts;" and James Fallows, "The Great Airline War," *Texas Monthly*, Dec. 1975.

40 Robert E. Bedingfield, "Braniff Defends Promotion Fares," *New York Times*, May 6, 1975; Fallows, "The Great Airline War;" Jones, "2 Airlines Accused of Illegal Gifts."

41 David P. Doherty to Thomas F. McBride, letter, Mar. 19, 1975, Securities and Exchange Commission Historical Society.

42 *Securities and Exchange Commission v. Minnesota Mining & Manufacturing*, Civil No. 3-7529 (W.D. Minn. filed Jan. 31, 1975), SEC Litigation Release No. 6711 (Jan. 31, 1975); and *Securities and Exchange Commission v. Phillips Petroleum Co.*, Civil No. 75-0308 (D.D.C. filed Mar. 31, 1975), SEC Litigation Release No. 6770 (Mar. 31, 1975).

43 *Securities and Exchange Commission v. Gulf Oil Corp.*, Civil No. 75-0324 (D.D.C. filed Mar. 11, 1975), SEC Litigation Release No. 6780 (Mar. 11, 1975).

44 "Gulf Admits $10 Million Donations," Boston Globe, Mar. 12, 1975; Eileen Shanahan, "Gulf Oil Accused by SEC of Hiding $10-Million Fund," *New York Times*, Mar. 12, 1975; and "Again, Political Slush Funds," *Time Magazine*, Mar. 24, 1975, 81.

45 Stanley Sporkin, interview by the author.

46 *Securities and Exchange Commission v. Gulf Oil Corp.*, Civil No. 75-0324 (D.D.C. filed Mar. 11, 1975). See also Shanahan, " Gulf Oil Accused by SEC of Hiding $10-Million Fund;" "Gulf Admits $10 Million Donations."

47 Newspapers primarily focused on the fact that in addition to going to Nixon, much of that money had also gone to as many as two dozen U.S. congressional candidates during the 1970 election year. Byron E. Calame, "Gulf Oil Struck Out as a Driller But Was a 'Gusher' on Political Scene," *Wall Street Journal*, Apr. 3, 1975.

48 Frederick Andrews, "Price Waterhouse Knew United Brands Paid Bribe but Didn't Require Disclosure," *Wall Street Journal*, Apr. 11, 1975.

49 "United Brands Posts Big Loss From Operations," *Wall Street Journal*, Mar. 28, 1975.

50 Stephen Sansweet, interview by the author, on file with the author. Interview details were confirmed by files concerning Honduras, box 4, National Security Advisor Presidential Country Files For Latin America, 1974-1977, Gerald R. Ford Library; and Ambassador Philip Sanchez to Secretary of State Henry Kissinger, telegram, Apr. 15, 1975, State Department Cables, Central Foreign Policy Files, National Archives, College Park, MD.

51 Henry Kissinger to All American Republic Diplomatic Posts, telegram, May 15, 1975, State Department Cables, Central Foreign Policy Files, National Archives, College Park, MD.

52 Bralove, "Power Struggle."

53 "U.S. Raps United Brands as Payoff Probe Widens," *Los Angeles Times*, Apr. 11, 1975.

54 Henry Kissinger to American Embassies in Tegucigalpa, Guatemala, San Jose, Panama, and Quito, telegram, Mar. 31, 1975, "Honduras - State Department Telegrams: To SECSTATE - EXDIS," box 4, National Security Advisor Presidential Country Files For Latin America, 1974-1977, Gerald R. Ford Library.

55 Henry Kissinger to American Embassies.

56 American Embassy in Tegucigalpa to Secretary of State, telegram, Apr. 1, 1975, Honduras - State Department Telegrams to SECSTATE NODIS, box 4, Presidential Country Files for Latin America, Gerald R. Ford Presidential Library.

57 Henry Kissinger to All American Republic Diplomatic Posts, telegram, May 15, 1975, State Department Cables, Central Foreign Policy Files, 1973–1976, National Archives, College Park, MD.

58 Kenneth Bacon et al., "Buying Favor: United Brands Paid Bribe of $1.25 Million to Honduran Official," *Wall Street Journal*, Apr. 9, 1975.

59 "SEC to Push Bribes Probe Despite Internal Opposition," *Hartford Courant*.

60 Bacon et al., "Buying Favor."

61 *Securities and Exchange Commission v. United Brands Co.*, Civil No. 75-0509 (D.D.C. filed Apr. 9, 1975), SEC Litigation Release No. 6827 (Apr. 10, 1975), SEC Litigation Release No. 7251 (Jan. 27, 1976).

62 *Securities and Exchange Commission v. United Brands Co.*, Civil No. 75-0509 (D.D.C. filed Apr. 9, 1975). Kenneth Bacon and Mary Bralove, "United Brands Accused by SEC of Second Payoff: Agency's Civil Suit Alleges Firm Also Paid $750,000 to Officials in Europe," *Wall Street Journal*, Apr. 10, 1975.

63 Bacon et al., "Buying Favor."

64 Kenneth Bacon, "U.S. Looks for Possible Criminal Charges in United Brands' Payment in Honduras," *Wall Street Journal*, Apr. 16, 1975.

65 Jacoby et al., *Bribery and Extortion*, 55.

66 Robert Lenzner, "Something's Fishy Here," *Boston Globe*, Apr. 16, 1975. See also Richard E. Mooney, "Foiling Corporate Cover-Ups," *New York Times*, Apr. 13, 1975.

67 American Embassy Tegucigalpa to Secretary of State, Apr. 9, 1975, State Department Cables, Central Foreign Policy Files, 1973–1976, National Archives, College Park, MD.

68 American Embassy Tegucigalpa to Secretary of State, Apr. 1, 1975, Honduras - State Department Telegrams to SECSTATE NODIS, box 4, Gerald R. Ford Presidential Library.

69 "Honduras May Sue Wall Street Journal Over Bribery Case," *Buenos Aires Latin*, Apr. 15, 1975.

70 Robert J. Cole, "S.E.C. Suit Links a Honduras Bribe to United Brands," *New York Times*, Apr. 10, 1975.

71 Alan Riding, "Honduran Army Ousts Leader Named in Bribery Case in U.S.," *New York Times*, Apr. 23, 1975.

72 "General Staff Member Discusses Reasons Behind Coup," Paris: *Agence France-Presse*, Apr. 23, 1975.

73 Riding, "Honduran Army Ousts Leader Named in Bribery Case in U.S."

74 "Banana Bribers Get Ultimatum," *Chicago Tribune*, May 16, 1975. For more information, see American Embassy in San Jose to Secretary of State, telegram, May 1, 1975, regarding alleged United Brands Bribe Attempt in Costa Rica.

75 Bacon and Bralove, "United Brands Accused by SEC of Second Payoff."

76 Staff Reporter, "Senate Panel Will Study United Brands Bribe Case," *Wall Street Journal*, Apr. 11, 1975.

77 Staff Reporter, "Senate Panel Will Study United Brands Bribe Case," *Wall Street Journal*.

78 Frank Church to Raymond Garrett, letter, Apr. 18, 1975, series 2.2, box 14, folder 4, Frank Church Papers. See also "Senate May Call Bribery Hearings on United Brands," *New York Times*, Apr. 17, 1975. By early May, the Senate inquiry revealed that Gulf Oil had paid at least $4 million in undisclosed bribes to foreign officials (the final number would be much higher). Those revelations set off public furor in Venezuela and Ecuador, where Gulf maintained holdings. "Gulf Oil Admits It Gave Foreign Officials $4 Million," *Los Angeles Times*, May 2, 1975.

79 Byron E. Calame, "Investigation of Gulf Oil's Political Fund Said to Be Reopened by Watergate Office," *Wall Street Journal*, Apr. 22, 1975.

80 *Securities and Exchange Commission v. Northrop Corp.*, Civil No. 75-0563 (D.D.C. filed Apr. 16, 1975), SEC Litigation Release No. 6839 (Apr. 16, 1975).

81 "Northrop Is Accused of Campaign Abuses," *Chicago Tribune*, Apr. 17, 1975; Curry, "Bribes by the Millions;" and Jack Egan, "SEC Extends Slush Fund Probe to Foreign Dealings," *Los Angeles Times*, May 4, 1975.

82 Eileen Shanahan, "S.E.C. Says Northrop Kept $30-Million Secret Fund," *New York Times*, Apr. 17, 1975.

83 Egan, "SEC Extends Slush Fund Probe to Foreign Dealings."

84 Richard D. James, "Castle & Cooke Concedes It Made Payoffs to Foreign Officials, Reversing Its Stand," *Wall Street Journal*, Nov. 27, 1975.

CHAPTER TWO: RISE OF THE ANTIBRIBERY ETHIC

85 Even Stanley Sporkin, in retelling his involvement years later, would further this narrative. Sporkin, "The Foreign Corrupt Practices Act–Then and Now;" and Sporkin, "Origins of the FCPA."

86 Ellen Gutterman, "Easier Done Than Said: Transnational Bribery, Norm Resonance, and the Origins of the US Foreign Corrupt Practices Act," *Foreign Policy Analysis* 11, no. 1 (2015): 122.

87 Timothy Martin, "The Development of International Bribery Law," Natural Resources and Environment 14, no. 2 (1999): 95-102; and Richard McCormick, "The Discovery that Business Corrupts Politics: A Reappraisal of the Origins of Progressivism," *American Historical Review* 86, no. 2 (1981): 256, note that "the fear that business corrupted politics exerted only minor influence in the late nineteenth century" and that when they recognized corruption, "ordinary people seemed to have blamed 'bad' politicians . . . and to have considered the businessmen guiltless."

88 "The Great Moral Issue of the Campaign: Cortelyou and Corruption," *New York World*, Nov. 5, 1904.

89 "An Open Letter to President Roosevelt on His Speech of Acceptance." *New York World*, July 20, 1904.

90 McCormick, "The Discovery," 256-73.

91 Alton B. Parker, "Political Corruption by the Trusts" (speech, Oct. 24, 1904) ("I am persuaded the time to begin the fight against those who would control the results of election contests for their private corporate interests, as distinguished from the public interest, is now, and whatever the result of the election may be, it should be continued until the evil is checked.").

92 John T. Noonan, *Bribes* (University of California Press, 1982), 625.

93 Henry F. Pringle, *Theodore Roosevelt, A Biography* (Cornwall Press, 1934), 355-356.

94 Tillman Act, Pub. L. No. 59-36, 34 Stat. 864 (1907).

95 Theodore Roosevelt, "The New Nationalism" (speech, Aug. 31, 1910), *Theodore Roosevelt Association Journal* 33, Theodore Roosevelt Digital Library, Dickinson State University.

96 Publicity of Political Contributions Act, 2 U.S.C. Section 241 (1910).

97 Publicity Act, Pub. L. No. 61-274, 36 Stat. 822 (1910).

98 Frank Anechiarico and James B. Jacobs, *The Pursuit of Absolute Integrity* (University of Chicago Press, 1996), 21.

99 *Newberry v. United States*, 256 U.S. 232 (1921).

100 McCormick, "Discovery," 273.

101 Laton McCartney, *The Teapot Dome Scandal* (Random House, 2008).

102 McCartney, *Teapot Dome Scandal*, 109.

103 McCartney, *Teapot Dome Scandal*, 109, remarks that the arrangements with Sinclair signified "a notable departure on the part of the government in seeking partnership with private capital for the working of government-owned natural resources."

104 One fabrication was that his socialite friend Ned McLean, famous owner of the *Washington Post* and the *Cincinnati Enquirer*, had given him the money. But when Walsh questioned McLean, he uncovered that in the lead-up to the Senate inquiry, McClean sent a series of frantic, cryptic messages to his contacts in Washington implying a cover-up, using code words like "Jaguar" to mean Senator Walsh and "the Big Bear" to refer to himself. As the hearings wore on, Fall seemed to only dig himself deeper into the hole. When Edward Doheny came forward to testify that actually he had lent Fall the money well before Fall had been appointed Secretary of the Interior, this again proved false, as the IOU that Doheny presented to show Fall's innocence was a blatant forgery. Doheny hadn't even bothered to have the document signed or written in Fall's handwriting. McCartney, *Teapot Dome Scandal*.

105 McCartney, Teapot Dome Scandal.

106 Under Prohibition, liquor could be sold solely for medical purposes, and only if the Department of Justice granted the seller a special medical permit. In exchange for issuing these medical permits, Daugherty had taken kickbacks from bootleggers all across the country. McCartney, *Teapot Dome Scandal*.

107 McCartney, *Teapot Dome Scandal*.

108 McCartney, *Teapot Dome Scandal*.

109 *Munitions Industry: Hearing Before the S. Special Comm. Investigating the Munitions Indus. Pursuant to S. Res. 206 A Resolution to Make Certain Investigations Concerning the Manufacture and Sale of Arms and Other War Munitions*, 73rd Congress 2503, 2849 (1934).

110 *Munitions Industry*, 73rd Congress 2538.

111 President Franklin Roosevelt, sensing that another war was likely inevitable, is said to have begun undermining the work of the committee while secretly working on a project to sell the British fifty destroyers. Matthew Ware Coulter, *The Senate Munitions Inquiry of the 1930s: Beyond the Merchants of Death* (Greenwood Press, 1997).

Notes | 303

112 See Bills H.R. 263, 66th Cong., 1st Sess., (1919); H.R. 5632, 67th Cong., 1st Sess., (1921); H.R. 6871, 68th Cong., 1st Sess., (1924); H.R. 4459, 69th Cong., 1st Sess. (1925); H.R. 5563, 70th Cong., 1st Sess., (1927); H.R. 9027, 70th Cong., 1st Sess., (1928); and H.R. 9769, 71st Cong., 2nd Sess. (1930). See also Coulter, Senate Munitions Inquiry.

113 Federal Corrupt Practices Act of 1925, 43 Stat. 1070.

114 Mark Grossman, *Political Corruption in America: An Encyclopedia of Scandals, Power, and Greed* (ABC-CLIO, 2003), 408.

115 John J. Wallis, Price V. Fishback, Shawn E. Kantor, "Politics Relief and Reform: Roosevelt's Efforts to Control Corruption and Political Manipulation during the New Deal," in *Corruption and Reform: Lessons from America's Economic History*, ed. Edward L. Glaeser and Claudia Goldin (University of Chicago Press, 2006), 343-372.

116 For more on this topic, see Philip Taft, "Corruption and Racketeering in the Labor Movement," *Bulletin* 38 (New York State School of Industrial and Labor Relations, 1958).

117 In his book entitled *The Enemy Within*, written after his Senate work investigating labor, Bobby Kennedy described what he saw as the interplay between criminals, legitimate businesses, and corrupt local politicians: "Evidence developed by the Committee showed that gangsters today control steel companies, laundry and dry-cleaning establishments, frozen food operations, and many other kinds of business. Hoodlums living reputable lives in Los Angeles have major vice and gambling holdings in the Midwest. They seek to corrupt and do corrupt public officials to an alarming extent." Robert F. Kennedy, *The Enemy Within* (Da Capo Press, 1960).

118 Ronald Goldfarb, *Perfect Villains, Imperfect Heroes: Robert F. Kennedy's War Against Organized Crime* (Random House, 1995).

119 Craig M. Bradley, "Anti-Racketeering Legislation in America," *American Journal of Comparative Law* 54, supplement (Fall 2006): 671-692.

120 Goldfarb, *Perfect Villains, Imperfect Heroes.*

121 Robert F. Kennedy, "Robert Kennedy Defines the Menace," *New York Times*, Oct. 13, 1963.

122 William Beecher, "Crime Crackdown: Robert Kennedy Plans Multi-Agency Drive Against Top Racketeers," *Wall Street Journal*, Jan. 23, 1961.

123 Kennedy, "Robert Kennedy Defines the Menace."

124 Kennedy, "Robert Kennedy Defines the Menace."

125 C. David Heymann, *RFK* (Penguin Books, 1998).

126 Heymann, *RFK*.

127 *United States v. Kubacki*, 237 F. Supp. 638 (E.D. Pa. 1965).

128 "Reading, Pa., Mayor Indicted," *Hartford Courant*, July 8, 1963.

129 *United States v. Addonizio*, 451 F.2d 49 (3d Cir. 1971), cert denied, 405 U.S. 936 (1972).

130 Bradley, "Anti-Racketeering Legislation."

131 "Former Newark Mayor Addonizio Gets 10-Year Sentence for Extortion," *Boston Globe*, Sept. 23, 1970.

132 John Kenny would eventually be sentenced in 1971 to eighteen months in jail. *United States v. Kenny*, 462 F.2d 1205 (2d Cir. 1972).

133 John S. Gawey, "The Hobbs Leviathan: The Dangerous Breadth of the Hobbs Act and Other Corruption Statutes," *Notre Dame Law Review* 87, no. 1 (2011): 383-420; and Charles F.C. Ruff, "Federal Prosecution of Local Corruption: A Case Study in the Making of Law Enforcement Policy," *Georgetown Law Journal* 65, no. 5 (1977): 1171.

134 Noonan, *Bribes*, 586.

135 Organized Crime Control Act of 1970, Pub. L. No. 91-452, 84 Stat. 937.

136 "Nixon Finally Gets the Crime Bill He Wanted." *New York Times*, Oct. 18, 1970.

137 In 1974, the federal Second Circuit Court of Appeals ruled that RICO also applied to foreign corporations, ensuring that proceeds of domestic corrupt activities could not then be invested in foreign enterprises. *United States v. Parness*, 503 F.2d 430, 439 (2d Cir. 1974), cert. denied, 419 U.S. 1105 (1975).

138 For the first time, financial institutions, private businesses, and individuals were now required to document all transfers of money in or out of the country over $5,000. Bank Records and Foreign Transactions Act, 12 U.S.C. § 1829(b), §§ 1951 to 1959.

139 Bennett I. Deutsch, "The Tax Treatment of Illegal Payments after Alex v. Commissioner," *Columbia Law Review* 79, no. 3 (1979).

140 *United States v. Isaacs*, 493 F.2d 1124, 1149-52 (7th Cir. 1974), cert. denied, 417 U.S. 976 (1974).

141 Susan B. King and Robert L. Peabody, "Control of Presidential Campaign Financing," *Proceedings of the Academy of Political Science* 32, no. 1 (1975): 184.

142 Elmer B. Staats, "Impact of the Federal Election Campaign Act of 1971," *Annals of the American Academy of Political and Social Science* 425, no. 1 (1976): 100.

143 Don Irwin, "Johnson Asks New Legislation on Campaign Spending, Gifts," *Los Angeles Times*, May 27, 1966.

144 Robert C. Albright, "Talky Senate May Deliver Yet," *Washington Post*, May 15, 1967.

145 "Time for Action on Ethics," *Los Angeles Times*, Apr. 2, 1967.

146 King and Peabody, "Control."

147 John W. Gardner, "To Control Campaign Costs," *New York Times*, Nov. 23, 1970.

148 *Common Cause v. Democratic Nat'l Comm.*, 333 F.Supp. 803 (D.D.C. 1971).

149 S. J. Micciche, "An End to Campaign Skulduggery?" *Boston Globe*, Jan. 24, 1971.

150 Joel L. Fleishman and Carol S. Greenwald, "Public Interest Litigation and Political Finance Reform," *Annals of the American Academy of Political and Social Science* 425 (1976): 114-123.

151 Robert Deindorfer, "John Gardner's Common Cause: Thousands Are Joining His Crusade for a Better America," *Boston Globe*, Nov. 22, 1970.

152 John Hanrahan, "Dowdy Convicted in Bribe Case," *Washington Post*, Dec. 31, 1971.

153 "TO PASS S. 382," Senate Vote #182 in 1971 (92nd Congress), Roll Call Votes, GovTrack, https://www.govtrack.us/congress/votes/92-1971/s182.

154 "The American Presidency Project," UC Santa Barbara, http://www.presidency.ucsb.edu/ws/?pid=3725. For more information, see Ben A. Franklin, "Nixon Signs a Law to Curb Spending on Campaigns," *New York Times*, Feb. 8, 1972.

155 Congress would quickly follow up on FECA by passing the Revenue Act of 1971, which allowed tax payers to contribute one dollar of their tax credit to a public fund to finance presidential elections.

Notes | 305

156 Franklin, "Nixon Signs a Law to Curb Spending on Campaigns," *New York Times*.

157 Morton Mintz, "Early Contributors to Nixon Disclosed," *Washington Post,* Sept. 29, 1973.

158 Mintz, "Early Contributors to Nixon Disclosed," *Washington Post*.

159 Fred Emery, *Watergate: The Corruption of American Politics and the Fall of Richard Nixon* (Touchstone, 1994), 109.

160 David Vogel, *Fluctuating Fortunes: The Political Power of Business in America* (Basic Books, 1989), 115.

161 *Common Cause v. Finance Committee to Re-elect the President*, Civ. Action No. 1780-72 (D.D.C. 1972). Two years later, after those unlawful donations were revealed, Nader's Project on Corporate Responsibility would file shareholder derivative suits against Gulf Oil and others seeking to recover unlawful political contributions. Robert Pitofsky, "Beyond Nader: Consumer Protection and the Regulation of Advertising," *Harvard Law Review* 90, no. 4 (1977): 661-701.

162 Morton Mintz, "Early Contributors to Nixon Disclosed," *Washington Post*.

163 Fleishman and Greenwald, "Public Interest Litigation and Political Finance Reform."

164 When one of the defendants was asked his occupation, for example, he'd answered simply, "anti-communist."

165 Emery, *Watergate*, 151.

166 Ronald P. Kane and Samuel Butler III, "Improper Corporate Payments: The Second Half of Watergate," *Loyola University Chicago Law Journal* 8, no. 1 (1976): 1.

167 Kane and Butler, "Improper Corporate Payments."

168 Emery, *Watergate*, 377.

169 Steve Emmons, "Hinshaw Convicted on 2 Counts of Receiving Bribes," *New York Times*, Jan. 27, 1976.

170 John V. Dowdy (D-TX), convicted of conspiracy, perjury, and promoting bribery; Bertram L. Podell (D-NY), convicted of conspiracy and conflict of interest; Frank J. Brasco (D-NY), convicted of conspiracy to accept bribes; Angelo D. Roncallo (R-NY), indicted for extorting political contributions; Andrew J. Hinshaw (R-CA), convicted of bribery and misappropriation of public funds; Henry J. Helstoski (D-NJ), indicted for bribery; James F. Hastings (R-NY), convicted of receiving kickbacks and mail fraud; Edward J. Gurney (R-FL), indicted for violating campaign finance laws and soliciting bribes; Richard A. Tonry (D-LA), pleaded guilty to illegal campaign contributions; Edward A. Garmatz (D-MD), indicted on bribery charges; Wendell Wyatt (R-OR), pleaded guilty to violating campaign spending laws; James R. Jones (D-OK), pleaded guilty to failing to report campaign contribution; Richard T. Hanna (D-CA), pleaded guilty to defrauding the government; Daniel Brewster (D-MD), indicted for solicitation and acceptance of bribes; George Hansen (R-ID), pleaded guilty to violating campaign finance laws; Otto E. Passman (D-LA), indicted for bribery and income tax evasion; and Joshua Eilberg (D-PA), pleading guilty to illegally receiving compensation. For further reporting, see Jonathan J. Cooper, "Members of Congress Charged With a Crime, 1798 – 2008," *Washington Independent*, July 29, 2008.

171 For example, Frank Clark (D-PA) pleaded guilty to mail fraud and income tax evasion; Daniel J. Flood (D-PA) pleaded guilty to mail fraud and tax evasion; Cornelius Gallagher (D-NJ) pleaded guilty to tax evasion; Martin B. McKneally (R-NY) pleaded guilty to tax evasion; and J. Irving Whalley (R-PA) was convicted of mail fraud, obstruction of justice, and payroll abuse.

172 United States Department of Justice, Criminal Division, Public Integrity Section, *Report to Congress on the Activities and Operations of the Public Integrity Section for 1981* (April 1982).

173   Noonan, *Bribes*, 601.

174   Noonan, *Bribes*.

175   US DOJ, *Report to Congress*.

176   Kane and Butler, "Improper Corporate Payments."

177   Fleishman and Greenwald, "Public Interest Litigation and Political Finance Reform."

178   Conference of the United States, 1971, H.R. Doc. No. 93-103 (1973).

179   In *Buckley v. Valeo*, 422 U.S. 1 (1976) the court upheld all the provisions of the 1971 act except for the limitation on expenditures.

180   Zephyr Teachout, *Corruption in America* (Harvard University Press, 2014), 210.

181   In 1976, James Risser, a reporter for the *Des Moines Register* earned a Pulitzer Prize for his exposé on large-scale corruption in the American grain exporting trade, right around the same time that federal grand juries were nearing a vote on bribery indictments involving a separate scandal of federal meat inspectors in over fifteen states.

182   In 1972, the Knapp Commission Report on Police Corruption was released, revealing that during 1971, more than half of New York City's 29,600 police officers were involved in corruption. That report inspired the Oscar-nominated movie *Serpico* staring Al Pacino the following year.

183   Noonan, *Bribes*, 501.

184   Milton S. Gwirtzman, "Is Bribery Defensible?" *New York Times Magazine*, Oct. 5, 1975, 19.

185   Noonan, *Bribes*, 584.

186   Julian E. Zelizer, *On Capitol Hill: The Struggle to Reform Congress and Its Consequences, 1948-2000* (Cambridge University Press, 2004), 117-118.

187   "Nixon Finally Gets the Crime Bill He Wanted." *New York Times*.

188   James Rosen, *The Strong Man: John Mitchell and the Secrets of Watergate* (Doubleday, 2008), 74-75.

189   Joseph Volz, "Jersey City Officials Indicted," *Newsday*, Nov. 17, 1970.

190   James M. Naughton, "How Agnew Bartered His Office to Keep from Going to Prison," *New York Times*, Oct. 23, 1973.

191   "30th Anniversary of Spiro Agnew Resignation," Sept. 30, 2003, by American History TV, C-SPAN, http://www.c-span.org/video/?178436-1/30th-anniversary-spiro-agnew-resignation.

192   Robert L. Heilbroner et al., *In the Name of Profit* (Warner Books, 1973), 94.

193   Gwirtzman, "Is Bribery Defensible?" *New York Times Magazine*.

194   For example, Walter Sterling Surrey, "The Foreign Corrupt Practices Act: Let the Punishment Fit the Crime," *Harvard International Law Journal* 20, no. 2 (1979), notes that "a new sense of morality and a concomitant schizophrenia" contributed to passage of the FCPA.

195   Frank H. Roberts and Fred M. Abbott, *The Law of Questionable Foreign Payments: Implications for American International Business* (Southwestern Legal Foundation, 1982), 123.

196   Duane Windsor and Kathleen A. Getz, "Multilateral Cooperation to Combat Corruption: Normative Regimes Despite Mixed Motives and Diverse Values," *Cornell International Law Journal* 33, no. 3 (2000): 743.

197 For example, Gutterman, "Easier Done," 1-20, notes that "[t]he FCPA arose as a result of Watergate-related revelations about foreign corrupt practices undertaken by major U.S. corporations, the ethical resonance of which led legislators to proceed with the Act, regardless of countervailing material strategic trade considerations." See also Kevin E. Davis, *Between Impunity and Imperialism: The Regulation of Transnational Bribery* (Oxford University Press, 2019), 38-39 notes that "Congress intended the FCPA to make a moral statement" and that many scholars "characterize the FCPA as an expression of 'post-Watergate morality.'"

198 For example Gregory K. Smith et al., "Foreign Corrupt Practices Act," *American Criminal Law Review* 28, no. 3 (1991): 541 writes "[t]he Watergate scandal was the genesis for the FCPA."); Donald R. Cruver, *Complying with the Foreign Corrupt Practices Act: A Guide for Doing Business in the International Marketplace* (Quorum Books, 1999) states that "[b]efore Watergate, no one had expressed official concern about bribery of foreign officials by American nationals, and no specific law forbade the practice."); Don Zarin, *Doing Business Under the Foreign Corrupt Practices Act* (PLI Press, 2011), § 1-1 notes that "[t]he Foreign Corrupt Practices Act (FCPA or Act) is a by-product of the Watergate scandal."; Criminal Division, U.S. Department of Justice and Enforcement Division, U.S. Securities and Exchange Commission, *A Resource Guide to the U.S. Foreign Corrupt Practices Act* (Nov. 14, 2012), stating "Congress enacted the FCPA in 1977 after revelations of widespread global corruption in the wake of the Watergate political scandal."; and Kevin E. Davis, "Why Does the United States Regulate Foreign Bribery: Moralism, Self-Interest, or Altruism?," *NYU Annual Survey of American Law* 67 (Mar. 2012): 497, notes that "[t]he FCPA was passed in direct response to evidence uncovered in the course of investigations sparked by the Watergate scandal."

199 Michael Schudson, *Watergate in American Memory: How We Remember, Forget, and Reconstruct the Past* (Basic Books, 1992).

200 Anechiarico and Jacobs, *The Pursuit of Absolute Integrity*, 7.

201 Anechiarico and Jacobs, *The Pursuit of Absolute Integrity*, 8.

202 Noonan, *Bribes*, 600. Alse see Ruth A. Miller, *The Erotics of Corruption: Law, Scandal, and Political Perversion* (State University of New York Press, 2008).

203 The list of those who were ultimately exposed during this decade is long. Wayne Hays (D-OH) was alleged to have had an affair with his secretary, Elizabeth Ray. Wilbur Mills (D-AR.), powerful Chairman of the House Ways and Means Committee and presidential hopeful in 1972, was caught having a relationship with Washington stripper Fanne Foxe. John Young (D-TX) was found having an affair with a female member of his staff. Robert D. Leggett (D-CA) fathered two children outside of marriage with his congressional secretary. Allan Howe (D-UT), Fred Richmond (D-NY), and Joe Waggonner (D-LA) were all three arrested on separate prostitution charges. And perhaps most famously, Ted Kennedy (D-MA) was involved in the death of a woman with whom it was suspected he was also having an affair in Chappaquiddick, Massachusetts.

204 Zelizer, *On Capitol Hill*.

205 Kate Galbraith, "A. Carl Kotchan, Lockheed Executive, Dies at 94," *New York Times*, Dec. 22, 2008.

206 Robert Lindsey, "Kotchian Calls Himself the Scapegoat," *New York Times*, July 3, 1977.

207 Frank Church "Multinational Corporations and East Asia: The Foreign Policy Implications of the Lockheed Affair" (speech, Harvard East Asia Conference, Oct. 15, 1976).

208 Louis Heren, "The Oily Smell of Corruption that Finally Put Teapot Dome into American Folklore," *The Times*, June 14, 1975.

209 *Corporate Rights and Responsibilities: Hearing Before the S. Comm. on Com.*, 94th Cong. 32 (1976) (statement of Dr. Gordon Adams, Dir. of Mil. Rsch., Council on Econ. Priorities)

210 Anthony Sampson, "Lockheed's Foreign Policy," *New York Magazine*, Mar. 15, 1976, 56.

CHAPTER THREE: OF PROFITS AND PATRIOTISM

211 Frank Vogl, *Waging War on Corruption* (Rowman & Littlefield 2012), 163.

212 LeRoy Ashby and Rod Gramer, *Fighting the Odds: The Life of Senator Frank Church* (Washington State University Press, 1994); and Frank Church to John Sparkman, letter, Feb. 27, 1975, series 2.2, box 14, folder 4, Frank Church Archives.

213 For example, while on his first trip to the East Coast to visit his older brother in colonial Annapolis, it's said that Frank left dismayed and repulsed by the opulence of wealthy homes he saw surrounding the naval academy. Ashby and Gramer, *Fighting the Odds*, 14.

214 Ashby and Gramer, *Fighting the Odds*, 28.

215 Ashby and Gramer, *Fighting the Odds*, 38.

216 To get from one location to the next, Bethine, his wife, would sit in the front seat of their battered Kaiser to drive while Frank lay in the back, punching away at a typewriter to prepare his next stump speech. Ashby and Gramer, *Fighting the Odds*, 57.

217 Geoffrey T. Hellman, "Does Anyone Look His Age?" *New Yorker*, July 16, 1960.

218 Ashby and Gramer, *Fighting the Odds*, 103.

219 Ashby and Gramer, *Fighting the Odds*, 95.

220 Bill Hall, *Frank Church, D.C. & Me* (Washington State University Press, 1995), 82.

221 Memorandum, "Relations of the Government of Chile with ITT," Mar. 1973, Multinational Corporations, 10.6, box 4, folder 8, part 3, Frank Church Papers.

222 Frank Church, "Multinational Corporations and East Asia."

223 Ashby and Gramer, *Fighting the Odds*, 423.

224 Carl Marcy and Pat Holt to Senators J. William Fulbright, Frank Church, and Clifford Case, memorandum, May 2, 1972, series 10.6, box 4, folder 8, part 2, Frank Church Archives.

225 In 1957, Humphrey had invited Church to speak at a Minneapolis-area Civil Rights dinner. When Civil Rights advocates threatened to picket the dinner, Church felt that Humphrey deserted him. Ashby and Gramer, Fighting the Odds, 92-93.

226 Carl Solberg, *Hubert Humphrey: A Biography* (W.W. Norton & Co., 1984), 469.

227 Ashby and Gramer, *Fighting the Odds*, 258.

228 Ashby and Gramer, *Fighting the Odds*, 375.

229 *Overseas Private Insurance Corporation (OPIC): Hearing Before the Subcomm. on Multinational Corp. of the S. Comm. on Foreign Rel.*, 93rd Cong. 318 (1973).

230 Jack Blum, interview by author, Oct. 11, 2012, on file with author.

231 As proof of Blum's "insider" status, his resume listed Senator Philip Hart as a reference, as well as other notable names, including Hannah Arendt and Harlan Blake.

232 Jerome I. Levinson, *Who Makes American Foreign Policy?: A Witches Brew* (Signature Book Printing, 2004), 19.

233 "Chile Embassy Burglarized," *Washington Post*, May 17, 1972.

234 A notorious Cold War liberal, Jackson was one of the few remaining Democrats still in favor of the war in Vietnam. Robert David Johnson, *Congress and the Cold War* (Cambridge University Press, 2006), 196.

235 Jerome I. Levinson, interview by the author, on file with the author.

236 *International Telephone and Telegraph Co. and Chile, 1970-1971: Hearing Before the Subcomm. on Multinational Corp. of the S. Comm. on Foreign Rel.*, 93rd Cong. 427 (1973) (testimony of Charles A. Meyer, Former Assistant Secretary of State for Latin American Affairs).

237 Levinson, interview.

238 Laurence Stern, "ITT Head Affirms Fund Offer," *Washington Post*, Apr. 3, 1973.

239 "ITT and CIA: Uneasy Riders," *Washington Post*, Apr. 5, 1973.

240 Frank Church U.S. Senator, Idaho, news release, April 13, 1973, Frank Church Papers and Frank Church to Sam Liner (constituent), letter, April 11, 1973, Frank Church Papers.

241 Ashby and Gramer, *Fighting the Odds*, 431.

242 *International Telephone and Telegraph Co. and Chile, 1970-1971: Hearing Before the Subcomm. on Multinational Corp. of the S. Comm. on Foreign Rel.*, 93rd Cong. 427 (1973) (testimony of Harold S. Geneen, Chairman and Chief Executive, ITT).

243 Laurence Stern, "ITT and CIA on Chile: A Semblance of Influence on Policy," *Washington Post*, Apr. 1, 1973.

244 For example, see Luzviminda Bartolome Francisco and Jonathan Shepard Fast, *Conspiracy for Empire: Big Business, Corruption and the Politics of Imperialism in America, 1876-1907* (Foundation for Nationalist Studies, 1985).

245 Note, however, that for a brief period in the 1930s, conflicts in other parts of the world would erode these common interests, pitting the U.S. government's desire to remain neutral against corporate cupidity. In one example case, Curtiss-Wright Export Corporation was fined $10,000 for selling machine guns to Bolivia for use in the Chaco war, a border dispute with Paraguay. By involving themselves in the Chaco, U.S. Secretary of State Cordell Hull charged that American arms manufacturers, for the sake of profit, were helping to carry on a "useless and sanguinary conflict"—one that would eventually lead to over 100,000 deaths. In much the same vein, the 1936 Senate Munitions Hearings found that arms manufacturers and financiers were to blame for warmongering in Europe, and in the years leading up to the war, President Franklin Roosevelt's administration would continue to struggle to prevent U.S. businesses from selling their goods to European governments, including Italy and Germany. *United States v. Curtiss-Wright Export Corp.*, 299 U.S. 304 (1936); Stephen Breyer, *The Court and the World* (Alfred A. Knopf, 2015), 26; and Robert Burk, *The Corporate State and the Broker State* (Harvard University Press, 1990).

246 Nicolas Spulare, *The American Economy* (Cambridge University Press, 1995), 22; and Frank Church, "Inquiry on the Multinational Corporation and Its Relationship to United States Foreign Policy" (speech, Business Financing Conference, New York, NY, Dec. 5, 1972).

247 Richard J. Barnett and Ronald E. Müller, *Global Reach: The Power of Multinational Corporations* (Simon & Schuster, 1974), 79.

248 Judith Stein, Pivotal Decade: *How the United States Traded Factories for Finance in the Seventies* (Yale University Press, 2010), 11.

249 Anthony Sampson, *The Sovereign State of ITT* (Stein & Day, 1973), 114.

250 Based on information from data for GDP in 1970, Countries Compared, NationMaster, https://www.nationmaster.com/country-info/stats/Economy/GDP-in-1970; and data for 1970, Fortune 500, CNN Money, https://money.cnn.com/magazines/fortune/fortune500_archive/full/1970.

251 Frank Church, "Remarks Before General Foods Executives" (speech, April 22, 1977).

252 Heilbroner, *In the Name of Profit*, 201. Out of the largest 200,000 manufacturing companies in 1967, only 0.1% shipped 42% of all manufactured goods by value. John Kenneth Galbraith, *The Essential Galbraith* (HMH, 2001), 122.

253 Melvin Kranzberg et al., eds., *Science Technology and Warfare* (University Press of the Pacific, 2001), 162. The arrangement was certainly true for General Motors as well; the company was the U.S. military's single biggest contractor that year based on the size of the order.

254 Kennedy's Secretary of Commerce, Luther Hodges, unsuccessfully sought to reform the Business Advisory Council, an organization dating back to Franklin Roosevelt's time to formalize relations between government and the private sector, resulting in the council's vote to break off all official ties with the White House and change its name. Subsequently, Kennedy angered industry leaders by employing the media to shame steel companies from raising prices. Vogel, *Fluctuating Fortunes*, 17-21.

255 John F. Kennedy, special message to congress on protecting consumer interest, Mar. 15, 1962, JFKPOF-037-028, box 037, collection "Papers of John F. Kennedy. Presidential Papers. President's Office Files," Digital Archives, John F. Kennedy Presidential Library and Museum.

256 When Nader was invited in 1966 by Senator Robert Kennedy to appear before Congress, newspaper reports revealed that General Motors had hired private detectives to intimidate him from testifying. The scandal would instantly launch Nader into the public limelight, where he would continue to stoke concerns about corporate misconduct on everything from the meat industry and baby foods to insecticides and mercury poisoning.

257 These included the Fair Packaging and Labeling Act (1966), the National Gas Pipeline Safety Act (1968), the Consumer Credit Protection Act (1968), the Truth in Lending Act (1968), the Occupational Safety and Health Act (1970); and the Consumer Product Safety Act (1972).

258 For more on this idea, see Marver Bernstein, *Regulating Business by Independent Commission* (Princeton University Press, 1955); and Gary Gerstle, *The Rise and Fall of the Neoliberal Order* (Oxford University Press, 2022), 159.

259 Vogel, *Fluctuating Fortunes*, 55. Similarly, when a group of university students gathered in Port Huron, Michigan in 1962 to issue a manifesto declaring the birth of a "New Left" movement, among their complaints was the fact that concentration of wealth in large corporations had bred excessive conformity and crushed individuality.

260 Martin Luther King, Jr., "Beyond Vietnam" (address, Clergy and Laymen Concerned About the War in Vietnam, Riverside Church, New York, NY, April, 4, 1967).

Notes | 311

261 In voicing their anger, some would even adopt "shock" tactics, as when a group of young men calling themselves the Guerrilla Art Action Group entered the lobby of the Museum of Modern Art in 1969 with bull blood in plastic bags hidden under their clothes. The men began wrestling on the museum's floor bathed in blood. The staged fight had been orchestrated as a protest against the Rockefeller family, which owned the museum and had interests in several military contractors operating in Vietnam. By the end of the decade, targeting corporations had become a common tactic among social activists, even when the social harm had nothing to do with the United States, as was the case when Union Carbide was boycotted for continuing to operate within the apartheid governments of Rhodesia and South Africa.

262 Stein, *Pivotal Decade*, 38.

263 Stein, *Pivotal Decade*.

264 "Unions Decry Use of Foreign Labor," *New York Times*, July 14, 1971.

265 "Democrats Strongly Back Consumer, Labor in Platform Unfriendly to Big Business," Wall Street Journal, June 28, 1972; John B. Judis, *The Paradox of American Democracy* (Routledge, 2000), 114.

266 Leonard Silk and David Vogel, *Ethics and Profits: The Crisis of Confidence in American Business* (Simon and Schuster, 1976), 21-22.

267 *Corporate Rights and Responsibilities*, 94th Cong. 247-48 (statement of James B. Farley, President, Booz, Allen & Hamilton); and Vogel, Fluctuating Fortunes, 114.

268 John Kenneth Galbraith, "Power and the Useful Economist," *American Economic Review* 63, no. 2 (1973): 1-12.

269 Diplomats from Chile, along with representatives from seventy-six other developing countries met in the fall of 1967 in Algiers, forming the group that would become known within the United Nations as the Group of 77. Over the next decade, they would propose a catalog of reforms aimed at stopping these perceived exploitative practices by multinational corporations and their home states.

270 Other cultural markers of the time included *America Inc.*, a 1971 best-selling book by Morton Mintz and Jerry Cohen.

271 Bruce Schulman, *The Seventies: The Great Shift in American Culture, Society, and Politics* (Da Capo Press, 2001), 51.

272 Between September 1974 and September 1975, top corporate executives from firms such as IBM, Exxon, Bechtel, and Hughes Tool held eight three-day meetings to explore the current and future role of business in U.S. society. Stein, *Pivotal Decade*.

273 "Pacific Basin Charter on International Investments, A Declaration of Basic Principles" adopted May 19, 1972, Pacific Basin Economic Council Fifth General Meeting, Wellington, New Zealand.

274 Clinard and Yeager, *Corporate Crime*, 205-206.

275 William Breit, "Galbraith and Friedman: Two Versions of Economic Reality," *Journal of Post Keynesian Economics* 7, no. 1 (Autumn, 1984): 18-29.

276 Frank Church, "The Multinational Corporation—A Trial Balance" (speech, Houston, TX, Mar. 2, 1973), series 10.6, box 4, folder 12, Frank Church Archives.

277 "Allende's Last Words," *Sydney Tribune*, Oct. 9, 1973.

278 Allende's death spurred reactions, some of them violent, across the Western world. In the early morning hours of September 28, a telephone operator at the New York Times received an anonymous phone call announcing that a bomb was about to go off in ITT's midtown Manhattan office. "This is retaliation of the ITT crimes they committed against Chile," the young man announced shortly before the small, homemade device exploded in the building's ninth-floor closet. Fortunately, no one was injured. "Headliners: A Message for I.T.T.," *New York Times*, Sept. 30, 1973.

279 The flow of money from U.S.-headquartered companies to Europe was designed to avoid a ceiling on interest rates that banks located in the United States could pay on time deposits, as well as reserve requirements imposed by the Federal Reserve Board. For a full explanation, see Raymond Vernon and Debora Spar, *Beyond Globalism: Remaking American Foreign Economic Policy* (The Free Press, 1989), 97.

280 Ashby and Gramer, *Fighting the Odds*, 456.

281 Levinson, *Who Makes American Foreign Policy?*, 202; Ashby and Gramer, *Fighting the Odds*, 455; and Jerome Levinson to Charles Percy, memorandum, April 5, 1976, series 10.6, box 4, folder 8, part 3, Frank Church Papers.

282 Levinson, interview.

283 123 Cong. Rec. H14519 (1977) (statement of Rep. Michael Harrington of Mass. on H.R. 3815).

284 *Multinational Corporations and United States Foreign Policy: Hearings before the S. Comm on Multinational Corporations*, 94th Cong. 1 (1976).

285 Ashby and Gramer, *Fighting the Odds*, 458.

286 Byrone E. Calame, "Stonewalling it at Gulf Oil," *Wall Street Journal*, Apr. 18, 1975

287 *Multinational Corporations and United States Foreign Policy* (statement of B.R. Dorsey, Chairman of the Board, Gulf Oil Corp.).

288 In actuality, the SEC reporter had misheard Dorsey during his testimony. He had in fact said, "several hundred million dollars," not "$700 million."

289 National Security Advisor Presidential Country Files for Venezuela, Box 6, State Department Telegrams: From SECSTATE–EXDIS, Gerald R. Ford Library.

290 Multinational Corporations and United States Foreign Policy (statement of B.R. Dorsey, Chairman of the Board, Gulf Oil Corp.).

291 That deal had apparently involved a $200,000 bonus to defray the costs that Park incurred on a trip to the United States in 1969 to meet with President Nixon.

292 The revelations are said to have even prompted South Korea's President Park to declare martial law and impose a twenty-four-hour blackout on all newspapers.

293 Gulf Oil Corporation, Report of the Special Review Committee of the Board of Directors of Gulf Oil Corporation (Form 8-K) (Dec. 30, 1975), 132.

294 Gulf Oil Corporation, Report.

295 *Multinational Corporations and United States Foreign Policy*.

296 *Multinational Corporations and United States Foreign Policy*.

Notes | 313

297 Whatever his motivations, Dorsey's fate would be decided six months later when Gulf concluded its monthslong internal investigation led by the acclaimed lawyer and former World Bank President, John J. McCloy. McCloy's 400-page report concluded that Dorsey, while perhaps unaware of the U.S. payments, "was not sufficiently alert and should have known that Wild was involved in making political contributions from an unknown source." As for the overseas payments, McCloy found that regardless of their legality, "such important and potentially serious decisions should not be made by management alone, without discussion with the Board." Two weeks later, Gulf's board voted unanimously to terminate Dorsey, marking a shameful end to his four-decades-long career with the company. Gulf Oil Corporation, Report, 270-78.

298 *Corporate Rights and Responsibilities* (statement of Adams).

299 State Department Washington DC to Secretary of State, telegram, April 9, 1975, 1975STATE139965, Central Foreign Policy Files, 1973-79, RG 59, National Archives.

300 *Corporate Rights and Responsibilities: Hearing Before the S. Comm. on Com.*, 94th Cong. 4 (1976) (opening statement of Sen. Durkin).

301 *Protecting the Ability of the United States to Trade Abroad: Hearing Before the Subcomm. on Int'l Trade of the S. Comm. on Fin.*, 94th Cong. 16 (1975) (testimony of Frank Church).

302 David W.P. Elliot, *The Vietnamese War: Revolution and Social Change in the Mekong Delta, 1930-1975* 2 (M.E. Sharpe, 2002).

303 Jack Anderson, "Corruption is Saigon's Major Foe," *Washington Post*, Feb. 27, 1968.

304 Joel Brinkley, *Cambodia's Curse: The Modern History of a Troubled Land* (Public Affairs, 2011).

305 Gwirtzman, "Is Bribery Defensible?" *New York Times Magazine*.

306 *Corporate Rights and Responsibilities: Hearing Before the S. Comm. on Com.*, 94th Cong. 4 (1976) (opening statement of Sen. Durkin).

307 Lloyd Shearer, "Sen Frank Church—Dark Horse Candidate for the Presidency," *Boston Globe*, Sept. 21, 1975.

308 Ashby and Gramer, *Fighting the Odds*, 458; and Sampson, *The Arms Bazaar*, 273.

309 Levinson, *Who Makes American Foreign Policy?*, 202.

CHAPTER FOUR: BLOODLETTING

310 Levinson, *Who Makes American Foreign Policy?*, 203.

311 By 1949, Northrop was left with only two sellable products: the F89 fighter and the winged Snark, an intercontinental missile.

312 "A Place in Space," *Time Magazine*, Oct. 27, 1961, 91.

313 "A Place in Space," *Time Magazine*.

314 Robert Lindsey, "The New Adventures of Tom Jones," *New York Times*, Sept. 19, 1976.

315 Ernst & Ernst, *Report on Special Investigation of Northrop Corporation and Subsidiaries* (Ernst & Ernst, 1975), 460.

316 Thomas V. Jones, interview by Peter Westwick, Aerospace Oral History Project, The Huntington Library, Feb. 16, 2010, https://hdl.huntington.org/digital/collection/p15150coll7/id/23308.

317 Ernst & Ernst, *Report*, 484.

318 Jack Egan, "The Spotlights Fall on 2 Aircraft Makers," *Washington Post*, June 15, 1975.

319 William H. Jones, "Northrop's Man in the Middle East," *Washington Post*, June 7, 1975.

320 *Political Contributions to Foreign Governments: Hearing Before the Subcomm. on Multinational Corp. of the S. Comm. on Foreign Rel.*, 94th Cong. 107 (1975) (opening statement of Sen. Frank Church, Chair, S. Subcomm. on Multinational Corp.).

321 Ernst & Ernst, *Report*, 840.

322 *Political Contributions to Foreign Governments*.

323 In 1971, the United States had agreed to equip and modernize the Royal Saudi Airforce through a long-range, multibillion-dollar program to sell the Saudi government F-5 planes. Northrop was designated as prime contractor for the entire program, which meant that it was required to disclose to the U.S. military all of its third-party agents, including Khashoggi. Ernst & Ernst, *Report*, 897.

324 Robert Smith, "A High Official in France Was on Northrop Payroll," *New York Times*, June 7, 1975.

325 *The Activities of American Multinational Corporations Abroad: Hearings Before the Subcomm. on Int'l Econ. Pol'y of the H.R. Comm. on Int'l Rel.*, 94th Cong. 101 (1975) (memorandum "Agents' Fees in the Middle East" approved by the Department of Defense).

326 Department of State to Saudi Arabia Jeddah, telegram, "Corruption in Saudi Arabia: Northrop," June 3, 1975, 1975STATE129754_b, State Department Cable, Public Library of US Diplomacy.

327 Department of State to Egypt Cairo, telegram, "Corruption in Saudi Arabia: Northrop," June 4, 1975, 1975STATE129804_b, State Department Cable, Public Library of US Diplomacy.

328 Jack Egan, "Northrop Apologizes on Saudi Bribe," *Wall Street Journal*, June 10, 1975.

329 "Foreign Letters to Northrop Reflect Consultant Ties," *New York Times*, June 7, 1975.

330 It is unclear whether Stehlin's death was a suicide or not. Boulton, *The Grease Machine*, 171.

331 Levinson, *Who Makes American Foreign Policy?*, 203.

332 Levinson, interview.

333 Ernst & Ernst, *Report*, 582.

334 Thomas V. Jones, interview.

335 *Political Contributions to Foreign Governments*, 94th Cong. 14 (remarks of Sen. Charles Percy, Member, S. Subcomm. on Multinational Corp.).

336 Jack Egan, "The Spotlights Fall on 2 Aircraft Makers," *Washington Post*.

337 *Political Contributions to Foreign Governments*, 94th Cong. 184 (statement of Thomas Jones, President, Northrop Corp.).

338 Jack Egan, "Oversight Cited by Northrop: Didn't Bar Payments, Jones Says," *Washington Post*, June 11, 1975.

339 *Political Contributions to Foreign Governments*, 94th Cong. 165 (remarks of Sen. Charles Percy, Member, S. Subcomm. on Multinational Corp.).

340 Boulton, *The Grease Machine*, 5-6.

341 Harold D. Watkins, "Overseas Activities Probed: Lockheed Denies Northrop-Type Deals," *Los Angeles Times*, June 12, 1975.

Notes | 315

342   The House voted for the Guarantee by the thinnest of margins: 192–189. The vote came out 49–48 in favor of Lockheed. With a single exception, all of the senators with Lockheed-related plants in their state voted in favor of the loan guarantees, while all of those in states with McDonnell Douglas or GE plants in their states voted against it.

343   P.D. Ring to Arthur Burns, memorandum, Oct. 8, 1975 (on file with the author).

344   *Lockheed Aircraft Corporation: Hearings Before the Subcomm. on Multinational Corp. of the S. Comm. on Foreign Rel.*, 94th Cong. 5 (1976) (documents from Arthur Young & Company and the Lockheed Aircraft Corporation Relating to Agent's Fees and Foreign Political Contributions).

345   At the time, many defense contractors, including Lockheed, refused to appear at the hearings. Jonathan Kasparek, *Proxmire: Bulldog of the Senate* (Wisconsin Historical Society Press, 2019), 206.

346   Jay G. Sykes, *Proxmire* (R. B. Luce, 1972), 239-240.

347   Robert Smith, "Proxmire Says Lockheed Bribed Foreign Officials," *New York Times*, Aug. 11, 1975.

348   Frank Church to William Proxmire, letter, Aug. 15, 1975, series 2.2, box 14, folder 6, Frank Church Archives.

349   Boulton, *The Grease Machine*, 264–5.

350   James Rowe, "Lockheed Paid $22 Million in Foreign Gifts," *Washington Post*, Aug. 2, 1975.

351   Jerry Landauer, "Lockheed Data on Payoffs in L-1011 Sales Overseas Is Sent to Senate Unit by Mistake," *Wall Street Journal*, Sept. 15, 1975.

352   "Suicide Note Left by Lockheed Officer," *New York Times*, Aug. 27, 1975.

353   *The Activities of American Multinational Corporations Abroad*, 94th Cong. 180 (statement of Philip A. Loomis Jr., Commissioner, Securities and Exchange Commission).

354   Levinson, interview.

355   Blum, interview.

356   Gwirtzman, "Is Bribery Defensible?" *New York Times Magazine*.

357   Walter E. Hanson, "Peer Review, Illegal Payments, and Lawyers' Letters," *Management Accounting* 58 (Oct. 1976): 15.

358   Stanley Sporkin, interview by Irving Pollack, Securities and Exchange Commission Historical Society, Sept. 23, 2003. See also Sommer, "The Slippery Slope of Materiality."

359   Evans, "Truth or Consequences."

360   Lewis D. Solomon and Leslie G. Linville, "Transnational Conduct of American Multinational Corporations: Questionable Payments Abroad," *Boston College Law Review* 17, no. 3 (1976): 303.

361   *The Activities of American Multinational Corporations Abroad*, 94th Cong. 180–82 (statement of Loomis).

362   *The Activities of American Multinational Corporations Abroad*, 94th Cong. 181 (statement of Loomis).

363 Corporate cases arising from the Watergate investigation include: *Securities and Exchange Commission v. Phillips Petroleum Co.*, Civil No. 75-0308 (D.D.C. filed Mar. 31, 1975); SEC Litigation Release No. 6770 (Mar. 31, 1975); *Securities and Exchange Commission v. Sanitas Service Corp.*, Civil No. 75-0520 (D.D.C. filed Apr. 10, 1975); SEC Litigation Release No. 6829 (Apr. 11, 1975); SEC Litigation Rel No. 6952 (June 30, 1975); *Securities and Exchange Commission v. Ashland Oil, Inc.*, Civil No. 75-0794 (D.D.C. filed May 16, 1975); SEC Litigation Release No. 6890 (May 19, 1975); *Securities and Exchange Commission v. General Refractories Co.*, Civil No. 75-0809 (D.D.C. filed May 21, 1975); SEC Litigation Release No. 6898 (May 21, 1975); SEC Litigation Release No. 6128 (June 11, 1975); and SEC Litigation Release No. 7098 (Sept. 24, 1975).

364 Office of the White House Press Secretary, news release, Oct. 2, 1975.

365 Sommer shared many of the same beliefs as Garrett regarding overseas bribery. In a speech he gave a few days after his own retirement six months later, Sommer warned that it was not "the role of the Commission to clean up corporate corruption throughout the world" and that "the credibility of the commission and its standing among professionals and among business people [had] been seriously compromised" by the investigations. Vogl, "SEC under Fire."

366 Roderick Hills, interview by Ralph Gerrara, Securities and Exchange Commission Historical Society, Dec. 20, 2002, https://www.sechistorical.org/collection/oral-histories/hills1222002Transcript.pdf.

367 *Securities and Exchange Commission v. Lockheed Aircraft Corp.*, 404 F. Supp. 651 (D.D.C. 1975).

368 Rogers & Wells to Henry Kissinger, letter, Nov. 19, 1975, box 22, Edward C. Scmults Files.

369 Henry Kissinger to Edward Levi, letter, Nov. 28, 1975 (on file with the author).

370 "Court Orders Lockheed to Give the SEC Full Custody of Foreign Payments Data," *Wall Street Journal*, Dec. 16, 1975.

371 "Strauss, die Gangster und die Wahrheit," *Der Spiegel,* Feb. 22, 1976, http://www.spiegel.de/spiegel/print/d-41279567.html.

372 Netherlands State Department to Secretary of State, telegram, Feb. 17, 1976, box 9, Presidential Country Files for Europe & Canada.

373 Germany Bonn to Secretary of State, telegram, "Lockheed," Dec. 23, 1975, 1975BONN20720_b, State Department Cable, Public Library of US Diplomacy.

374 Blum, interview.

375 Donnie Radcliffe, "White House Christmas Party for Congress: What a Difference a Year Makes." *Washington Post*, Dec. 19, 1975.

376 "Ex-Humphrey Aide Gets Prison Term, $5,000 Fine," *Los Angeles Times*, June 26, 1975.

377 "Possible 1968 Hughes Donation Is Acknowledged by Humphrey," *New York Times*, Mar. 20, 1974. See also Archibald Cox, "Charges Illegal Gift to Humphrey," *New York Times*, Oct. 20, 1973; and "Milk Co-Op Aide Pleads Guilty to Campaign Gifts," *Wall Street Journal*, July 24, 1974.

378 Rachel Patterson, "Humphrey Putting Finances in Order as Interest Grows in Possible Candidacy," *Boston Globe*, Apr. 25, 1976.

379 Ellen Proxmire, *One Foot in Washington: The Perilous Life of a Senator's Wife* (R. B. Luce, 1963), 11.

380 *Abuses of Corporate Power: Hearings Before the Subcomm. on Priorities and Econ. in Gov't of the Joint Econ. Comm.*, 94th Cong. 32 (1976) (statement of Hon. Roderick M. Hills, Chairman, Securities and Exchange Commission).

381 *Abuses of Corporate Power.*

382 In the Hague, Blum had caught up with Hans Teengs Gerritsen, a Lockheed consultant who'd fought alongside the Netherlands' Prince Bernhard during World War II. In Zurich, Blum had tried interviewing Fred C. Meuser, Lockheed's former Director of Sales, but was rebuffed by Swiss authorities who told him that he'd risk being arrested under the Swiss Penal Code. Department of State to Italy Rome, telegram, "Lockheed: Swiss Press Interview with Senate Committee Investigator," Feb. 27, 1976, 1976STATE047904_b, State Department Cable, Public Library of US Diplomacy.

383 Boulton, *The Grease Machine*, 268.

384 Bill Hall, *Frank Church*, 53.

385 In contrast to the approach taken by the Subcommittee on Multinational Corporations, the Senate Munitions Inquiry of 1934 made it a practice of entering into the congressional record the names of foreign government officials accused of accepting bribes from U.S. companies. This led to a slew of formal complaints issued by governments in Mexico, Argentina, Peru, Bolivia, Chile, and Great Britain as well as the cancellation of several contracts with American companies. These reprisals contributed to the overall undermining of the inquiry in the eyes of the American public. John Edward Wiltz, *In Search of Peace: The Senate Munitions Inquiry, 1934-1936* (Louisiana State University Press, 1963), 153-159.

386 *Multinational Corporations and United States Foreign Policy: Hearing Before the Subcomm. on Multinational Corp. of the S. Comm. on Foreign Rel.*, 94th Cong. 315 (1976) (statement of Sen. Percy).

387 Lockheed Aircraft Corporation.

388 Robert Shaplen, "Annals of Crime: The Lockheed Incident–II," *New Yorker*, Jan. 30, 1978, 74.

389 Japan Tokyo to Secretary of State, telegram, "Press Reactions to Lockheed Revelations," Feb. 6, 1976, 1976TOKYO01885_b, State Department Cable, Public Library of US Diplomacy.

390 Japan Tokyo to Department of State, telegram, "Ambassador's Statement in Response to Queries Concerning Lockheed," Feb. 6, 1976, 1976TOKYO01891_b, State Department Cable, Public Library of US Diplomacy.

391 Levinson, *Who Makes American Foreign Policy?*, 201.

392 "[H]aving had relationships in Japan over a period of 28 years, and probably having made at least a dozen trips there," Percy said, "at least in the industries in which I engaged, that was not a practice in Japan." Multinational Corporations and United States Foreign Policy, 94th Cong. 369 (1976) (question by Sen. Percy during testimony of A. Carl Kotchian, President, Lockheed Aircraft Corp.).

393 *Multinational Corporations and United States Foreign Policy*, 94th Cong. 349–50 (testimony of Kotchian).

394 Levinson, *Who Makes American Foreign Policy?*, 209-210.

395 Paul Kemezis, "Disclosures by Lockheed Shake Dutch and Japanese," *New York Times*, Feb. 8, 1976.

396 At the time, the Dutch government had recently contracted with Lockheed for the F-104 Starfighter as well as the Orion antisubmarine aircraft.

397 Netherlands The Hague to Belgium Brussels, Department of State, France Paris, Germany Bonn, Italy Rome, Japan Tokyo, Luxembourg, North Atlantic Treaty Organization (NATO), Secretary of State, Sweden Stockholm and United Kingdom London, telegram, "Lockheed Payments Upset Dutch," Feb. 9, 1976, 1976THEHA00670_b, State Department Cable, Public Library of US Diplomacy.

398   Netherlands The Hague to Belgium Brussels, telegram.

399   Netherlands The Hague to Belgium Brussels, telegram.

400   President Ford Committee Records, International Bribery Inquiry Folder, box G16, Gerald R. Ford Presidential Library.

401   Boulton, *The Grease Machine*, 271.

402   Jerome I. Levinson, *Who Makes American Foreign Policy?*, 214-225.

403   AmEmbassy Tokyo to Assistant Secretary Habib, telegram, NSA Trip Briefing Books and Cables of Henry Kissinger, box 31, Gerald R. Ford Presidential Library.

404   Edward Schmults, memorandum to the President, "Questionable Foreign Payments by U.S. Companies," Feb. 24, 1976, box C36, Gerald R. Ford Presidential Library.

405   "Corporate Bribe-Givers Face New Scrutiny by the IRS and a Ford Panel," *Wall Street Journal*, Feb. 11, 1976.

406   "Ford Sets Inquiry Into Overseas Practices of U.S. Firms as Bribery Reports Mount," *Wall Street Journal*, Feb. 11, 1976.

407   Gerald R. Ford to Takeo Miki, letter, Mar. 11, 1976, Michigan Yearbook of International Legal Studies.

408   Department of State to New Zealand Wellington, telegram, "Briefing Memorandum–Japanese Concern About Lockheed Disclosures," Feb. 22, 1976, 1976STATE042838_b, State Department, Public Library of US Diplomacy.

409   *Oversight on the Lockheed Loan Guarantee: Hearings Before the S. Comm. on Banking, Hous. & Urb. Aff.*, 94th Cong. 14 (1976) (Sen. William Proxmire, Chairman, during testimony of William Simon, Secretary of the Treasury and Chairman of the Emergency Loan Guarantee Board).

410   Foreign Pay-Offs/U.S. Companies (1)-(6), Kenneth A. Lazarus Files, box 51, TA 7, Gerald R. Ford Presidential Library.

411   Japan Tokyo to Commander in Chief US Pacific Command, telegram, "Lockheed Affair: New York Times Advertisement," Apr. 2, 1976, 1976TOKYO04902_b, State Department Cable, Public Library of US Diplomacy.

412   Levinson, *Who Makes American Foreign Policy?*, 214-225.

413   Levinson, *Who Makes American Foreign Policy?*, 225.

414   Bill Hall, *Frank Church*, 115.

415   Bill Hall, *Frank Church*, 124.

416   "Ford Sets Inquiry Into Overseas Practices of U.S. Firms as Bribery Reports Mount," *Wall Street Journal*.

417   Ann Crittenden, "Closing In on Corporate Payoffs Overseas," *New York Times*, Nov. 15 1976.

418   Lloyd N. Cutler, Global Interdependence and the Multinational Firm, (New York: Foreign Policy Association, 1978), 18.

419   The subsidiary charged the payments to an undeveloped leasehold and then deposited the laundered funds in a Swiss bank account, which Ashland could draw upon to pay off politicians around the world.

420   Jack Anderson and Les Whitten, "Four Firms Gave Politicians $8 Million," *Washington Post*, Mar. 22, 1976.

Notes | 319

421 Solberg, *Hubert Humphrey*, 453.
422 Elizabeth Drew, "A Reporter in Washington, D.C.: Spring Notes–II," *New Yorker*, Sept. 12, 1976, 45.
423 F. Forrester Church, *Father and Son* (Harper & Row, 1985), 121.
424 Italy Rome to Commander in Chief European Command Vaihingen Germany, Defense Intelligence Agency, Department of State, Documents Officer Allied Forces Southeastern Europe, Italy Milan, Italy Naples, North Atlantic Treaty Organization (NATO) and Secretary of State, telegram, "Lockheed Scandal: Smoke Without Fire? No One Burned, But Everyone Asphyxiated Just the Same?," Apr. 29, 1976, 1976ROME06981_b, State Department Cable, Public Library of US Diplomacy.
425 Netherlands The Hague to Belgium Brussels, Denmark Copenhagen, Department of State, France Paris, Germany Bonn, Ireland Dublin, Italy Rome, Japan Tokyo, Luxembourg, North Atlantic Treaty Organization (NATO), Secretary of State, Switzerland Bern, U.S. Mission to European Union (formerly EC) (Brussels) and United Kingdom London, telegram, "Lockheed and the Prince," Feb. 27, 1976, 1976THEHA01077_b, State Department Cable, Public Library of US Diplomacy.
426 Netherlands The Hague to Belgium Brussels telegram, "Lockheed and the Prince.".
427 Boulton, *The Grease Machine*, 268.
428 An interesting side note is that Maeno had obtained his pilot's license in order to play the role of a soldier in his soft-core pornographic movies. At the time of the attack on Kodama, Maeno's latest film, "Tokyo's Madame Emmanuelle," was showing in a downtown theater in New York, and after his death, briefly attained a cult following. Richard Halloran, "Japan Seeks Motive in Crash Into Lockheed Agent's Home," *New York Times*, Mar. 24, 1976.
429 In July, the Japanese Supreme Court granted Kotchian immunity, an extremely rare occurrence in Japan to that point. Even so, Kotchian fought the proceedings under U.S. law, ultimately losing on appeal. The U.S. Supreme Court declined to intervene on the case. Shaplen, "Annals of Crime: The Lockheed Incident–II," 74.
430 A. Carl Kotchian, "The Payoff: Lockheed's 70-Day Mission to Tokyo," *Saturday Review*, July 1977, 7.
431 Kotchian subsequently wrote a book, entitled "Lockheed Sales Mission: Seventy Days in Tokyo," which was largely based on exclusive interviews he gave to Yoshio Murakami, a correspondent for the Asahi newspapers. The book was never published in English, although parts of it were later reprinted in the *Saturday Review*. Kotchian, "The Payoff."
432 Robert Shaplen, "Annals of Crime: The Lockheed Incident–I," *New Yorker*, Jan. 23, 1978, 48.
433 Kotchian, "The Payoff," 7.
434 Steven Hunziker and Ikuro Kamimura, *Kakuei Tanaka: A Political Biography of Modern Japan* (Times Books International, 1996), 90.
435 Kotchian, "The Payoff," 8.
436 Shaplen, "Annals of Crime: The Lockheed Incident–I," 71.
437 Shaplen, "Annals of Crime: The Lockheed Incident–I," 74.
438 "Mr. Tanaka and Lockheed," Washington Post, Aug. 21, 1976.

439 Japan Tokyo to China Hong Kong, China United States Liaison Office Peking, Commander United States Forces Japan, Commander in Chief US Pacific Command, Italy Rome, Netherlands The Hague, Philippines Manila, Secretary of State, South Korea Seoul and Taiwan Taipei City, telegram, "Reaction to Tanaka's Arrest," July 28, 1976, 1976TOKYO011364_b, State Department Cable, Public Library of US Diplomacy.

440 Japan Tokyo to China United States Liaison Office Peking, Commander United States Forces Japan, Commander in Chief US Pacific Command, Italy Rome, Netherlands The Hague, Philippines Manila, Secretary of State, South Korea Seoul and Taiwan Taipei City, telegram, "Arrest of Former Prime Minister Tanaka," July 27, 1976, 1976TOKYO011294_b, State Department Cable, Public Library of US Diplomacy.

441 Hunziker and Kamimura, *Kakuei Tanaka*, 136.

442 President Ford, Henry A. Kissinger and Brent Scowcroft, memorandum of conversation, National Security Adviser's Memoranda of Conversation Collection, Gerald R. Ford Presidential Library.

443 Church, "Multinational Corporations and East Asia."

444 Shaplen, "Annals of Crime: The Lockheed Incident—I," 56.

445 Jerome Alan Cohen, "Japan's Watergate: Made in U.S.A," *New York Times*, Nov. 21, 1976. Note that the truth was somewhat more complicated. Although the LDP would fair badly in the 1976 elections, Tanaka somehow still managed to hold onto his electoral seat and would remain in politics for many more years to come, wielding much the same level of power behind the scenes as he had as Prime Minister. In 1983, a judge found him guilty of "forfeiting the people's trust in public offices," sentencing him to four years in prison and a fine of 500 million yen, but even then, Tanaka walked free for several more years while the decision went up on appeal. That is not to say that no real change in Japanese politics came out of the Lockheed affair. Before the December election, a group of Japanese politicians calling themselves the "New Liberal Club" would break away from the LDP promising a new, more transparent model of politics. As part of their efforts, Japan's Diet would pass a package of legislative proposals designed to prevent another Lockheed. Kiichi Miyazawa, the director of Japan's Economic Planning Agency who would later serve as Prime Minister from 1991 to 1993 observed at the time, "Lockheed accelerated the generational change that is taking place in Japan. In time, a more vocal society will emerge."

446 "Prince Bernhard and the Lockheed Payments," *The Financial Times*, Aug. 27, 1976.

447 *Foreign Payments Disclosure: Hearings Before the Subcomm. on Consumer Prot. and Fin. of the H.R. Comm. on Interstate & Foreign Com.*, 94th Cong. 726 (1976) (statement of Theodore C. Sorensen).

448 *Hearings Before the S. Comm. on Banking, Hous. & Urb. Aff.*, 94th Cong. (1976) (statement of Elliot L. Richardson).

449 Frank Church, "The Multinational Corporation: A Trial Balance" (speech, Houston, TX, Marc. 2, 1973), series 10.6, box 4, folder 12, Frank Church Papers.

450 Division of Enforcement to SEC Commission, memorandum, "Voluntary Program," Jan. 7, 1977, Securities and Exchange Commission Historical Society, https://www.sechistorical.org/museum/galleries/rev/rev04a.php. See also Unlawful Corporate Payments Act of 1977: *Hearings Before the Subcomm. on Consumer Prot. and Fin. of the H.R. Comm. on Interstate and Foreign Com.*, 95th Cong. 25 (1977) (statement of Dr. Gordon Adams, Dir. of Mil. Rsch., Council on Econ. Priorities).

451 Acting Commissioner of Internal Revenue to Acting General Counsel, memorandum, "Corporate Slush Funds—Illegal Foreign Payments," Mar. 9, 1977, Securities and Exchange Commission Historical Society, https://www.sechistorical.org/collection/papers/1970/1977_0309_IRSCorporate.pdf.

452 Ashby and Gramer, *Fighting the Odds*, 459.

CHAPTER FIVE: LEGISLATING MORALITY

453 *Foreign Corrupt Practices Act: Hearing Before the Subcomm. on Oversight and Investigations of the H.R. Comm. on Interstate and Foreign Com.*, 96th Cong. 2 (1979) (opening statement of Rep. Bob Eckhardt).

454 *Multinational Corporations and United States Foreign Policy*, 94th Cong. 13 (statement of B.R. Dorsey, chairman of the board, Gulf Oil Corp.).

455 A bill to give the Secretary of State responsibility for monitoring the overseas business activities of American companies in order to detect any violations of Federal law and to make it unlawful for an American company to bribe any foreign official, H.R. 7539, 94th Cong. (June 3, 1975).

456 *The Activities of American Multinational Corporations Abroad*, 94th Cong. 17 (statement of Michael F. Butler, Vice President and General Counsel, Overseas Private Investment Corporation. In his statement, Mark B. Feldman, Deputy Legal Advisor, Department of State, also noted that extraterritorial application of U.S. was often viewed by other governments as a sign of U.S. arrogance.

457 *The Activities of American Multinational Corporations Abroad*, 94th Cong. 22 (1975) (statement of Mark B. Feldman, Deputy Legal Advisor, Department of State).

458 *Lockheed Bribery: Hearings Before the S. Comm. on Banking, Hous. & Urb. Aff.*, 94th Cong. 34 (1975) (statement Of D. J. Haughton, Chairman of the Board, Lockheed Aircraft Corp.).

459 *The Activities of American Multinational Corporations Abroad*, 94th Cong. 24 (statement of Feldman).

460 Munitions Industry: Hearing Before the S. Special Comm. Investigating the Munitions Indus. Pursuant to S. Res. 206 A Resolution to Make Certain Investigations Concerning the Manufacture and Sale of Arms and Other War Munitions, 73rd Congress 2488 (1934).

461 "Pay-offs Hurt Pro-Business Swing," *Baltimore Sun*, Feb. 22, 1976. For further discussion, see Lewis Solomon and Leslie Linville, "Transnational Conduct of American Multinational Corporations: Questionable Payments Abroad," B*oston College Industrial and Commercial Law Review* 17, no. 3 (1976): 305.

462 Gwirtzman, "Is Bribery Defensible?" *New York Times Magazine*.

463 J. Jefferson Staats statement on behalf of the U.S. Chamber of Commerce to the Senate, Committee on Banking, Housing and Urban Affairs described in "History of S. 305 and H.R. 3815" in American Enterprise Institute Legislative Analysis: Criminalization of Payments to Influence Foreign Governments (American Enterprise Institute for Public Policy Research, 1977).

464 At the time, 26 U.S.C. § 162(c) provided that bribes and kickbacks, including payments to government officials, could not be deducted in computing taxable income if the payment (wherever made) would be unlawful under U.S. law if made in the United States. An often-cited example for the applicability of antitrust law was the SEC's discovery that General Tire and Rubber had been bribing government officials in Morocco and Chile to keep Goodyear off the local market. *The Activities of American Multinational Corporations Abroad*, 94th Cong. 87 (statement of Donald I. Baker, Deputy Assistant Att'y Gen., Antitrust Div., Dep't of Just.). See also *United States v. Sisal Sales Corporation*, 274 U.S. 268 (1927); *Occidental Petroleum Corp. v. Buttes Gas & Oil Co.*, 331 F. Supp. 92 (C.D. Cal. 1971); and *Unlawful Corporate Payments Act of 1977*, 95th Cong. 25 (statement of Adams).

465 Roderick M. Hills, "Address to the NY Bar Association" (New York, NY, Mar. 15, 1976).

466 In the absence of specific guidelines, few believed that U.S. corporations were under any real obligation to disclose such payments. For example, in a letter dated April 9, 1976, one accounting firm wrote Chairman Hills that "it [was] difficult to convince clients of the need to disclose when the accountant can only point to speeches given by SEC officials or published reports of the actions of others. This becomes even more difficult when legal counsel advises their clients that the Federal Securities Laws and Regulations apparently do not require the types of disclosures that are being advocated informally by the Commission and its staff." Roderick Hills to Peat, Marwick, Mitchell & Co. (Certified Public Accountants), letter, April 9, 1976.

467 IRS Commissioner Donald Alexander noted that: "The tax laws are not the appropriate instrument for the resolution of this problem of basic morality." The Activities of American Multinational Corporations Abroad, 94th Cong. 39 (statement of Donald C. Alexander, Comm'r, Internal Revenue Serv.).

468 *The Activities of American Multinational Corporations Abroad*, 94th Cong. 55 (statement of Alexander).

469 *Protecting the Ability of the United States to Trade Abroad*, 94th Cong. 16.

470 *Protecting the Ability of the United States to Trade Abroad*, 94th Cong. 21.

471 Office of Senator William Proxmire, Wisconsin, news release, Mar. 12, 1976, Collection of Manuscript Division, Library of Congress.

472 "It is clear from the Senate Resolution 265 that our initiative for a multilateral approach will be considered credible in the Congress only if these proposals describe an international agreement binding on governments," wrote Deputy Secretary of State Bob Ingersoll in an internal memorandum addressed to Kissinger. "A less emphatic initiative would simply not slow down the drive of Church and others for unilateral U.S. solutions based on prosecution in the U.S. for crimes committed overseas." Department of State to Secretary of State, telegram, "Action Memorandum: Corrupt Practices: Lockheed Case: My Testimony Before Proxmire Subcommittee, March 3 (S/S No. 7604304)" Mar. 2, 1976, 1976STATE050342_b, State Department Cable, Public Library of US Diplomacy.

473 Ed Schmults to Bill Seidman, memorandum, June 4, 1976.

474 Brent Scowcroft, memorandum to the President, June 9, 1976.

475 Elliot Richardson, memorandum to the President, "Questionable Payments Abroad," June 3, 1976.

476 Elliot Richardson, memorandum to the President, "Questionable Payments Abroad," June 3, 1976.

477 H.R. 7539, 94th Cong. (June 3, 1975); H.R. 11987, 94th Cong. (Feb. 19, 1976); S. 3133, 94th Cong. (Mar. 11, 1976); S. 3150, 94th Cong. (Mar. 16, 1976); S. 3379, 94th Cong. (May 5, 1976); S. 3418, 94th Cong. (May 12, 1976); H.R. 13870, 94th Cong. (May 18, 1976); H.R. 13953, 94th Cong. (May 21, 1976); H.R. 14358, 94th Cong. (June 4, 1976); H.R. 14340, 94th Cong. (June 11, 1976); S. 3664, 94th Cong. (July 2, 1976); S. 3741, 94th Cong. (Aug. 6, 1976); H.R. 15149, 94th Cong. (Aug. 10, 1976); H.R. 15481, 94th Cong. (Sept. 8, 1976); H.R. 1602, 95th Cong. (Jan. 10, 1977); S. 305, 95th Cong. (Jan. 18, 1977); H.R. 3815, 95th Cong. (Feb. 22, 1977); and H.R. 7543, 95th Cong. (June 1, 1977). See also H.R. 7563, 94th Cong. (June 3, 1975); H.R. 9860, 94th Cong. (Sept. 25, 1975); H.R. 10144, 94th Cong. (Oct. 9, 1975); H.R. 10612, 94th Cong. (Nov. 6, 1975); S. 2662, 94th Cong. (Nov. 13, 1975); S. 2839, 94th Cong. (Dec. 19, 1975); H.R. 11532, 94th Cong. (Jan. 27, 1976); H.R. 11963, 94th Cong. (Feb. 18, 1976); S. 3151, 94th Cong. (Mar. 16, 1976); H.R. 13680, 94th Cong. (May 11, 1976); S. 3439, 94th Cong. (May 14, 1976); H.R. 14681, 94th Cong. (July 1, 1976); H.R. 3603, 95th Cong. (Feb. 16, 1977); and H.R. 9878, 95th Cong. (Nov. 1, 1977).

478 Tax Reform Act, H.R. 10612, 94th Cong. (Nov. 6, 1975).

479 Specifically, the bill sought to prohibit payments "for the purpose of inducing that individual to use his influence ... to obtain or maintain business for or with the issuer." S. 3133, 94th Cong. (Mar. 11, 1976).

480 Beginning in the 1940s, the courts developed the notion that the "scheme to defraud" prong under the Mail Fraud Statute extended to the intangible rights of citizens to honest public services. *Shushan v. United States*, 117 F.2d 110 (5th Cir. 1941), overruled by United States v. Cruz, 478 F.2d 408 (5th Cir. 1973) and *United States v. George*, 477 F.2d 508, 513 (7th Cir. 1973). See also Pub. L. No. 87-849, 76 Stat. 1119 (1962). By the 1970s, the idea that the public had a right to "honest and faithful services" and that the mail fraud statute could be used to prosecute when they'd been defrauded of that right became widely accepted practice. *United States v. George*, 477 F.2d 508, 513 (7th Cir. 1973).

481 S. 3133, 94th Cong. (Mar. 11, 1976).

482 122 Cong. Rec. S12099 (1976) ("Why Not Disclose Bribes," statement by Senator Proxmire).

483 Sporkin, "The Worldwide Banning of Schmiergeld," 269.

484 Sporkin, "The Worldwide Banning of Schmiergeld."

485 Roderick Hills, interview.

486 In the letter, Hills said that he opposed S. 3133's criminalization provisions on the basis that it would require the SEC to get involved in sensitive overseas activities which had "important implications for international trade in commerce," as well as the $1,000 disclosure provision, which he viewed as unnecessarily rigid. Ralph C. Ferrara, "Saints and Sinners: The Legislative Approach to Questionable and Illegal Corporate Payments: SEC & IRS Requirements," *New York Law Journal* 2 (1976): 99.

487 Roderick Hills to William Proxmire, letter, Mar. 18, 1976, Securities and Exchange Commission Historical Society.

488 Levinson, interview.

489 Richard Burt, "Foreign Relations Committee's Influence at Lowest Point in 20 Years," *New York Times*, Nov. 23, 1977.

490 Humphrey had apparently gotten Senate Majority Leader Mike Mansfield to refer the draft bill to Proxmire. Levinson, *Who Makes American Foreign Policy?*, 230-231.

491 S. 3379, 94th Cong. (May 5, 1976).

492 "Mr. Tanaka and Lockheed," *Washington Post*.

493 Richard Lyons, "Senate Acts to Curtail Bribes and Kickbacks in Arms Sales," *New York Times*, Feb. 6, 1976.

494 Elliot Richardson to L. William Seidman and Brent Snowcroft, memorandum, June 8, 1976, Kissinger-Snowcroft West Wing Office Files, box 22, folder "Questionable Corporate Payments Abroad–Meeting, June 9, 1976," Gerald Ford Archives.

495 Teachout, *Corruption in America*, 183.

496 Teachout, *Corruption in America*, 217.

497 An Act to Prevent Frauds Upon the Treasury of the United States, 10 Stat. 170 (1853). See also Cong. Globe, 32nd Cong., 2nd Sess. 392 (1853); and Teachout, *Corruption in America*, 116. *Evans v. United States*, 504 U.S. 255 (1992) prohibits the giving of something of value to an official with the intent of influencing behavior "under color of official right."

498 Contemporary examples of this prophylactic approach abound at both the state and local level. In New Hampshire, for example, gifts of over twenty-five dollars to state executive and legislative officials are banned. N.H. Rev. Stat. Ann. §15-B:3 (2016). Florida has a flat ban on all gifts of any value to state and local officials by lobbyists or lobbyist employers. Fla. Stat. §112.3215(6)(a) (2024).

499 Church, *Father and Son*; and Church, "Remarks Before General Foods Executives."

500 During his time in the Senate, for example, Church championed the normalization of relations with communist China and later, President Carter sent him to Cuba to discuss normalizing relations with Fidel Castro.

501 Ken McLean, interview by Anita Hecht, Wisconsin Historical Society, Sept. 11, 2009.

502 Sykes, *Proxmire*.

503 Kasparek, Jonathan, *Proxmire, Bulldog of the Senate*, (Wisconsin Historical Society Press, 2019), 219.

504 Samantha Power, "A Problem From Hell": *America and the Age of Genocide* (Basic Books, 2002), 165-166.

505 Proxmire, *One Foot in Washington*, 20.

506 *Escott v. BarChris Construction Corp.*, 283 F.Supp. 643 (S.D.N.Y. 1968).

507 *Regulatory Reform—Securities and Exchange Commission: Hearing Before the Subcomm. on Oversight and Investigations of the H.R. Comm. on Interstate and Foreign Com.*, 94th Cong. 577 (1976) (testimony of Abraham J. Briloff, Distinguished Professor of Accountancy, Baruch College).

508 Clinard and Yeager, *Corporate Crime*, 192.

509 *Ernst & Ernst v. Hochfelder*, 425 U.S. 185 (1976).

510 American Institute of Certified Public Accountants, *Statement on Auditing Standards* (American Institute of Certified Public Accountants, 1973), 320.28.

511 SEC, Annual Report of the SEC for the Fiscal Year Ended June 30, 1975 (1975) discussing Regulation S-X published as part of the Accounting Series Releases.

512 *Prohibiting Bribes to Foreign Officials: Hearings Before the S. Comm. on Banking, Hous. & Urb. Aff.*, 94th Cong. 1-2 (1976).

513 *Prohibiting Bribes to Foreign Officials*, 94th Cong. 4 (statement of Roderick M. Hills, Chairman, SEC).

514 Richardson to Seidman and Snowcroft, memorandum.

515 Lockheed/Coca Cola, Carter Quote File, box H28, President Ford Committee Records, Series H: Research Office Files, 1973-76, Gerald R. Ford Presidential Library.

516 Edward Levi to President Gerald Ford, memorandum, May 24, 1976, Arthur F. Burns Papers, box E43, folder "Senate Committee on Banking Housing and Urban Affairs," Gerald R. Ford Presidential Library.

517 Eliot Janeway, "That 'Payola' Is Not Really Necessary," *Washington Star* (Feb. 22, 1976) in Arthur F. Burns Papers, box E43, Senate Committee on Banking Housing and Urban Affairs, Gerald R. Ford Presidential Library.

518 Elliot Richardson, memorandum to the President, "Questionable Payments Abroad," June 3, 1976.

519 Brent Scowcroft to Henry Kissinger, memorandum, June 10, 1976.

520 Elliot Richardson to William Proxmire, letter, June 11, 1976, providing comments on S. 3133.

Notes | 325

521 Elliot Richardson, memorandum to the President, "Questionable Corporate Payments Abroad," June 8, 1976, Gerald R. Ford Presidential Library.

522 122 Cong. Rec. S18603 (1976) (quoting "Pious Evasions," *New York Times*, June 16, 1976); and "Mr. Tanaka and Lockheed" *Washington Post*.

523 "Mr. Tanaka and Lockheed," *Washington Post*; "Ford Draws Church's Criticism," *New York Times*, June 17, 1976; Press Release by Senator William Proxmire, June 14, 1976; and 122 Cong. Rec. S18622 (1976).

524 George Ball, a Senior Managing Partner at Lehman Brothers and former Under Secretary of State in the Kennedy and Johnson administrations, opined that full disclosure was the most effective deterrent and had the added benefit of discouraging the "cupidity of foreign officials." *Foreign and Corporate Bribes: Hearings Before the S. Comm. on Banking, Hous. & Urb. Aff.*, 94th Cong. 41 (1976) (statement of George Ball, Lehman Brothers). Leonard Meeker, of the Center for Law and Social Policy, similarly testified that "a mandatory program of disclosure ought to be a top priority" in passing any new legislation. *Foreign and Corporate Bribes*, 94th Cong. 65 (statement of Leonard C. Meeker, Ctr. for L. and Soc. Pol'y).

525 Ashby and Gramer, *Fighting the Odds*, 229.

526 122 Cong. Rec. S18622.

527 S. Rep. No. 94-1301 (1976) to accompany S. 3664.

528 Richard Darman to Mansfield D. Sprague, memorandum, "Summary of Congressional Activities on Multinational Corporations, April 5-9, 1976," Kenneth A. Lazarus Files, box 51, Gerald R. Ford Presidential Library and Museum.

529 S. Rep. No. 94-1031 (1976), 8.

530 S. Rep. No. 94-1031.

531 122 Cong. Rec. S30324 (1976).

532 The word "corruptly" was meant to connote the same meaning as required under domestic bribery law 18 U.S.C. § 201(b). "The word 'corruptly' connotes an evil motive or purpose such as is required under 18 U.S.C. § 201(b) which prohibits domestic bribery. As in 18 U.S.C. § 201(b), the word 'corruptly' indicates an intent or desire to wrongfully influence the recipient. It does not require that the act be fully consummated or succeed in producing the desired outcome." S. Rep. No. 94-1301 (1976) to accompany S. 3664.

533 S. Rep. No. 94-1031.

534 122 Cong. Rec. S30330 (1976).

535 122 Cong. Rec. S30334 (1976).

536 122 Cong. Rec. S30423 (1976).

537 122 Cong. Rec. S30421 (1976).

538 122 Cong. Rec. S30421.

539 122 Cong. Rec. S30420 (1976).

540 Levinson, interview.

541 Frank Church to John Sparkman, letter, Oct. 1, 1976, series 2.2, box 14, folder 12, Frank Church Papers.

542 Church had apparently been on Carter's short list of early contenders and had even won a straw poll taken by the Carter family itself, but was unliked by others on Carter's staff. Ultimately, Carter went with Walter Mondale, whose close relationship with labor and the Jewish community played better to his political weaknesses. Peter Bourne, *Jimmy Carter: A Comprehensive Biography* (Scribner, 1997), 331; and Stuart Eizenstat, *President Carter: The White House Years* (St. Martin's Press, 2018), 90-91.

543 Bill Hall, *Frank Church*, 55.

544 Douglas Brinkley, *Gerald R. Ford* (Henry Holt & Co., 2007), 139.

545 Eizenstat, *President Carter*.

546 "1976 Democratic Party Platform," July 12, 1976, American Presidency Project, UC Santa Barbara, https://www.presidency.ucsb.edu/documents/1976-democratic-party-platform.

547 Jimmy Carter, "Meeting of Oct. 16, 1973," box 16, series 1.1, Trilateral Commission records, Rockefeller Archive Center.

548 To combat post-Watergate fears of an imperial presidency, Carter would do away with a slew of White House traditions, including the uniforms Nixon had used to dress the White House guards, the use of government cars for his staff, and the practice of playing "Hail to the Chief" upon his arrival. Schulman, *The Seventies*, 122.

549 At one point, the energy problem had gotten so bad that cities across the Northeast and Midwest, including Detroit, were forced to reduce electric voltage and dim lights for part of the day.

550 "Statement of U.S. Government Position on Illicit Payments," Mar. 10, 1977, Securities and Exchange Commission Historical Society. https://www.sechistorical.org/collection/papers/1970/1977_0310_PositionIllicit.pdf

551 Elliot Richardson, memorandum to the President, "Questionable Corporate Payments Abroad," Jan. 18, 1977, Library of Congress.

552 *Foreign Corrupt Practices and Domestic Foreign Investment Disclosure: Hearings Before the S. Comm. on Banking, Hous. & Urb. Aff.*, 95th Cong. 2 (1977) (opening statement of Sen. Proxmire).

553 Bob Woodward, "White House Reviewing Intelligence Operations," *Washington* Post, Feb. 18, 1977; and Department of State to Nairobi Kinshasa, telegram, "Wash Post Alleges Cia Payments to Mobutu and Kenyatta" Feb. 19, 1977, 1977STATE038948_c, State Department Cable, Public Library of US Diplomacy.

554 *Foreign Corrupt Practices and Domestic Foreign Investment Disclosure*, 95th Cong. 70 (statement of W. Michael Blumenthal, Sec't of Treasury).

555 Lloyd Cutler, "Plain Talk About Fancy Bribes" (speech, Trilateral Commission, Ottawa, Canada, Spring 1976). Two years later, after the FCPA was eventually enacted and the criminalization approach formally adopted, Cutler expressed doubt, saying "that anyone could be successfully prosecuted under such a law seems most unlikely." Lloyd N. Cutler, *Global Interdependence*, 46.

556 Paul Sabin, "'Everything has a price': Jimmy Carter and the Struggle for Balance in Federal Regulatory Policy," *Journal of Policy History* 28, no. 1 (2016).

557 Securities Exchange Act Release No. 34-13185 (Jan. 19, 1977), 42 FR 4854 (Jan. 26, 1977). The SEC eventually adopted Regulation 13B-2, but it would not become effective until March 23, 1979. The sections regarding false or misleading statements to auditors were removed but then reinserted after passage of Sarbanes-Oxley in 2003.

558 *Foreign Corrupt Practices and Domestic Foreign Investment Disclosure*, 95th Cong. 305.

559 *Markup Session on S.305, Corporate Bribery*, S. Comm. on Banking, Hous. and Urban Affairs, 95th Cong. (1977).

560 *Markup Session* on *S.305*.

561 *Markup Session on S.305*.

562 U.N. Comm'n Transnat'l Corp., Rep. on the Resumed Second Session & Third Session, U.N Doc. E/C.10/32 (1977).

563 Department of State to Secretary of State, telegram, "Status of the United States Initiative on Illicit Payments" May 7, 1977, 1977STATE104406_c, State Department Cable, Public Library of US Diplomacy.

564 See R. Heath Larry (chairman, National Association of Manufacturers) to William Proxmire, letter, Mar. 15, 1977, Securities and Exchange Commission Historical Society, warning that preemptive action by the United States would be "counterproductive to building the international cooperation necessary to achieve a real multilateral approach" and Ad Hoc Committee on Foreign Payments, *Report on Questionable Foreign Payments by Corporations: The Problem and Approaches to a Solution* (Association of the Bar of the City of New York, 1977) advising against "any solution attempted unilaterally through legislative action" in favor of "diplomatic initiatives in the United Nations."

565 *Unlawful Corporate Payments Act of 1977*, 95th Cong. 196.

566 *United States v. Esquenazi*, No. 11-15331 (11th Cir. 2014).

567 Harrington warned that a "shift from international corporate bribery to international corporate political contributions [was] hardly a solution to the problem of corporate payments." 123 Cong. Rec. S.14575 (statement of Rep. Michael Harrington of Mass. on H.R. 3815).

568 "The Committee intends that the courts shall recognize a private cause of action based on this legislation . . . on behalf of persons who suffer injury as a result of prohibited corporate bribery." House Report to Accompany H.R. 3815, H.R. Rep. No. 95-640 (1977). Hills' successor at the SEC, Harold Williams, also favored the inclusion of a private right of action into the bill. *Unlawful Corporate Payments Act of 1977*, 95th Cong. 196 (statement of Harold M. Williams, Chairman, SEC).

569 For example, see 15 U.S.C. § 15 (antitrust) and 18 U.S.C. § 1964 (Racketeer Influenced and Corrupt Organizations (RICO)).

570 Conference Report to Accompany S.305, H.R. Rep. No. 95-832 (1977); and *Foreign Corrupt Practices and Domestic Foreign Investment Disclosure*, 95th Cong. 215 (Wallace E. Olson, President, American Institute of Certified Public Accountants, to Wiliam Proxmire, letter, Mar. 24, 1977).

571 These provisions largely originated out of the Ashland Oil review committee report to the SEC, which had found that the company's internal audit division had either cooperated directly in concealing the payments or failed to sufficiently review the book categories used by the accountants to conceal the bribes. Clinard and Yeager, *Corporate Crime*, 192.

572 For a summary of the amendment and the rationale used, see "Senator Adlai Stevenson III Amendments to S.305, Foreign Corrupt Practices Act of 1977," Apr. 6, 1977, Securities and Exchange Commission Historical Society.

573 Terry E. Bathen, "A Congressional Response to the Problem of Questionable Corporate Payments Abroad: The Foreign Corrupt Practices Act of 1977," *Law & Policy in International Business* 10, no. 4 (1978): 1253.

574 "Saints and Sinners Concluded: The Foreign Corrupt Practices Act," *Corporate Conduct Overseas: The U.S. Criminal Laws and International Codes*, eds. W. Surrey and R. von Mehren (Practicing Law Institute, 1978). For an example of the administration's position, see *Unlawful Corporate Payments Act of 1977*, 95th Cong. 175 (statement of W. Michael Blumenthal, Sec'y of the Treasury).

575 123 Cong. Rec. S38466 (1977). Note, however, that even after enactment of the FCPA, the SEC asserted that courts should recognize an implied private right of action "on behalf of persons who suffer injury as a result of prohibited corporate bribery." Securities Exchange Act Release No. 34-14478, Notification of Enactment of Foreign Corrupt Practices Act, 43 Fed. Reg. 7752, 7754 (1978); and Special Counsel Frederick B. Wade to Raymond Garcia, Emergency Comm. For American Trade, letter, May 16, 1978, Federal Securities Law Reporter (CCH, 1978), ¶ 81,701.

576 123 Cong. Rec. S38466, H38779 (1977).

577 Daily Diary of President Jimmy Carter, Dec. 19, 1977, Jimmy Carter Presidential Library and Museum, National Archives.

578 Quoted in Schulman, *The Seventies*, 124-25.

579 In January 1980, for example, PBS would air a popular ten-part documentary miniseries hosted by Friedman lauding the miracle of free-market capitalism and inveighing against almost all forms of government intervention.

580 Rick Perlstein, *Reaganland: America's Right Turn, 1976–1980* (Simon & Schuster, 2020), 286.

581 General Motors, for example, found itself pleading for government protection from Japanese imports, and Chrysler, the country's ninth-largest corporation, found itself on the verge of bankruptcy. Vogel, Fluctuating Fortunes, 9; and Perlstein, *Reaganland*, 676-677.

582 For example, early in 1978, Carter formed the Regulatory Review Group (RARG) to recommend ways of reducing the cost of future regulation; a few months later, he issued an executive order requiring all regulatory agencies to prepare detailed analysis of any future regulatory rules costing more than $100 million per year. Vogel, Fluctuating Fortunes, 172.

583 *Business Accounting and Foreign Trade Simplification Act: Joint Hearings on S. 708 Before the Subcomm. on Securities and the Subcomm. on International Finance and Monetary Policy of the Senate Comm. on Banking, Housing and Urban Affairs*, 97th Cong. 1st Sess. 414 (1981) (testimony of William Dobrovir).

584 Soon after enactment of the FCPA, President Carter would instruct the DOJ to formulate guidelines to ensure that its enforcement did not impede the ability of American companies to compete overseas; a special White House Export Disincentive Task Force concluded that the FCPA was costing the United States $1 billion per year in lost trade. Gutterman, "Easier Done," 115.

585 Bathen, "A Congressional Response;" and Perlstein, *Reaganland*, 724.

586 For example, see Philip Shabecoff, "Big Business on the Offensive," *New York Times*, Dec. 9, 1979.

587 In circumventing the finance restrictions imposed by FECA, corporations copied a tactic first adopted by labor unions, which commonly used political action committees as vehicles to funnel contributions to candidates after passage of the Smith-Connally Act of 1943 prohibiting direct labor-union contributions in federal elections.

588 The Supreme Court validated the independent expenditure strategy in a suit filed by Common Cause with the FEC involving the Republican PAC called Americans for Change. *Common Cause v. Schmitt*, 512 F. Supp. 489 (D.D.C. 1980), 455 US 129 (1982).

589 "Machinists Complain on Corporate Political Action," *New York Times*, Oct. 10, 1979.
590 "Political Action Groups Set '78 Spending Pace," *New York Times*, May 13, 1979; and Perlstein, *Reaganland*, 893.
591 All told, seven members of Congress were eventually convicted of bribery and sentenced to jail.
592 Zelizer, *On Capitol Hill*.
593 Noonan, *Bribes*, 699.
594 Daily Diary of President Jimmy Carter.
595 Statement on Signing S. 305 into Law, Dec. 20, 1977, 13 Weekly Comp. Press. Docs. 1909 (Dec. 26, 1977).
596 "Carter Approves Bill on Corporate Bribes," *New York Times*, Dec. 21, 1977

EPILOGUE

597 Data for DOJ and SEC Enforcement Actions per Year, Foreign Corrupt Practices Act Clearinghouse, Stanford Law School, https://fcpa.stanford.edu/statistics-analytics.html?tab=1.; see also Wesley A. Cragg and William Woof, "The US Foreign Corrupt Practices Act and its implications for the Control of Corruption in Political Life," Business and Society Review, 107:1 (Dec. 17 2002), 17 (noting that following the inauguration of President Reagan, enforcement patterns changed and enforcement of the FCPA was relaxed, funding for the two principal enforcement agencies was considerably reduced, and efforts by the administration to alter the provisions of the Act were initiated).
598 Thomas Gladwin and Ingo Walter, "The Shadowy Underside of International Trade," *Saturday Review*, July 9, 1977, 22, quoting Charles Bowen, former chairman of Booz Allen and Hamilton, a leading management consulting firm.
599 S. 2763, *A bill to amend and clarify the Foreign Corrupt Practices Act of 1977*, (1980); S. 708, *A bill to amend and clarify the Foreign Corrupt Practices Act of 1977*, (1981), S. 414, *A bill to amend and clarify the Foreign Corrupt Practices Act of 1977*, (1983), S. 430, *A bill to amend and clarify the Foreign Corrupt Practices Act of 1977*, (1985).
600 Foreign Corrupt Practices Act Amendments of 1988, H.R. 4848, Pub. L. No. 100-418, 102 Stat. 1107, 100th Cong. (1988) (enacted August 23, 1988).
601 The American Bar Association, for example, founded the Central and East European Law Initiative (CEELI) in 1990. Through CEELI, scores of American lawyers and judges traveled to the former Soviet bloc to assist in drafting new laws, as well as running workshops focused on Western-style legal education and judicial development. Notably, many of these ABA efforts were spearheaded by key holdovers from the Carter administration, including Lloyd Cutler, Carter's former White House counsel, and Homer Moyer, who worked in the general counsel's office of the U.S. Department of Commerce in the 1970s. Both became leading anticorruption experts in the later parts of their careers. M. M. McKeown, "The ABA Rule of Law Initiative Celebrating 25 Years of Global Initiatives," *Michigan Journal of International Law* 39, no. 1 (2018): 117, 121.
602 Michael Johnston and Scott Fritzen, *The Conundrum of Corruption: Reform for Social Justice* (Routledge, 2021), 127.
603 James D. Wolfensohn, "People and Development: Annual Meetings Address by James D. Wolfensohn, President (English)" (speech, Annual Meetings of the World Bank and the International Monetary Fund, Washington, D.C., October 1, 1996).

604 Kirsten Lundberg, "High Road or Low? Transparency International and the Corruption Perception Index (Case Number 1658)," *Harvard Kennedy School* (Aug. 1, 2002).

605 OECD Convention on Combatting Bribery of Foreign Public Officials in International Business Transactions, 37 I.L.M. 1 (1998).

606 House Report No. 105-802 Oct. 8, 1998–International Anti-Bribery and Fair Competition Act of 1998.

607 Note that the OECD Convention recognizes that in some countries, (mainly in civil law countries), criminal sanctions may not apply to corporations. In those situations, the Convention requires those countries to impose appropriate monetary sanctions and other penalties.

608 Council of Europe, Criminal Law Convention on Corruption, Jan. 27, 1999, Eur. T.S. No. 173; African Union Convention on Preventing and Combatting Corruption, July 11, 2003, 43. I.L.M. 5; United Nations Convention against Corruption, Oct. 31, 2003, 2349 U.N.T.S. 41.

609 Davis, *Between Impunity and Imperialism*, 41.

610 See e.g., Final Report, Global Forum on Fighting Corruption: Safeguarding Integrity Among Justice and Security Officials (Washington, D.C., February 24, 1999), https://1997-2001.state.gov/global/narcotics_law/global_forum/global_forum_report.pdf.

611 Lanny Breuer, "International Criminal Law Enforcement: Rule of Law, Anti-Corruption, and Beyond" (speech, Council on Foreign Relations, May 4, 2010).

612 Breuer, "International Criminal Law Enforcement."

613 Data for DOJ and SEC Enforcement Actions per Year.

614 Data for DOJ and SEC Enforcement Actions per Year.

615 Joe Palazzolo, "FCPA Inc.: The Business of Bribery," *Wall Street Journal*, Oct. 2, 2012.

616 Johnston and Fritzen, two corruption scholars, aptly summarize this transformation over the span of the last thirty-odd years as follows: "At the advent of the 2020s, anti-corruption efforts have attained a size, diversity, and global scope that few could have envisioned in the 1980s. It commands extensive human, economic, and analytical resources. Research, teaching, institutions, and training programs have sprung up in many parts of the world, treaties and mutual monitoring processes have been created, and data are readily available from a wide range of sources. Corruption is entrenched as a mainstream concern for international organizations, and as a frequent focus for journalists." Johnston and Fritzen, *The Conundrum of Corruption*, 9.

617 John Kerry, "Remarks at Anti-Corruption Summit Plenary" (speech, London, U.K., May 12, 2016).

618 "Squeaky-Clean Europe Is More Corrupt Than You Think," *Economist*, September 12, 2024, 41; Gillian Dell and Andrew McDevitt, *Exporting Corruption 2022: Assessing Enforcement of the OECD Anti-Bribery Convention* (Transparency International, 2022); OECD, *OECD Foreign Bribery Report: An Analysis of the Crime of Bribery of Foreign Public Officials* (OECD Publishing, 2014), https://doi.org/10.1787/9789264226616-en.

619 Dell and McDevitt, *Exporting Corruption* 2022.

620 State of implementation of the United Nations Convention against Corruption, UN Office of Drugs and Crime (2015) (noting that "few States parties have introduced or taken steps towards establishing as criminal offences the bribery of foreign public officials and officials of public international organization.") (p.22).

621 Dell and McDevitt, *Exporting Corruption* 2022.

622 Johnston and Fritzen, *The Conundrum of Corruption*, 5.

623 Jennifer Arlen and Samuel W. Buell, "The Law of Corporate Investigations and the Global Expansion of Corporate Criminal Enforcement," *Southern California Law Review* 93, no. 4 (2020).

624 Under a DPA, the government could bring formal charges against a company but would refrain from prosecuting in exchange for the company's concession to pay fines and undertake compliance reforms. First used by U.S. prosecutors against corporations in the early 1990s, DPAs became a favorite tool of the DOJ and SEC after the collapse of Arthur Andersen in 2002. Part of their appeal was that DPAs allowed prosecutors to go after corporate malfeasance without endangering a company's corporate license to operate (and potentially the livelihoods of its employees). Insofar as DPAs provided a path to bypass public prosecution before a judge, companies too saw them as an attractive alternative, often agreeing to settle corruption charges brought against them even where the government's evidentiary proof may have otherwise been too weak to hold up in court.

625 *Restoring Balance: Proposed Amendments to the Foreign Corrupt Practices Act, U.S. Chamber Institute for Legal Reform* (October 2010), https://openairblog.wordpress.com/wp-content/uploads/2011/10/us-chamber-of-comm-amending-the-fcpa.pdf.

626 For example, see Dave Michaels, "SEC Chairman Scolds Weak Anticorruption Enforcement Abroad," *Wall Street Journal*, Sept. 9, 2019.

627 Data for DOJ and SEC Enforcement Actions per Year; and Charles F. Smith and Brittany D. Parling, "'American Imperialism': A Practitioner's Experience with Extraterritorial Enforcement of the FCPA," *University of Chicago Legal Forum* 237 (2012), 239.

628 Fritz Heimann & Mark Pieth, *Confronting Corruption: Past Concerns, Present Challenges, and Future Strategies*, (Oxford U. Press, 2018), 212.

629 Data for DOJ and SEC Enforcement Actions per Year.

630 For example, see Andrew Ceresney, "Remarks at 31st International Conference on the Foreign Corrupt Practices Act' (speech, National Harbor, MD, November 19, 2014), "We will continue our efforts to level the playing field for companies doing business abroad and hold corrupt actors accountable when they fail to play by the rules;" Trevor N. McFadden, "Acting Principal Deputy Assistant Attorney General Trevor N. McFadden Speaks at Anti-Corruption, Export Controls & Sanctions 10th Compliance Summit" (speech, Washington, D.C., April 18, 2017), "the Fraud Section's FCPA prosecutions are intended to level the playing field for honest businesses that are undercut by businesses that engage in corrupt behavior;" Rod Rosenstein, "Deputy Attorney General Rosenstein Delivers Remarks at the 34th International Conference on the Foreign Corrupt Practices Act" (speech, Oxon Hill, MD, November 29, 2017), remarking that "Corporate America should regard law enforcement as an ally. We support the rule of law, which establishes and safeguards a vibrant economic marketplace for your products and services."

631 Lauren Cohen and Bo Li, "The Political Economy of Anti-Bribery Enforcement," Working Paper No. w29624 (NBER, December 2021), using statistical analysis techniques to show that FCPA enforcement actions against foreign firms spike over 20 percent in the year leading up to U.S. elections, with no similar pattern for U.S.-domiciled firms; Steven Arrigg Koh, "The Criminalization of Foreign Relations," *Fordham Law Review* 90, no. 2 (2021): 739, arguing that aggressive extraterritorial prosecution of the FCPA is reflective of America's larger domestic mass incarceration problems, and that unchecked prosecutorial authority leads not only to bias against people of color, but against foreign nationals as well.

632 Smith and Parling, "'American Imperialism,'" 249.

633 Nor was this the first time that GE had sought to acquire distressed European companies caught in the crosshairs of DOJ FCPA investigations, including UK-based companies Amersham plc (acquired in 2003) and Vetco Gray (acquired in 2007). Kron's colleagues included William Pomponi, Frederic Pierucci, and Lawrence Hoskins. Pomponi died in 2016 while awaiting sentencing; Pierucci served a thirty-month sentence, after which he wrote a memoir claiming that he had been the victim of American economic warfare; and Hoskins eventually had his FCPA conviction overturned on appeal.

634 For example, see, Matthew Stephenson, "The OECD Rightly Rejects Claims That U.S. FCPA Enforcement Is Improperly Politicized." *Global Anticorruption Blog*, November 24, 2020, https://globalanticorruptionblog.com/2020/11/24/the-oecd-rightly-rejects-claims-that-u-s-fcpa-enforcement-is-improperly-politicized/.

635 U.S. Department of Justice, "Alstom Pleads Guilty and Agrees to Pay $772 Million Criminal Penalty to Resolve Foreign Bribery Charges," press release, December 22, 2014, https://www.justice.gov/archives/opa/pr/alstom-pleads-guilty-and-agrees-pay-772-million-criminal-penalty-resolve-foreign-bribery.

636 Kenneth A. Blanco, "Acting Assistant Attorney General Kenneth A. Blanco Speaks at the Atlantic Council Inter-American Dialogue Event on Lessons From Brazil: Crisis, Corruption and Global Cooperation" (speech, Washington, D.C., July 19, 2017).

637 Dom Phillips, "Brazil's New Hero Is a Nerdy Judge Who Is Tough on Official Corruption," *Washington Post*, Dec. 23, 2015.

638 Phillips, "Brazil's New Hero Is a Nerdy Judge Who Is Tough on Official Corruption," *Washington Post*.

639 At the time, people marched in the streets of Brazil wearing masks and t-shirts bearing Moro's likeness, while in the United States, he was given a flattering interview by Anderson Cooper on *60 Minutes* and invited to give the commencement speech at the University of Notre Dame's graduation. Other audiences included ones at the Woodrow Wilson International Center for Scholars and a black-tie event hosted by the Cato Institute honoring recipients of the Milton Friedman Prize for Advancing Liberty.

640 In 2019, the Brazilian Supreme Court blocked an attempt by the US DOJ to provide the taskforce with a $687 million payment from fines levied against Petrobras that, instead of going to the National Treasury, would have gone to a private anticorruption foundation tied to Transparency International's Brazil chapter. Brian Mier, "Transparency International: Brazil Court Opens Investigation of Anti-Corruption NGO," *Brasil Wire*, Apr. 14, 2022.

641 For example, a 2024 survey found that the number of Brazilians saying that the FCPA and other anticorruption laws have helped curb the risk of corruption decreased by almost 25 percent since 2020. See 2024 Latin America Corruption Survey (Miller & Chevalier 2024), 10.

642 Congressman Hank Johnson, "Rep. Johnson, Colleagues Ask DOJ for Answers on Brazil Corruption & Persecution of Former President Lula da Silva," press release, August 21, 2019, https://hankjohnson.house.gov/media-center/press-releases/rep-johnson-colleagues-ask-doj-answers-brazil-corruption-persecution; and Congressman Hank Johnson, "Rep. Johnson, Colleagues Ask A.G. Garland for Answers on DOJ Role in Brazil Probe and Persecution of Former President Lula da Silva," press release, June 7, 2021, https://hankjohnson.house.gov/media-center/press-releases/rep-johnson-colleagues-ask-ag-garland-answers-doj-role-brazil-probe-and.

643 "The Trouble with America's Extraterritorial Campaign Against Business," *Economist*, January 17, 2019.

Notes | 333

644 Transparency International Corruptions Perceptions Index 2023, https://images.transparency-cdn.org/images/CPI-2023-Report.pdf, noting that amidst a general, worldwide weakening of justice systems, corruption was thriving with impunity across the globe.

645 See Davis, *Between Impunity and Imperialism*, 244, noting that "the most important elements of the regime have been designed by members of the OECD, a group of wealthy countries, which is in turn dominated by the largest and wealthiest countries of all, most notably the United States [while] other actors are systematically excluded from key decision-making processes, including decisions in individual enforcement actions, decisions about overall enforcement strategy, and decisions about the overall legal framework of the anti-bribery regime." See also Rochelle Terman, *The Geopolitics of Shaming: When Human Rights Pressure Works and When It Backfires* (Princeton University Press, 2023, suggesting that the OECD Working Group's use of a "name and shame" technique has been shown in other contexts to be heavily biased and often counterproductive; and Stéphane Bonifassi, S., et. al, "The Role of Victims in Negotiated Settlements" The International Academy of Financial Crime Litigators Working Paper No 2., https://financialcrimelitigators.org/publications, pointing out that even when foreign bribery laws are enforced, most of the confiscated corporate proceeds and disgorged profits go to the treasury of the prosecuting countries, not to the countries where the bribes actually occurred, nor to the people most harmed by them.

646 Although the prohibition of "passive bribery" has been recognized for some time by Article 16(2) of the UN Convention Against Corruption, few if any countries have chosen to implement it.

647 Thomas Firestone and Drago Kos, "With the Foreign Extortion Prevention Act, America Puts the World on Notice," *FCPA Blog*, February 1, 2024.

648 The threat of punitive retaliation against the United States is nontrivial given the recent spate of cases involving U.S. congressmen accepting bribes from foreign parties. In 2024 alone, New Jersey Senator Bob Menendez was found guilty for accepting bribes from businesses with Egyptian ties, while Texas representative Henry Cuellar was charged in a yearslong bribery scheme involving a Mexican bank and Azerbaijani oil company.

649 For example, a 2022 global survey found that for the first time ever, people from developing countries felt more favorably toward China (62 percent) than toward the United States (61 percent). Roberto Foa, Margot Mollat, Han Isha, Xavier Romero-Vidal, David Evans, and Andrew Klassen, *A World Divided: Russia, China and the West* (Bennett Institute for Public Policy, University of Cambridge, 2022), doi:10.17863/CAM.90281.

650 For example, see Vineeta Yadav and Bumba Mukherjee, *The Politics of Corruption in Dictatorships* (Cambridge University Press, 2016), noting that authoritarian regimes are not always synonymous with corruption and that corruption levels actually decreased between 1985 and 2010 in a sampling of authoritarian regimes.

651 John Githongo, "Thirty Years of Anti-Corruption: A Personal Reflection," *The Elephant*, February 23, 2024, https://www.theelephant.info/reflections/2024/02/23/thirty-years-of-anti-corruption-a-personal-reflection/.

652 His efforts to expose large-scale corruption within the Kenyan government led to Githongo's exile to the UK and resulted in a fast-paced political thriller written about his life in 2009 that received plenty of well-deserved media attention. He has since remained active in the anticorruption space, serving as a member of Transparency International's Global Council and a chairman and board member of several African governance organizations. In 2022, he received a lifetime award from the United Nations Office on Drugs and Crime for his dedication to fighting corruption.

653 Githongo, "Thirty Years of Anti-Corruption."

654 See, generally, Francis Fukuyama, *The End of History and the Last Man* (Free Press 1992).

655 Ralph Nader correctly observed this when testifying before Congress in 1976, noting that the "recent avalanche of disclosed corporate crime was set off by small, flukish rocks." *Abuses of Corporate Power*, 94th Cong. 101 (1976) (prepared statement of Ralph Nader).

656 For more on this, see Johnston and Fritzen, *The Conundrum of Corruption*, noting that "[t]he worst corruption situations were seen as occurring mostly 'out there,' in the developing world, while those in affluent societies, and those countries' contributions to corruption elsewhere, were initially accorded much less importance."

657 For example, see Sampson, *The Arms Bazaar*, 285–86, noting that "[m]ultinationals are so big, they wield so much money, that it upsets the local equilibrium." They become "themselves major actors in the play of politics; and actors of a very blundering kind, like bulls in china shops. They do not simply follow[ ] the 'custom of the country' [but] creat[e] new customs."

658 See, generally, Eisinger, *The Chickenshit Club*.

659 See Christiaan Keulder, *Africans See Growing Corruption, Poor Government Response, But Fear Retaliation If They Speak Out: Afrobarometer Dispatch No. 488* (Afrobarometer, November 10, 2021).

660 Yuen Ang, *China's Gilded Age* (Cambridge University Press, 2020).

661 Frank Vogl, "Corruption and the Global Debt Crisis" (speech, George Mason University, May 15, 2024).

662 Jorgen Anderson et al., "Elite Capture of Foreign Aid: Evidence from Offshore Bank Accounts," Policy Research Working Paper No. 9150 (World Bank Group, February 2020).

663 David Lowenthal, *The Past is a Foreign Country* (Cambridge U. Press, 1985), 209.

664 International Anti-Corruption Prosecutorial Taskforce, Founding Statement (March 20, 2025), https://www.gov.uk/government/publications/international-anti-corruption-prosecutorial-taskforce.

665 *United States v. Aluminum Company of America* (Alcoa), 148 F.2d 416 (2nd Cir. 1945).

666 Vernon and Spar, *Beyond Globalism*, 116.

667 Robert H. Bork, *The Antitrust Paradox: A Policy at War with Itself* (Basic Books, Inc., 1978).

668 ABA Section of Antitrust Law, Competition Laws Outside the United States, p. 14 (2001).

669 Marek Martyniszyn, "Extraterritoriality in EU Competition Law" in Nuno Cunha Rodrigues (ed), *Extraterritoriality of EU Economic Law* (Springer 2021).

670 *Protecting the Ability of the United States to Trade Abroad*, 94th Cong. 8 (statement of Frank Church).

671 *McDonnell v. United States*, 579 U.S. 550 (2016); Snyder v. United States, 603 U.S. 1 (2024).

INDEX

Abscam 260

accounting and internal controls 222, 224, 226

    See also Foreign Corrupt Practices Act

Addonizio, Hugh 67–68

Agnew, Spiro 69–70, 82, 85–86, 89

All Nippon Airways 175, 180, 191–195

Allende, Salvador 100, 105–109, 116, 119

American Airlines 29, 78, 158

American Ship Building Company 24, 30

Anderson, Jack 100, 103, 105, 133

anticorruption bills
    H.R. 3815 252, 254
    H.R. 7539 204–205
    S. 305 244–246, 249
    S. 3133 211–213, 221–222, 232, 234
    S. 3379 214–216, 221, 232, 234
    S. 3418 222, 224–225, 232
    S. 3664 232, 235–237, 240–241, 244
    S. 3741 226, 229

antitrust law 51, 103, 207–208, 253, 287–289

Arms Export Control Act 200

Arthur Young & Company 148, 150, 153, 155–156, 162, 170–171

Ashland Oil 30, 78, 187

Bacon, Kenneth 34, 37

Bahamas 30–31, 42, 60, 124, 126–128, 130

Baker, Robert "Bobby" 70–71

Banks Records and Foreign Transactions Act (Bank Secrecy Act) 69, 218

Barrientos, René 123, 129

Biden, Joseph 154, 239, 277

Black, Eli 8, 17, 19–21, 33–34, 37, 40, 43, 47, 93, 121, 256, 283
    early work 14
    family 10, 12
    funeral 18
    problems at work 18
    religious beliefs 14–15
    reputation 10, 13–15
    suicide 9, 11–13, 15–16

Blum, Jack 103, 137, 156, 160–164, 168, 240

Blumenthal, Michael 245–247, 249–250

Boeing Company 60, 90, 193, 219–220

Bolivia 44, 123, 129

books and records 212, 224, 235, 248, 250, 252, 254–255, 267
    See also Foreign Corrupt Practices Act

Borah, William E. 95, 97–99, 186, 221

Bralove, Mary 13, 15–16, 33, 37

Braniff Airways 28–30, 32, 43

Brazil 60, 273–275

Broe, William 106–108

Bryan, William Jennings 50

Cambodia 133

Carter, Jimmy 246
    1976 campaign 166, 185–188, 226–227, 240–242
    1980 campaign 260
    and antibribery legislation generally 230, 243, 247–248, 250, 255
    and the FCPA (*see* Foreign Corrupt Practices Act)

Case, Clifford 101, 216, 239

Castle & Cooke 37, 44, 187

Central Intelligence Agency 141, 253
    and bribery 172, 199–200, 245, 255
    and the Church Committee 104, 106, 165, 169–170
    and foreign policy 111
    and ITT 103–104, 106–107
    and Watergate 77, 79

Chacharis, George 65

Chile 100, 103–109, 132, 253
    coup 119, 233

China 96, 98, 164, 218
   and bribery 60, 270, 284
   rivalry with U.S. 279
Church, Frank 100-102, 118, 123, 151-152, 164, 246, 253
   1976 presidential campaign 134, 156-157, 165-166, 182, 185-188, 216, 240
   and antibribery legislation 204, 213-217, 226, 230, 232, 234-235, 237-240, 249, 254
   bribery investigations 41, 93, 145-147, 160, 169, 173, 176-179, 181
   corruption, views on 89, 131-134, 142, 197, 218-221, 290
   death 258
   early life 95-99
   and the Foreign Relations Committee 98, 120-121, 184-185, 214, 258
   and Teapot Dome 90
   and Vietnam 101, 218
   See also Hubert Humphrey; William Proxmire; the Subcommittee on Multinational Corporations
CIA. *See* Central Intelligence Agency
Civil Aeronautics Board (CAB) 27-29
the Cold War 98, 131, 206, 231, 233, 282, 285
Committee to Re-elect the President 23-25, 36, 75-77, 84, 124
Common Cause 72-74, 77, 79, 91, 246
Cooper, John Sherman 101-102
corporate social responsibility 26, 117
Corrupt-Practices Act 53, 91
Cortelyou, George 49, 75
Cortelyouism 50
Cox, Archibald 23, 79, 249
CRP. *See* Committee to Re-elect the President

Daugherty, Harry 58
Deferred prosecution agreements 271
DeFrancis, Frank J. 141, 145-146
Democratic National Convention 97-98, 231
Denby, Edwin 56

Department of Defense 34, 142, 199
Department of Justice 268, 270-271, 276-277, 290
   cooperation with Japanese 182-184
   corruption investigations 29, 65-68, 83, 123, 195
   and legislation 208, 230, 235-237, 250
   and organized crime 63, 67
   politicization 249, 272-275, 280
   resources 84
Department of the Interior 55-56
Department of State. *See* State Department
Dodd, Thomas J. 71
Doheny, Edward 57, 90
DOJ. *See* Department of Justice
Dorsey, Bob
   on legislation 129-130, 147, 204
   testimony of 93-94, 122-130
Douglas Company. *See* McDonnell Douglas
Dowdy, John 73-74
DPA. *See* deferred prosecution agreements

Eckhardt, Bob 58, 203, 252-253, 256
Emergency Loan Guarantee Board 149
Ernst & Ernst 42, 135, 137-138, 140, 142-143, 145-148, 223, 254
Evans, John 158
Exxon 44, 111, 117, 119, 130, 253

Facilitation payments. *See* grease payments
Fall, Albert 56, 59
FCPA. *See* Foreign Corrupt Practices Act
FECA. *See* Federal Election Campaign Act
Federal Corrupt Practices Act 54, 76, 124, 217, 246
   1910 adoption of 53
   1925 amendments to 61
   lack of enforcement 55, 61, 70-71
   lawsuits pursuant to 73, 77-78, 91, 158

Index | 337

Federal Election Campaign Act 83, 91, 259
    1971 adoption of 74
    1976 amendment to 81
    and Watergate 75–76
Ferrara, Ralph 16–20
Findley, William 148, 171–172
Forbes, Charles 58
Ford, Gerald 79, 159, 164–165, 243
    1976 presidential campaign 241–242
    and antibribery legislation 205, 208–210, 226–231, 238, 241, 245
    and Japan 181–184, 197
    and Watergate 79–80
    See also Task Force on Questionable Corporate Payments Abroad
Foreign Corrupt Practices Act 29, 54, 260, 268
    1988 amendments to 263
    accounting provision 248, 250, 255
    backlash against 259, 263, 271–272
    books and records provision 248, 254–255
    and the Carter administration 245–250, 257–259, 261
    conference committee 254–256
    criminal sanctions 248–249
    enforcement of 3–5, 249–250, 263, 268, 270–272, 276, 280
    executive order pause 2, 4, 280
    foreign officials, definition of 252, 255
    foreign subsidiaries, application to 255–256
    future of 278, 285–287, 290–291
    historiography of 48, 86–87
    House adoption 252–254, 256
    introduction of 244
    knowledge requirement 250
    lobbying against 252, 254
    naming of 91
    national security exception 255
    and the OECD Convention 3, 265–267, 270
    passage of 203–204, 256
    penalties 250, 255
    politicization 4–5, 272–275, 280
    and post-Cold War era 3, 264–267, 282
    and private right of action 249, 253, 256
    Senate adoption 250–251, 256
    signing of 257, 261
    and third-party agents 250, 263
    and Watergate 70, 86–88
Foreign Extortion Prevention Act (FEPA) 277–278
Foreign Military Sales Act 216
Foreign Relations Committee. *See* Senate Foreign Relations Committee
Friedman, Milton 118, 258, 264
Fukuyama, Francis 282–283
Fulbright, J. William 100–102, 104, 120, 214

Galbraith, John Kenneth 116, 118
Gardner, John W. 72–73
Garrett, Ray 20, 25, 42, 157, 159
Gelsthorpe, Edward 18–20
Geneen, Harold 102, 106–108, 119
General Motors 111–112, 134, 187, 272
Germany 44, 112, 114, 140–141, 160, 162, 171, 183, 251, 264
Gingery, William 27–29, 44
Globalization 1, 264, 267, 278–279, 281
Goldfarb, Ronald 63
Grease payments 233–234, 263
Gulf Oil Company 43, 213
    Bahamas fund 30–31, 124, 126–127
    bribes 44, 121–123, 127–129, 153, 187
    hearings 42, 93, 95, 121–134, 137, 144, 153, 166, 284
    SEC dealings 30–32, 37,
    stonewalling 123
    and Watergate 78, 123–124, 130
Gwirtzman, Milton 86

Harding, Warren 55–56, 58
Haughton, Daniel 148, 152–155, 159, 169
Hauser, Ernest 160–162, 164, 168–169
Hills, Roderick 159, 168, 207, 213, 222–225, 229, 235, 238, 248–249
  See also Proxmire, William
Hiyama, Hiro 189, 193, 195
Hobbs Anti-Racketeering Act 62, 65–68, 80, 84, 91, 217
Honduras
  banana tax 21
  coup 40
  political environment 39
  response to United Brands scandal 38–40
  and United Brands 19, 22, 26, 31, 34, 37, 121
House Committees
  Judiciary 64
  Standards of Official Conduct 71
House Subcommittee on International Economic Policy 155, 158
Hughes, Charles Evans 51
Humphrey, Hubert
  accepting bribes 166–167, 187
  and antibribery legislation 213–214, 258
  health problems 166, 258
  and Frank Church 94–95, 101–105, 120–121, 134, 165–166, 184–185, 188, 214
  and William Proxmire 167–168

Idris, Mohammad 132
Internal Revenue Service 30–31, 63, 69, 79, 200, 230
International Telephone and Telegraph Company 102, 104, 120–121, 131
  and Chile 100, 103, 105–109, 132, 253
  and multinationalism 111–112, 118
International Traffic in Arms Regulations 200

Interstate and Foreign Travel or Transportation in Aid of Racketeering Enterprises Act. *See* Travel Act
Iran 59, 111, 137, 141, 186
IRS. *See* Internal Revenue Service
Italy 44, 123, 128, 130–132, 135, 171, 176, 184, 188, 199, 218, 251, 253,
Itoh, Hiroshi 163, 195
ITT. *See* International Telephone and Telegraph Company

Jackson, Henry "Scoop" 104, 165
Japan 44, 60, 89, 114, 163–164, 169, 171–176, 178–184, 187, 189–192, 194–198, 218, 227, 251
Javits, Jacob 101–102, 105, 184
Johnson, Lyndon 70
  and campaign finance reform 71–72
  and Frank Church 98–99
Jones, Thomas 25, 137, 141, 154, 175–176
  becoming CEO 138–139
  and legislation 147
  lifestyle 139–140
  testimony of 144–148
Justice Department. *See* Department of Justice

Kasahara, Masanori 196
Kennedy, John 64–65, 83, 98, 112–113
Kennedy, Robert "Bobby" 62–65, 69, 84, 97–98
Kenny, John 67, 84
Kerner, Otto, Jr. 69
Khashoggi, Adnan 141–143, 145, 156
Kissinger, Henry 35, 160–161, 178, 181–182, 191, 196–197, 208, 210, 227, 229, 231, 245
Kodama, Yoshio 174
  assassination attempt 190
  criminal background 164
  indictment 189
  meeting with Lockheed 192
  political ties 173, 180
  right-wing ideology 163, 173

Index | 339

Korea 44, 123, 127–128, 135
Kotchian, Carl 89–90, 169, 174–176, 178–179, 182, 190–195
Kubacki, John 66–67

La Follette, Robert 56, 167, 221
Leone, Giovanni 178, 188, 199
Levi, Edward 161, 209, 227
Levinson, Jerome 103–104, 107, 121, 123, 130, 134–135, 137–138, 144, 155–156, 160, 170–171, 174, 177, 179, 185, 204, 214–215, 239–240
Libya 132, 187
Lockheed 168, 185–188, 199–200, 204, 209, 213, 218, 256
    and auditors, *see* Arthur Young & Company
    board of directors 148, 151
    and bribes 43, 89–90, 143, 153, 160–162, 163–164, 169, 171, 175–176, 191–194
    and government loans 149–150
    hearings 152, 154, 165, 170–172, 174–177
    and Japan 173, 178–181, 189–190, 197–198
    and Northrop 140, 146–147
    payment methods 171–172, 194
    stonewalling 154–156, 159, 174, 183–184, 227
Loomis, Philip A. 155, 158, 160
López Arellano, Oswaldo 34–35, 37, 39–40

Mail Fraud Statute
    and foreign bribery legislation 212
    and honest services fraud 69
Marubeni Corporation 163, 175, 189, 191–195
materiality 157, 207, 212, 226
McClellan Committee 62–63, 97–98
McClellan, John 68, 97
McCone, John 106

McDonnell Douglas 175, 186, 193
McGovern, George 77, 99, 102
Mexico 56, 57, 59, 60, 178, 283
Miki, Takeo 180–182, 189–190, 195, 197
Minnesota Mining and Manufacturing (3M) 30, 78
Mitchell, John 67, 75, 83–85, 249
Mobil 44, 119, 130
morality 3–5, 15–16, 47, 49, 82, 64, 94, 157, 200, 203, 205, 207, 217–219, 231, 236, 245, 257, 260, 279, 281–282, 285, 290
    See also post-Watergate morality
movies
    Murder on the Orient Express 9
    Network 93, 116–117
    On the Waterfront 62
    Serpico 82
muckrakers. 50, 219, 282–283

Nader, Ralph 76, 113
neoliberalism
    ascendancy 258, 264
    backlash against 4, 278
    ideological roots 117–118
The Netherlands 44, 131, 140, 160, 168–169, 171, 176–177, 184, 188–189, 198, 218, 288
The New Deal 62, 95, 258
New Left movement 114n259
New Right movement 258
New York Life Insurance Company 51
Nixon, Richard 151, 159, 182–183, 191, 242, 249, 283
    1972 election 75–77
    and campaign finance reform 70, 72, 74, 86
    and illegal campaign contributions 23–24, 30, 36, 78, 123–124, 128, 130,
    resignation 79, 80, 115
    and law enforcement 67, 83, 84

Nol, Lon 133
Noonan, John, Jr. 68, 82–83, 88, 91 260
Northrop Corporation 90, 139
    Congressional inquiry into 135, 137–138, 144–148, 153, 165, 200, 246
    consultants 140–142
    cover-up 25, 143
    fallout 43, 147–148
    and Lockheed 146–147, 149, 156, 204, 209, 213
    SEC dealings 25, 30, 42–43
Nye, Gerald 60, 90

OECD. *See* Organization for Economic Co-operation and Development
OECD Convention on Combating Bribery of Foreign Public Officials in International Business Transactions 266–267, 270, 281
Organization for Economic Co-operation and Development 3, 170, 209, 228, 265–266, 270, 278, 282
Okubo, Toshiharu 191–195
Operation Car Wash 273–275
OPIC. *See* Overseas Private Investment Corporation
Organized Crime Control Act 68, 74
    See also RICO
Osano, Kenji 180, 192
Overseas Private Investment Corporation 106, 108

Pan American Petroleum 56–59, 90
Panama 21, 32, 41, 110, 290
Park, Chung-hee 123, 127–128
Parker, Alton B. 48–49, 51
Percy, Charles 102–103, 120, 143, 147, 170, 176, 216, 239, 284
Phillips Petroleum Co. 30, 187
Pieth, Mark 266, 271–272
political action committees (PACs) 259

Pollack, Irving 16–17, 25
post-Watergate morality 47, 82–83, 85–87, 89–90, 156, 206
Powell, Adam Clayton, Jr. 71
Pratt, John 159–162, 168
PriceWaterhouse 32–33, 38
Prince Bernhard 160, 169, 177, 188–189, 198–199
Progressive era 48–50, 53, 56, 112, 167
Proxmire, William 137, 158, 209
    and antibribery legislation 211–218, 221–222, 224–226, 228–237, 239–241, 254, 256
    bribery, attitude toward 219
    and Frank Church 152, 213
    and Jimmy Carter 243
    and Lockheed 151–152, 154, 183, 198
    reputation 219–221
    and Roderick Hills 168, 213, 248–249
    See also Humphrey, Hubert
Pulitzer, Joseph 49–51

Qaddafi, Muammar 132

Repenning, Werner 161–162
Republican National Convention 54, 231
Richardson, Elliot 78, 181, 209–210, 227–229, 235, 245
RICO 68–69, 75, 80, 83–84, 88, 91, 253
Rogers, William 36, 151, 153, 156, 160–161
Roosevelt, Archibald "Archie" 57–58
Roosevelt, Franklin 62, 95
Roosevelt, Kermit, Jr. 141
Roosevelt, Theodore 48–52, 56, 58, 75, 141

Sansweet, Stephen 32–33, 37, 39
Saudi Arabia 44, 119, 141–143, 156
Savy, William 140
SEC. *See* Securities and Exchange Commission
Securities and Exchange Act 23, 36, 244, 340, 341

Index | 341

Securities and Exchange Commission 47, 121, 134, 149, 237, 261, 283–284
   and antibribery legislation 68, 207, 212–213, 215, 222–226, 229–230, 232, 235–236, 238, 248–249, 252, 254,
   cases brought 24, 30, 32, 37–38, 41–43, 159–161
   creation of 16
   disagreements within 25, 36, 157–158
   FCPA, enforcement of 268, 271–273, 290
   filings with 31, 76, 186–187, 200
   independence of 250
   investigations by 18–20, 22, 26–27, 29, 33, 35, 123–125, 154–155, 168
   Management Fraud Program 24, 30
   and Watergate 23–24, 87
   See also Foreign Corrupt Practices Act; voluntary disclosure program
Senate Committees
   Armed Services 104
   Banking, Housing, and Urban Development 151, 232
   Finance 72
   Foreign Relations, *see* Senate Foreign Relations Committee
   Judiciary 103
   On Ethics 71
   On Improper Activities in the Labor or Management Field, *see* McClellan Committee
   Public Lands and Survey 56
Senate Foreign Relations Committee 103, 152
   hearing room 93–94, 169, 174
   internal politics 101, 121, 184–185, 213–214
Senate Munitions Inquiry 59, 61, 206
Senate Subcommittees
   Administrative Practices and Procedures 27
   Mexican Affairs 59
   Multinational Corporations, *see* Senate Subcommittee on Multinational Corporations
   Privileges and Elections 77
   Western Hemisphere 100
Senate Subcommittee on Multinational Corporations
   and banking hearings 121
   and bribery hearings 42, 93, 121–123, 125–134, 169–172, 256
   demise of 239–240
   establishment of 100–103
   funding of 94, 120–121
   and ITT hearings 103–109, 118, 121
   and oil hearings 119–120, 122–123, 129
Simon, William 181, 208, 210, 227, 231
Sinclair, Harry 56, 58–59, 90
Sinclair Oil Corporation 56–59, 90
Sirica, John 78
slush fund 29, 30, 43, 78, 200, 248, 256
Smith-Connally Act 62
Solarz, Stephen 204–205, 208, 216
Sommer, Al, Jr. 157, 159
Sparkman, John 121, 152, 214, 240
Spong, William 101, 105
Sporkin, Stanley 20, 22, 25–26, 30–31, 36, 42, 87, 124, 151, 250, 284
   disclosures by 121, 125, 134–135, 256
   and legislation 212–213, 223–225
   reputation of 16–17
   and Watergate 23–24
Standard Fruit 21, 37
   See also Castle & Cooke
Standard Oil 51, 111
Stans, Maurice 75–76
State Department 60, 100, 274
   and antibribery legislation 200, 205, 227–230, 245
   and Lockheed 160–161, 174, 177–178, 182
   and Northrop 25, 42, 135, 143
   and United Brands 33, 35–36

Stehlin, Paul Marie 140, 143–144
Strauss, Franz Josef 160–161, 168
Supreme Court decisions 58
    Buckley v. Valeo (1976) 81
    Citizens United v. Federal Election Commission (2010) 291
    Ernst & Ernst v. Hochfelder (1976) 223, 254
    McDonnell v. United States (2016) 291
    Newberry v. United States (1921) 54
    Snyder v. United States (2024) 291
    United States v. Aluminum Company of America (1945) 288
    United States v. Brewster (1972) 81
Symington, Stuart 101, 109, 120

Taft, William Howard 56, 110
Taft-Hartley Act 62, 65
Tanaka, Kakuei 89, 169,
    arrest 195–196
    meeting with Marubeni 191–193
    political career 179–180
Task Force on Questionable Corporate Payments Abroad 181, 226
Teapot Dome 56–58, 61, 90, 283
    and foreign bribes 59
TI. *See* Transparency International
Tillman Act 52–54, 91
Tower, John 206, 233, 238, 241, 255
Transparency International 265–266, 270, 274, 280
Travel Act 64–66, 83, 88, 91
Trump, Donald 2, 4, 280, 287

United Brands 8, 11, 15, 39, 124
    board of directors 34
    bribe payments 20-22, 33–35, 41, 43–44, 87
    congressional inquiry 42
    SEC dealings 17–20, 22, 25–27, 31–32, 36–38
    reputation 25–26, 35, 41
    size 10
United States Grain Standards Act 82

Vietnam War 93, 99, 101–102, 104, 108–109, 114, 132–133, 135, 172, 205, 218
Vogl, Frank 94
voluntary disclosure program 158–159, 186, 200

Wakasa, Tokuji 193–195
Wall Street Journal 174, 182
    Gulf Oil leak 125
    investigation into Teapot Dome 55, 283
    investigation into United Brands 13, 15, 32–39, 41, 44, 87, 121, 256, 282–283
Walsh, Thomas 56
Walsh Committee 57–59
Watergate 24–25, 28, 70, 84, 146, 159, 182–183, 198, 244, 249, 283
    break-in 76–77
    hearings 22–23, 78
    memory of 48, 83, 87–88, 227
    Special Prosecution Office 42, 79–80, 123–124, 158, 182
    See also post-Watergate morality, Watergate babies
Watergate babies 205, 261
Waters, Robert 155
Whiteford, Bill 126–127
Wild, Claude 123
Wilson, Woodrow 47, 53–55, 91
World Bank 265–266, 269

ABOUT THE AUTHOR

Ken Koeberlein

Severin Wirz is an attorney specializing in U.S. and international anticorruption law. His career spans grassroots advocacy and high-stakes investigations—from advancing collective action initiatives with nonprofit organizations in East Africa to guiding Fortune 100 companies through complex cross-border enforcement matters. He currently serves as Director of Ethics & Compliance at Applied Materials, a leading semiconductor equipment manufacturer based in Silicon Valley. Previously, he was Senior Director of Anti-Corruption Compliance at TIAA, where he led global antibribery efforts across the financial services enterprise.

Severin is a frequent contributor to the field, with published articles on anticorruption compliance and editorial roles in key reference works, including *Practicing Under the U.S. Anti-Corruption Laws* and the series *How to Pay a Bribe: Thinking Like a Criminal to Thwart Bribery Schemes*.

READ MORE

This isn't the end of the story. Scan the QR code above for an interactive experience, including a timeline of pivotal events that led up to the passage of the Foreign Corrupt Practices Act.

ABOUT CCI PRESS

CCI Press is the publishing imprint of CCI Media Group LLC, parent company of Corporate Compliance Insights (CCI). CCI is the web's premier independent, global source of news and opinion for compliance, ethics, and risk.

Founded in 2010, CCI provides a knowledge-sharing forum and publishing platform for established and emerging voices in compliance and ethics and is a recognized creator, publisher, and syndication source for editorial and multimedia content for today's compliance professional.

www.ingramcontent.com/pod-product-compliance
Lightning Source LLC
Chambersburg PA
CBHW052131070526
44585CB00017B/1781